Conflict and Social Change Series

Series Editors
Scott Whiteford and William Derman
Michigan State University

Ancestral Rain Forests and the Mountain of Gold: Indigenous Peoples and Mining in New Guinea, David Hyndman

"I Am Destroying the Land!" The Political Ecology of Poverty and Environmental Destruction in Honduras, Susan C. Stonich

More Than a Living: Fishing and the Social Order on a Polynesian Atoll, Michael D. Lieber

Literacy, Power, and Democracy in Mozambique: The Governance of Learning from Colonization to the Present, Judith Marshall

Computing Myths, Class Realities: An Ethnography of Technology and Working People in Sheffield, England, David Hakken with Barbara Andrews

The Culture of Protest: Religious Activism and the U.S. Sanctuary Movement, Susan Bibler Coutin

Gender, Sickness, and Healing in Rural Egypt: Ethnography in Historical Context, Soheir A. Morsy

Life Is a Little Better: Redistribution as a Development Strategy in Nadur Village, Kerala, Richard W. Franke

¡Óigame! ¡Óigame! *Struggle and Social Change in a Nicaraguan Urban Community,* Michael James Higgins and Tanya Leigh Coen

Manufacturing Against the Odds: Small-Scale Producers in an Andean City, Hans C. Buechler and Judith-Maria Buechler

The Bushman Myth: The Making of a Namibian Underclass, Robert J. Gordon

Surviving Drought and Development: Ariaal Pastoralists of Northern Kenya, Elliot Fratkin

FORTHCOMING

The Myth of the Male Breadwinner: Women and Industrialization in the Caribbean, Helen I. Safa

Chicano and Mexican Communities in Rural California, Juan Vicente Palerm

Ancestral Rain Forests and the Mountain of Gold

Indigenous Peoples and Mining in New Guinea

David Hyndman

Westview Press

BOULDER • SAN FRANCISCO • OXFORD

Conflict and Social Change

Copyright © 1994 by Westview Press, Inc.

Published in 1994 in the United States of America by Westview Press, Inc., 5500 Central Avenue, Boulder, Colorado 80301-2877, and in the United Kingdom by Westview Press, 36 Lonsdale Road, Summertown, Oxford OX2 7EW

A CIP catalog record for this book is available from the Library of Congress.
ISBN 0-8133-7804-4

Printed and bound in the United States of America

The paper used in this publication meets the requirements of the American National Standard for Permanence of Paper for Printed Library Materials Z39.48-1984.

10   9   8   7   6   5   4   3   2   1

Contents

Tables, Figures, and Plates

Acknowledgments

My personal and professional involvement with the Wopkaimin people goes back two decades. I first entered the ancestral rain forests of the Wopkaimin in 1973, and their warmth and hospitality made my fieldwork a time of profound growth. I particularly wish to thank Bini Abifagoim and his family for their genuine friendship and gracious assistance. This book fulfils my promise to Bini and the many families with whom I lived to tell their story--the way of life in their homeland, the unanticipated problems of resettlement and the resistance to threatened loss of land and culture.

The research presented here has been variously funded by the Australian Research Council, the Australian Academy of Social Sciences, the Australian National University, The University of Queensland, Natural Systems Research and the Ok Tedi Health and Nutrition Project.

David Hyndman

1

The Wopkaimin: A Fourth World at the Crossroads

Ecologically Rich/Economically Poor

Resource expropriation by the industrial world spins in ever–widening circles to locate materials to exploit. Increasingly, these invasions focus on the remote areas of the tropics where indigenous peoples of the Fourth World have endured through isolation. The Wopkaimin homeland in the mountains of westernmost Papua New Guinea (PNG) was occupied in 1981 by the Ok Tedi gold and copper mining project. Since then they have been swept into the tragic scenario of yet another ecologically affluent, but economically poor, Melanesian people undergoing massive cultural and ecological change (Nietschmann 1984).

Resource exploitation imposed from outside raises the question as to who should own and use resources (Stretton 1976:5). In the Wopkaimin case, the state declared itself to be resource owner, and the Wopkaimin were recognized only as landowners. The mining transnational as resource developer arrived in the Wopkaimin ancestral rain forests in the late 1960s, bringing a threat to the cultural, spatial and resource autonomy of the Wopkaimin. They can no longer rely on the continuity of their cultural management of resources which has long permitted sustainable utilization of a unique ecosystem with negligible impact on resources. Now many of the wild animals and plants of the region are no longer exclusively for internal production and circulation because they have become commodities to be sold in newly created markets. Moreover, local impact on land, air and water from the Wopkaimin kinship mode of

1

production was virtually negligible compared to the continuing pollution created by the Ok Tedi project. Land and water requirements for the Ok Tedi project take nearly 10 percent of Wopkaimin land and its ecological and cultural impact ramifies throughout the region.

Since I first did fieldwork among the Wopkaimin in 1973, I have come more and more to appreciate the ecological significance of their ancestral rain forests and their methods of resource control that have conserved their way of life, habitat and customary rights to their homeland. In the 1970s my study of how the subsistence–oriented Wopkaimin had long maintained the quality of their lands, water and resources was theoretically guided by subsistence–ecology. Some 700 Wopkaimin exercised the only effective control over a 1,000 km^2 ecosystem through their possession of a sophisticated and detailed understanding of local biota and environments and through their time–proven, ecologically and culturally adapted management of resources.

Formerly on the other side of the frontier of Australian colonialism and, after 1975, of the new state of PNG, the Wopkaimin were thrust into the world capitalist system in the 1980s with the arrival of the Ok Tedi mining project. In opposition to Wopkaimin resource control based on ancestral knowledge and techniques accumulated over thousands of years (Swadling 1983) of testing and experimentation was the enormity of one of the world's largest open cut mines. The new competitive resource frontier ushered in a volatile clash between kinship and capitalist modes of production.

The Mountain Ok Cultural Sphere

New Guinea is the most environmentally complex and culturally diverse island in the Pacific. Within that diversity, authorities, nevertheless, find uniformities and integration which they have variously labeled "distinctive regional types" (Brown 1978:272), "cultural regionalism" (Bulmer, S. 1982:175), "regional cultures" (Chowning 1982:166), "areal cultures" (Schwartz 1962:89), and "original communities" (Watson 1980:vii). Features noted include trade, exchange and shared ceremonies. The homeland of the Mountain Ok peoples constitutes one of three cultural spheres (Hyndman and Morren 1990) in the Highlands and it shares the attributes of an areally extensive "original community" as defined by Watson (1980:viii).

The headwaters of the Fly and Sepik Rivers originate in the Mountain Ok cultural sphere (Figure 1.1), which constitutes a major ecological and cultural demarcation of the Highlands. Though areally extensive, it is not as densely populated as the Eastern or Western Highland cultural spheres. It is an ancient rain forested region that even covered the grassland corridor which once existed along the central cordillera until 12000 years ago (Swadling 1983; see Short *et al.* 1976:409, plate 374).

There are three kinds of groups to characterize the Mountain Ok peoples distributed around the Sepik Source Basin, Highland core, Mid-altitude fringe and Lowland fringe (Table 1.1; Figure 1.2). In the Highland core are the Telefolmin, Falamin, Ulapmin, and Tifalmin peoples of the Sepik Source Basin, with associated Highland core peoples, the Oksapmin and Bimin, to the east and the Ngalum/Sibilmin to the west. The Mid-altitude fringe peoples of the north slope are the Atbalmin, Am Nakai Miyanmin and the Dulanmin and of the south slope are the Wopkaimin, Kauwolmin, Fegolmin, Kamfegolmin, Angkeiakmin, Seltamanmin, Baktamanmin, Kwermin and Augobmin. In the northern Lowland fringe are the Sa Nakai Miyanmin and Ninataman Telefolmin and in the southern slopes are the Minomin–Aekyom.

The Wopkaimin: A People of the Mid–altitude Fringe

The Wopkaimin live in the Mid–altitude fringe of the Mountain Ok sphere (Figure 1.2). This distinct ecological zone between 500–1500 m comprises over 40 percent of the eastern half of the island (Allen 1983:9). Topographically, the Wopkaimin homeland extends from the foothills to the Barhman ranges of the central cordillera. They primarily live in Lower Montane *Araucaria*, oak and mixed rain forest wedged between Lowland Rain Forest and Midmontane beech and conifer forest. Their homeland receives over eight meters of rain every year, one of the highest rainfall areas on the island (Brookfield and Hart 1971:9–13).

The key features of Wopkaimin success have been small population size and a large territory in which both individuals and groups can easily move about to exploit abundant but patchily distributed wild foods and to cultivate *Colocasia* taro. Wild foods are diverse (Hyndman 1982a) and many plants that are original domesticates of New Guinea, such as sugar cane, pitpits, aibika, *Rungia* and *Pandanus*, are presently centered in the Mid–altitude fringe and this diversity contrasts with the poor resource base of the Upper Montane Rain Forest (Bulmer, S. 1982:194; Hope *et al.* 1983).

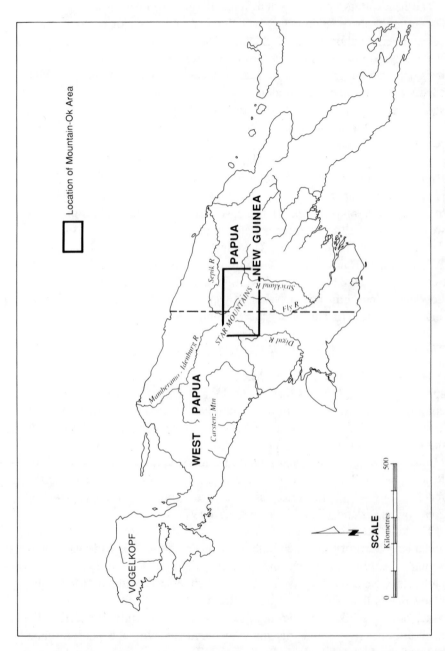

FIGURE 1.1 New Guinea and the location of Mountain Ok peoples.

Table 1.1 Population and Territory of Mountain Ok Peoples

People (Status and Zone)	Population[a]	Territory[b]	Density (km²)	Altitude[c] (meters)
Highland core				(1500–3000)
Ifitaman Telefolmin	1400	400	3.5	
Falamin	1000	250	4.0	1450
Ulapmin	350	230	2.9	1450
Tifalmin	650	240	2.7	1450
Oksapmin	6000	1000	6.0	1450
Bimin–Kuskusmin	1000	250	4.0	1750
Ngalumin/Sibilmin	10–15000	2600	3.8–5.8	1750 1450
Mid–altitude Fringe				(500–3000)
Atbalmin	2400	147	1.6	800–1600
Eliptaman Telefolmin	2100	930	2.3	1450
Fegolmin	1900	990	1.9	1450
Kamfegolmin	75	100	0.8	1450
Baktamanmin	200	207	0.9	1000
Am Nakai Miyanmin	1100	1380	0.8	600–1200
Wopkaimin	700	810	0.9	1450
Kauwolmin	600	400	1.5	1450
Angkeiakmin	600	860	0.7	1150
Kwermin	300	200	1.5	800–1400
Augobmin	?	200		?
Dulanmin	300	300	1.0	900
Seltamanmin	200	200	1.0	900
Lowland Fringe				(200–600)
Sa Nakai Miyanmin	500	1200	0.4	200–600
Ninataman Telefolmin	200	400	0.5	600
Sisimin (Hewa)	350	1000	0.3	600

[a]1980 Census of Papua New Guinea (except for Ngalum, for which see Power 1964).
[b]Planimeter measurements of Figure 1.2; approximations only.
[c]Mean altitude of settlements and gardens within territorial range.

As Mid–altitude fringe peoples the Wopkaimin are 'in between' in relation to extensive trade networks (Hughes 1977) because they are intermediate participants linking the Lowland Ningerum with the Highland

6

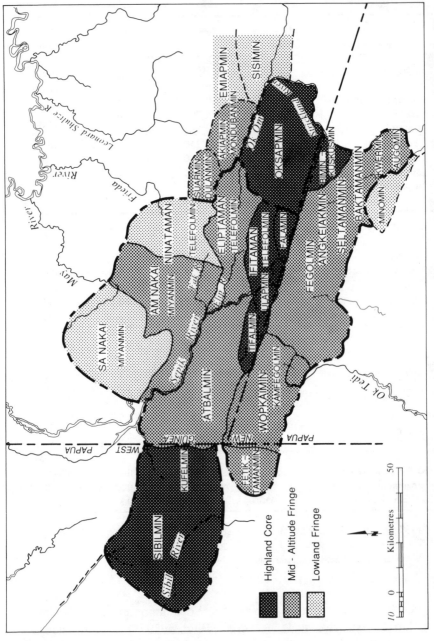

FIGURE 1.2 Core and fringe status of the Highland, Mid-altitude and Lowland Zones of the Mountain Ok.

Tifalmin. As middlemen they trafficked in prestige items such as plumes, capital goods such as stone tools and consumables such as tobacco.

Wopkaimin, and all Mountain Ok group designations commonly have a *min* suffix, meaning "people". Together the five contiguous Wopkaimin parishes consider themselves a common min people. The Fetiktaman, Beinglim, Kavorbang, Iralim and Migalsim parishes (Figure 1.3) are territorial and social groupings which have claims on and ultimate rights to use named and delimited hamlet, garden and rain forest resources. Thus, the parish is recognized as a clearly bounded, territorially discrete unit.

The Wopkaimin as a people are linked through the male Afek cult and their main temple, the *Futmanam*, is located in Bultem. Bultem is the most important hamlet of Iralim parish. The Kam Basin is the center of the Iralim parish and it is considered the heart of the Wopkaimin homeland (Figure 1.4).

Doing Research with the Wopkaimin

Fieldwork in the 1970s

In the 1970s my fieldwork spanned a total of 16 months that included one month in 1973, seven months in 1974, five months in 1975, one month in 1977 and two months in 1978. Craig (1967), Barth (1971) and William Clarke (pers com) observed that Bultem was the largest Wopkaimin settlement and noted that their most important cult house was permanently located there. After a week's reconnaissance, I discovered that the Bultem ritual center was not currently occupied, but I was invited to settle elsewhere in the Kam Basin. My house turned out to be the first one erected in Moiyokabip, a hamlet that grew to seven houses and was my home between 1973–1974 (Figure 1.4). The Wopkaimin regularly shift hamlets and I had another house built in Bakonabip where I lived between 1975 and 1978 (Figure 1.4).

From my base of operations in the Kam Basin, I primarily worked alone. However, intensive animal collection and specimen preparation took place in March 1974 when I worked in the field with the zoologist James Menzies and intensive plant collection and specimen preparation took place in February 1975 when I worked with the botanist David Frodin. I had returned to the University of Queensland when a team from the PNG Institute of Medical Research (IMR) conducted a health survey

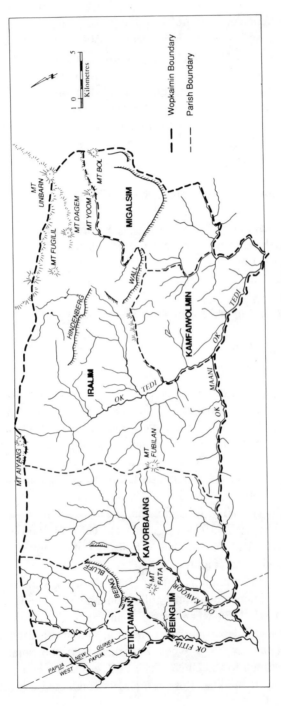

FIGURE 1.3 Wopkaimin Parishes.

9

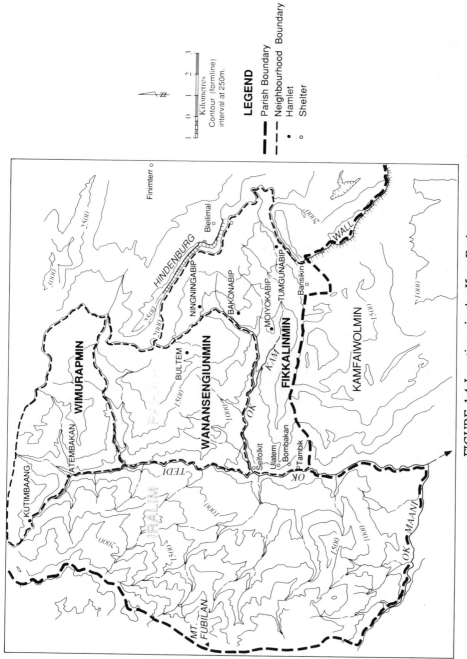

FIGURE 1.4 Locations in the Kam Basin.

LEGEND

Parish Boundary
Neighbourhood Boundary
• Hamlet
○ Shelter

Kilometres
0 1 2 3
Contour (formline) interval at 250m.

with the Wopkaimin in October 1975. On one three-week walkabout I familiarized myself with the greater Mountain Ok region and its peoples and met fellow anthropologists Dan Jorgensen (1981a), who was living with the Telefolmin, and Barbara Jones (1980), who was living with the Fegolmin.

I was a participant observer and also used unstructured interviews to fill general ethnographic notebooks. It was necessary to gain a general understanding of Wopkaimin social life before I could concern myself with measuring the appropriation of domesticated and non-domesticated resources and the temporal and spatial organization of subsistence activities. My study involved mapping hamlets, gardens and other resource zones and taking daily records of hamlet residents and food returns. Production, distribution and consumption in their kinship mode of production was measured in terms of energy expenditure and nutritional return for various activities and localities in reference to food species, resource zone, social group and type of resource.

Human behavior is a fundamental variable in the ethnographic analysis of subsistence ecology. It is difficult to provide the same data as ecologists contribute to the study of non-human ecosystems because of the importance of human culture and action, the limitation of time and resources and ethnographer competency in related fields of zoology, botany, nutrition and medicine. My use of technical field manuals and collaborative fieldwork was, I felt, a successful interdisciplinary fieldwork experience. As a fieldworker I was compelled to recognize things and images of things perceived by the Wopkaimin. Ecosystem perception is part of the cultural reason people behave in the way they do (Ellen 1982:209). Ethnobiology not only structures people's awareness of the environment but their utilization of the environment as well. Cognized and operationalized models, the interrelationship between matter and energy flows and information flows, are necessary to the ethnographic analysis of subsistence ecology. It allows the researcher to focus attention on the area where the unintentional rationality of the system articulates with the rationality of the producer (Godelier 1972:10–13).

Fieldwork in the 1980s

In the 1980s I had a total of 12 months' fieldwork that consisted of two months in 1980, four months in 1981, two months in 1982 and four months in 1985. I returned at the end of 1980 with a copy of my completed Ph.D. thesis (1979) and presented it to Bini Abifigoim, who was my principal research consultant and one of the few literate Wopkaimin men at that time. The Wopkaimin were expanding sago groves and hunting shelters at Finalbin and Woktemwanin along the Ok Tedi River into hamlets because it was rumored that PNG would soon permit the Ok Tedi mining project to begin on Mt Fubilan. In the Kam Basin most of the Wopkaimin were residing in Tumgunabip rather than Bakonabip and Bultem still remained unoccupied.

I was in Port Moresby when PNG and Ok Tedi Mining Limited (OTML) signed the contract in February 1981 to start gold mining at Ok Tedi. The Department of Minerals and Energy was distributing *The Impact of the Ok Tedi Project*, a consultants' report from Jackson *et al.* (1980). The negotiated agreement was for PNG to meet the cost of consultants to prepare the socioeconomic (Jackson *et al.* 1980) and cultural (Barth and Wikan 1983) impact reports, whereas OTML was to meet the cost of an Environmental Impact Statement (EIS). I was a professional EIS consultant through Natural Systems Research Ltd (NSR) from June to July 1981 and conducted interdisciplinary fieldwork with terrestrial and aquatic ecologists and an epidemiologist and we later produced several reports for the Ok Tedi EIS (Frodin and Hyndman 1982; Hyndman 1982b; Pernetta and Hyndman 1982).

In early 1982 I returned with Bill Anderson, an epidemiologist from IMR, for fieldwork in collaboration with the Ok Tedi Health and Nutrition Project under the direction of Professor John Lourie of the University of Papua New Guinea Medical School. Our hamlet survey indicated that over 40 percent of the Wopkaimin had migrated to Finalbin and Woktemwanin, which had grown into roadside villages on the Tabubil–Mt Fubilan access road. I was unable to return to the field again until 1985 when I had sufficiently recuperated from leg, foot and back injuries as the result of a motorcycle accident in late 1982 (Hyndman 1985). When I finally returned in early 1985 with the zoologist James Menzies, we encountered only 12 Wopkaimin still living in the Kam Basin. However, on my last research visit late in 1985 many of the Wopkaimin were beginning to decentralize out of their roadside villages to Bombakan, a new hamlet they were constructing in their Kam Basin homeland.

From Subsistence Ecology to Political Ecology

The historical development of human ecology has already been well summarized by Anderson (1973), Grossman (1977) and Ellen (1982). The ethnographic analysis of subsistence ecology is particularly concerned with subsistence–oriented indigenous peoples and comprehends people and environment as parts of a single system. The ecosystem becomes the primary unit of study and the researcher's "concern shifts from which part most influences the other to the structure of the whole system and how it operates and changes" (Clarke 1971:200). Nietschmann (1970:85) comprehensively defines a subsistence system as:

> the complex of functionally related resources and activities through which a group secures food for their own needs and by their own efforts, usually by the direct exploitation of their environment. The primary objective is food, whether it is from agriculture, horticulture, silviculture, hunting, fishing, gathering, animal husbandry, or any combination thereof. Production, distribution, and consumption of foodstuffs is generally performed by discrete social units, such as households or kin groups, with little circulation of labor or produce outside the social network.

The study of subsistence ecology in PNG has long attracted the attention of anthropologists and geographers, first in the Sepik (Lea 1964) and then in the Highlands (Bowers 1968; Brookfield and Brown 1963; Waddell 1972). Attention then focused on the Mid–altitude fringe, the rugged mountainous interior between Lowland and Highland New Guinea (Rappaport 1968; Townsend 1969; Clarke 1971; Buchbinder 1973; Dornstreich 1973; Hyndman 1979; Morren 1974). Peoples there, like the Wopkaimin, are hunter–horticulturalists whose staple food is *Colocasia* taro.

Rappaport's (1968) ecological analysis of the *kaiko* ritual of the Mid–altitude fringe Tsembaga Maring has become a classic in anthropology. His homeostatic explanation of the cultural regulation of environmental relationships attracted considerable criticism (Clarke 1971; Friedman 1975; McArthur 1977; Vayda and McCay 1977) and his defense (1984:299–479), unfortunately, has not adequately addressed the problems of calorific reductionism and neo–functionalism. Nonetheless, Rappaport inspired many ethnographies that operationalized cultural and biophysical interrelationships and gave a new dimension and sophistication to the analysis of subsistence ecology in PNG.

Nietschmann utilized subsistence ecology to study the complex and diversified subsistence system of the Miskito Indians on the Caribbean coast of Nicaragua (1973) and effectively extended the approach to analyze the socio–ecological impact of green turtles becoming a commodity to sell rather than a resource to share (1974). Later a "political ecology of fisheries" was successfully used by Nietschmann (1987a:8) to examine how Third and Fourth World peoples in the Pacific socio-ecologically responded to the tuna conflict incorporating them into the world capitalist system. Pacific Rim industrialized states, having worn out their continental shelf fisheries, ventured into the Pacific to catch migratory tuna without recognizing the 200-mile Exclusive Economic Zones (EEZ) of Pacific island states. Tradition of ownership of marine space and species provided the cultural and historic base for the EEZ claims in the Pacific and eventually forced a U.S. treaty recognizing that the fish and the fishing grounds belonged to the islanders.

Political ecology demonstrates the importance of evaluating ecological change in social terms and criticizes political economy for failing to take into account ecological processes underlying production. Schmink and Wood (1987:40) forwarded a "political ecology" of development to elucidate the Amazon case:

> Distinct forms of sociopolitical organization are based on different production principles. For our purposes two types are of special importance: those based on subsistence, or simple reproduction, and those based on expanded production and private accumulation. The relevance to political ecology stems from the markedly different implications the two forms of organization have in terms of human appropriation of the natural environment.

Blaikie and Brookfield (1987:17) take political ecology to combine the concerns of ecology and a broadly defined political economy and define "regional political ecology" as encompassing "interactive effects, the contribution of different geographical scales and hierarchies of socioeconomic organizations (e.g. person, household, village, region, state, world) and the contradictions between social and environmental changes through time."

Sheridan's (1988) ethnography of a peasant community in northwestern Mexico pioneers a political ecology perspective. Cucurpe, according to the Opata Indians, is the place 'where the dove calls'; the floodplain of the Rio San Miguel in northern Sonora, Mexico. However, Cucurpeno peasants, not Indians, now live where the dove calls. Sheridan sketches a 300-year frontier history where ethnic and geographical boundaries were very fluid. On the resource frontier a closed indigenous community ceased to exist by the 18th century but the Cucurpenos have held on to some of their corporate grazing lands in competition with miners and private ranchers up until the present time.

Sheridan's ethnography of contemporary Cucurpeno resource control takes political ecology to combine the approaches of political economy, which places Cucurpe in the modern world system, and cultural ecology, which examines Cucurpeno adaptation to environmental and demographic factors. The book provides a creative dialectic between local and external forces and brings forth the tensions between the household and the community as decision–making units, and that between the Cucurpenos and the state.

Adaptation to local environment determines corporate control of scarce resources more directly than the actions of external elites. The household is the basic unit of production, consumption and resource control; the corporate community only emerges in the control of certain resources. Cucurpenos are a community of interest, not of place. Sheridan's ethnography demonstrates that the peasant mode of production is characterized above all by the existence of the household as the fundamental unit of both production and consumption. Rangeland and irrigation water are beyond the control of fiercely economic independent households to control on their own, so corporate tenure becomes a limited adaptation to economic need.

Kinship and Capitalist Modes of Production

Political ecology conceptualizes the relationship between the Wopkaimin and mining in terms of a struggle between different modes of production, a kin–ordered subsistence–oriented mode of production and a capitalist mode of production. The goal of capitalist production is realization of a surplus, whereas the goal of kinship production is subsistence. Surplus realized in a kinship mode of production is appropriated for internal reciprocal exchange and ritual. According to Wolf (1982:91), relations of kinship can be seen as a means of committing social labor to the transformation of nature through appeals of filiation, marriage, consanguinity and affinity. Hence, we can speak of kin–ordered and subsistence–oriented indigenous people like the Wopkaimin as having a kinship mode of production.

The concept of subsistence production follows Godelier's (1979:17) distinction between a mode of subsistence and a mode of production. A mode of subsistence is the appropriation of natural and human–altered resources by a particular people in a specific historical period. A mode of production is characterized by social relations which determine the forms of access to resources and means of production, organizes labor processes and determines distribution and consumption of the products of social labor. Subsistence ecology, divorced as it was from the context of mode of production, was conceptually ahistorical. Subsistence ecology concentrated on the forces of production, the appropriation of resources in a specific historical period, and ignored social relations of production. Political ecology views Wopkaimin subsistence production as both mode of subsistence and mode of production, a totality, a kinship mode of production.

The kinship mode of production is a conceptual tool for understanding specific human relationships, it is not a stage of cultural or mode of production evolution. The kinship mode of production is non–capitalist rather than pre–capitalist. The Wopkaimin are not potential capitalists waiting for their mode of production to evolve from 'primitive communism' to capitalism so they can have a 'class struggle'. However, the expansion of capitalism with colonialism and neo–colonialism subordinates, utilizes and in some cases replaces other modes of production. Political ecology conceptualizes the relationship between indigenous peoples and the invading world capitalist system as a conflict between subsistence production for simple reproduction (kinship mode of production) and extended production for private accumulation (capitalist mode of production). The relationship between the Wopkaimin and mining, therefore has been a conflict between kinship and capitalist modes of production.

The expansion of mining meant that Wopkaimin lands and resources became commodities to be appropriated and exploited in capitalist production. Exchanges among systems differing in complexity of organization of the flow of material, information and energy is usually from the less highly organized to the more highly organized. On the Ok Tedi mining frontier it is the ecological equivalent of the rich get richer argument. Competition between capitalist modes of production (large systems) and kinship modes of production (small systems) has meant cultural and ecological disruption for the latter. The large system is so immensely different in scale and technology from the small system that the self–sufficient, internally regulated Wopkaimin subsistence system changed into a dependent, externally regulated economy with a degraded environment and culture.

Four Worlds of Experience and Action

As the mining resource frontier aggressively expands into Melanesia, it creates a clash of kinship and capitalist modes of production between nations and states. Models for Three Worlds (Worsley 1984) accept legitimacy of the state as the basic unit of analysis, ignoring the fact that there are many more nation peoples in the world than there are states which encapsulate them. As a result of indigenous people's struggles against state domination and incorporation into the world capitalist system, a Fourth World has emerged within the states of the First, Second and Third Worlds. An acknowledgment of the Fourth World is essential to a political ecology analysis of the relationship between indigenous peoples and extractive mineral development in New Guinea.

When First Nation peoples of North America attended the historic United Nations Environmental Conference in Sweden in 1972 they found they networked better with the Saami, Bretons and Basques, rather than the Third World delegates, and together they coined the term Fourth World for the indigenous nations of the world who are encapsulated within states (Weyler 1984). According to George Manuel, former president of the National Indian Brotherhood of Canada and the World Council of Indigenous Peoples, the Fourth World is "peoples who have special non-technical, non-modern exploitative relations to the lands which they still inhabit and who are disenfranchised by the nations within which they live" (Manuel and Posluns 1974). Indigenous peoples themselves are popularizing the term Fourth World and it is still being circulated for validation.

As a consequence of encapsulation, nations are self-conscious indigenous peoples with a specific homeland and tradition of place (Connor 1978). The Fourth World does not consist of minorities or ethnic groups but of nation peoples, which is an ideologically different proposition, with different levels of identity and political consciousness. The distinction is well summarized by McCall (1980:542):

A minority is a group seen by its members (or oppressors) as being part of the political subdivision that is the state, whilst an ethnic group sees itself in terms of cohesive, even blood-marked relatedness. The next stage of political (and ideological) consciousness is achieved when the same group begins to negotiate for recognition as a nation--a nation, it should be added, seeking to claim a contiguous territory.

Although media and academia regularly interchange state, nation and nation–state, the Fourth World sees fundamental distinctions between nations and states. Nations are geographically bounded territories of a common people, whereas states are centralized political systems, recognized by other states, that use civilian and military bureaucracy to enforce one set of institutions, laws and sometimes language and religion within its claimed boundaries (Nietschmann 1987b). Fourth World peoples derive their distinctive identity in large part from their different relations to land and productive processes, which "involves land and labour (the Fourth World), primary production in the form of farm or mineral wealth (the Third World), manufacturing industry (the Second World), and expertise (the First World)" (McCall 1980:545). Moreover, the Fourth World sees themselves as nation peoples on the basis of identity, ancestry, history, culture, institutions, territory, language, ideology and often religion. The Fourth World comprises nation peoples existing beneath the imposition of some 190 currently recognized states.

Fourth World reality, then, stems from consciousness of its peoples. It is not circumstances of birth alone but also what political action indigenous peoples take about it that creates the Fourth World. Self–determination is the power of the Fourth World to define themselves as indigenous peoples (Weaver 1984). Indigenous peoples and their nations are locked into states (Berger 1985) and the essence of the Fourth World is its encapsulating relationship within the First, Second and Third Worlds (Paine 1985). Most of the Fourth World have no wish to assimilate, refuse to be proletarianized and have a fierce desire to retain their identity, culture and land. Indigenous peoples assert persistent cultural identity systems in opposition to states through the process of shared land, language and identity symbols (Spicer 1971). In contrasting cultural environments, Fourth World nations regularly outlive states and their assimilation pressures, develop well–defined symbols, do not politically control other peoples and do not organize as a state (Spicer 1971).

There is no atlas for indigenous peoples homelands but Nietschmann (1987b) estimates there are 3,000–5,000 Fourth World nations who make up most of the world's distinct peoples and 50 percent of the land area. Bodley (1988) calculates that over 200 million indigenous peoples continue to exert a degree of homeland autonomy within states. Their distribution is global, which according to Burger (1987), consists of 2.5 million in North America, 25–30 million in Central and South America, 60,000 in Scandinavia, 51 million in India, 67 million in China,

28 million in the USSR, 11 million in Burma, 500,000 in Thailand, 6.5 million in the Philippines, 240,000 in New Zealand, 250,000 in Australia and at least 500,000 elsewhere in the Pacific.

Four Worlds of experience and action (McCall 1980) characterize the regional political ecology of mining in New Guinea. Melanesian nation peoples are victims of classic colonialism in Kanaky, which the French call their department of New Caledonia, internal colonialism in PNG and Third World recolonization in West Papua, which the Indonesians call their province of Irian Jaya. After invading the Western half of New Guinea, Indonesia created a mythical people, the Irianese, to obscure and outlaw Melanesian identity and their armed struggle for self-determination. However, Melanesian nations there identify as West Papuans and refer to their territory as West Papua. In New Guinea, a Fourth World perspective taken in front of the bulldozer blade from the forest looking out examines Melanesia nationalism and the incorporation of indigenous nations into the modern world system.

Political Ecology of the Wopkaimin

Indigenous peoples in Lowland and Highland PNG became incorporated into the world capitalist system earlier than those living in the Mid-altitude fringe. Boyd (1975) was the first to apply subsistence ecology to the analysis of socio-ecological change due to coffee cash cropping in the Highlands. Informed by Nietschmann's work, Grossman (1981) developed a "cultural ecology of economic development" to study the impact of cattle and coffee production on subsistence in the PNG Highlands. Grossman (1984) could more appropriately have characterized the Kapanara villagers as having a kinship, rather than a peasant mode of production (Gregory 1982; Sexton 1986), but his cultural ecology of economic development importantly brought together subsistence ecology and political economy in the ethnographic study of resource control in PNG.

The political ecology of the Wopkaimin will account for the ecological basis of their production and the present competition on the Wopkaimin resource frontier as a conflict between kinship and capitalist modes of production and as a struggle between two incompatible social systems, nations and states. Sheridan's (1988) ethnography was a political ecology of a peasant mode of production and resource control, whereas this ethnography is a political ecology of a kinship mode of production and resource control.

Following Godoy (1985), the political ecology of the Wopkaimin and the Ok Tedi mining project is divided into an economic base and a derivative sociopolitical and ideological superstructure. In terms of the economic base, mining development has been achieved by the invasion and annexation of indigenous peoples lands and resources. Although the elite sector of PNG benefits from the appropriation and exploitation of indigenous lands and resources, it is the transnationals like OTML who really profit. In terms of the derivative sociopolitical superstructure, mining requirements for capital, labor and food for workers as well as the physical output of the operation integrates surrounding regions into a single ecological/economic sphere (Godoy 1985:207). Finally, the superstructure of ideology constitutes the main Wopkaimin protest response to mining.

2

Ancestral Rain Forests: The Ethno-Ecological Basis of Production

The High Rainfall Zone of the Southern Mid-Altitude Fringe

The Ok Tedi River, the major western tributary of the Fly River drainage system, rises at 2900 m in the Star Mountains in the center of the island of New Guinea, flows through the rugged homeland of the Wopkaimin and ultimately meets the Fly River at 70 m at the d'Albertis Junction. The Ok Tedi headwaters are situated within the high rainfall regime of the southern Mid-altitude fringe (Figure 2.1). The Kam Basin ancestral homeland of the Wopkaimin commences at the Ok Tedi and Ok Kam junction at 600 m and rises to over 2200 m at the summit of the Hindenburg Wall (Figure 1.4). Above 2200 m, the Hindenburg Plateau extends northward to the slopes of the Bahrman Mountains.

One of the few regional ecological studies available for montane New Guinea is Gressitt and Nadkarni (1978) on Mount Kaindi near Wau which has a more seasonal, drier climate. There is no biogeographical literature for the southern Mid-altitude fringe west of Ok Tedi. Reports are available for Mt Sisa (Dwyer 1982) and Mt Karamui (Hide, Pernetta and Senabe 1984) to the east of Ok Tedi, but they are located on the northern edge of the zone. Hyndman and Menzies (1990) provide a comprehensive regional ecological analysis for the distinctive ecosystem of the upper Ok Tedi.

Continuously heavy rainfall characterizes the region (Brookfield and Hart 1971), with some of the highest rainfall recorded in New Guinea (McAlpine, Kieg and Falls 1983). Seasonal distribution of rainfall is low

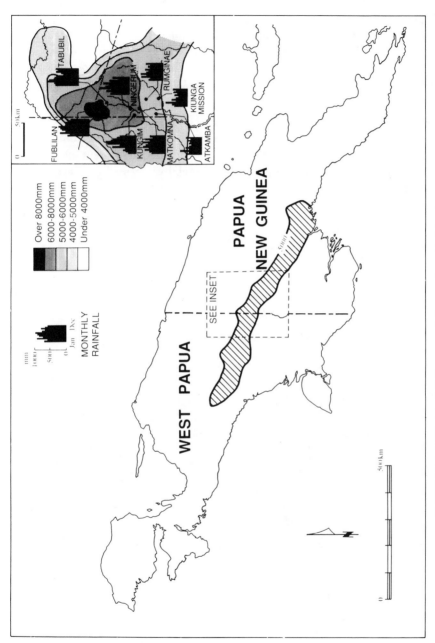

FIGURE 2.1 High rainfall zone of the southern Mid–altitude fringe.

with a single maximum (December–March) and minimum (May–August). From records taken in 1975, Tabubil (650 m) averages 7919 mm, Bakonabip (1400 m) 7190 mm and Mt. Fubilan (2200 m) 9104 mm of annual rainfall. The spread of average monthly temperatures in Tabubil is slight, with a high in April of 24.6° C and a low in August of 22.2° C and temperatures drop 1° C for every 200 m increase in elevation.

Characteristic vegetation in the Wopkaimin homeland is rain forest, interrupted by only occasional gardens. Hyndman and Menzies (1990) made botanical surveys in each distinctive floristic zone and compiled a complete listing of all plants collected and identified. Different mammals, birds, reptiles, amphibians and fish, especially "game" species, were collected with the Wopkaimin and Hyndman and Menzies (1990) provide a complete listing of all vertebrates collected and identified.

PLATE 2.1 Kam Basin, homeland of the Wopkaimin (photo courtesy of the author).

The Kam Basin Homeland: A Sense of Place

The Wopkaimin make a tripartite division of their homeland into an inner circle of hamlets (*abip*), bordered by gardens (*yon*) and encircled by rain forests (*sak*) (Figure 2.2). It is necessary to be "inside" a place to fully grasp it, which fundamentally contrasts the insiders' way of experiencing place and the outsiders' way of conventionally describing them (Buttimer 1980). As Cosgrove (1978:66) points out, "human ideas mould the landscape, human intentions create and mould places, but our own experience of space and place itself moulds human ideas." Space is abstract, but place is the past and present (Tuan 1975). The result of culture and life in society is shared images and experiences of place and landscape (Cosgrove 1978). It is therefore culture, and not landscape and topography alone that determines spatial limits. Ideology of spatial relations serves to organize sociopolitical action and cultural forms (Thornton 1980).

Thornton (1980) introduced the term "topology" for the structure of differentiation that must be imposed upon space before it can represent anything. The cultural creation of place requires appropriating landforms into a cultural frame by attributing to them specific values, differentiating space symbolically (topology) and making territory (Thornton 1980). Places achieve identity and meaning through human intention towards them and the relationships between those intentions and the physical setting and activities within it (Cosgrove 1978).

Throughout the New Guinea Mid–altitude fringe and Highlands, men retain game animal bones for a variety of technological, ornamental, decorative and ritual purposes (Bulmer 1976). Mountain Ok hunters regularly place game animal bones on display on the rear wall of men's houses (Barth 1975; Jorgensen 1981a; Pernetta and Hyndman 1982; Wheatcroft 1975). Such bone displays are commonly referred to as 'trophy collections' (Bulmer 1976) or 'trophy arrays' (Craig 1988). Some of the Wopkaimin moved residence within the Kam Basin from Moiyokabip to Bakonabip (Figure 1.4) in 1975 and they constructed a new men's house. Meat from animals sacrificed to the ancestors in the men's house went into hamlet sharing (*abipkagup*) and selected bones over the next ten years were used to gradually transform the rear wall of the men's house into an impressive relic and trophy array (Figure 2.3). Hunting and provisioning of meat is pre–eminent in men's lives and trophy and relic

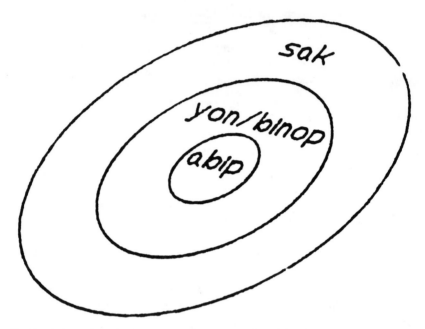

FIGURE 2.2 Wopkaimin construction of a cultural landscape.

FIGURE 2.3 Bakonabip men's house trophy array in 1985.

arrays are accumulated in the men's house as tangible expressions of success in hamlet sharing and sacrifice to the ancestors.

Lived place and time require home and a horizon of reach outward from the home (Buttimer 1980). Integration between the men's house dwelling and reaching out through hunting, sharing and sacrificing creates a Wopkaimin cultural expression of place. Culture informs the perception they have of place and the mental maps they form from filtered information flow. The perceived environment is always and wholly a cultural artifact (Brookfield 1969). By collecting, organizing, storing, recalling and manipulating trophy array information, the Wopkaimin transform environmental complexity into a single unified sense of place.

Mental maps (Gould and White 1974) are a product, an organized representation "that stands for the environment, that portrays it, that is both a likeness and a simplified model, something that is, above all, a mental image" (Downs and Stea 1977). Trophy arrays are a mode of representation of Wopkaimin mental maps and they are an important form of experience in providing the basis of perception (see Hyndman 1991a).

Trophy arrays act as mental map triggers to recall the characteristics of place. They act as ethnobiological models of animal resources in relation to human settlement and gardens (see Craig 1988). It takes many years to complete a trophy array, maintenance is often sporadic and identity of trophies is often masked by heavy coats of sooted cobwebs. Over a ten-year period, bones were grouped together in the Bakonabip trophy array (Figure 2.3) on the basis of shared characteristics. They are identity categories for a range of places and equivalence categories for the steep biotope gradient of the ancestral rain forests.

The Wopkaimin tripartite mental map is culturally imposed on the landscape (Figure 2.4). Ancestral relics (*manamem*) are stored in string bags centrally at eye level on the trophy array. They belong to the *abip* realm in the relatively long–term hamlet sites placed centrally in the homeland. Domestic pigs are fostered to select families residing a short distance from hamlets and mandibles from these animals are displayed beneath the ancestral relics. They are always slaughtered and butchered in the hamlet and sacrificed to the ancestors for continued success in pig raising. Wild pig bones are placed lower than domestic ones; they come from *gipsak*, the lowest zone of rain forest encircling the inner garden and hamlet zones. Wild boars are necessary for impregnating domestic sows and they threaten gardens. Marsupial mandibles are displayed highest off the floor, they primarily come from the mid to highest rain forests.

26

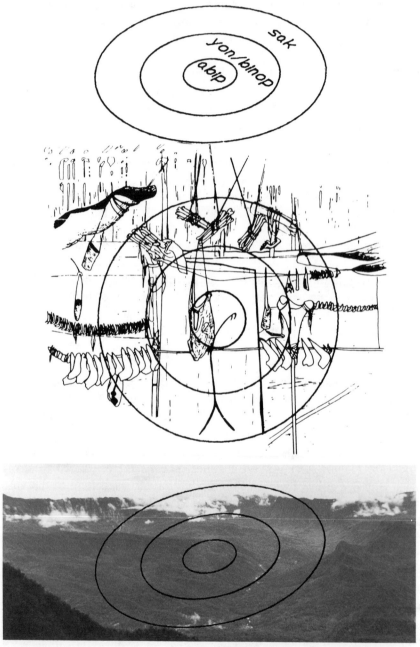

FIGURE 2.4 Wopkaimin cultural landscape imposed on the Kam Basin.

Cassowary pelvis and thigh bones are placed in association with the wild pigs and marsupials representing the co-existence of these animals in the outer rain forests.

Trophy arrays incorporate knowledge of the complex inter-relationships between place and time. They serve as a basis for interpretation and prediction because the kind of information they transmit is "cyclical, leading to a steady state in the perceived environment and resources sub-system" (Brookfield 1969:65). Trophy arrays are mental maps to carry the past forward as a way to interpret present conditions. With them the Wopkaimin are able to look ahead in both space and time to cope with what is likely to happen where. By generating reasonable expectations that relate time to space, they make appropriate decisions about resource use. Resources of a place are an evaluation of the perceived environment at a particular time (Brookfield 1969) and trophy arrays produce a mental map of place by using the stock of information available. Resource use of the past is displayed in the present to solve future problems.

Wopkaimin kinship relations of production are based on living with and appropriating the living resources of their 1000 km^2 of ancestral rain forests. The most basic discontinuities they recognize in nature are between hamlet (*abip*), gardens and secondary regrowth (*yon* and *binop*) and rain forest (*sak*). They also divide their homeland into four ecological zones according to biological community and cultural activity, which they term (1) *gip*, (2) *fakkam*, (3) *ilein*, and (4) *atinaang*. These zones, according to Paijmans (1976) floristic designation, correspond to (1) Foothill Rain Forest from 500 to 1,000 m, (2) Lower Montane Rain Forest from 1000 to 1800 m, (3) low altitude Midmontane Rain Forest from 1800 to 2200 m, and (4) Midmontane Rain Forest from 2200 to 3000 m (Figure 2.5). These prevailing divisions of nature based on altitude and biota are made by other Mountain Ok peoples as well (Barth 1975:29).

Cultural Appropriation of Ancestral Rain Forests

The Wopkaimin group rain forest (*sak*) and domesticated plants into the following mutually exclusive life-forms: trees and large epiphytes (*ass*); shrubs and small epiphytes (*assmankatep*); climbers and lianas (*soklein*) and herbs (*al*). In addition to these named life-form groupings, a rather large number of intermediate ethnobotanical ranks are linguistically

28

unnamed, though they are dealt with regularly and are unambiguously recognized. These unnamed intermediate rank groups include closely related generics like palms, gingers and pandans.

As with plants, the Wopkaimin group animals (Table 2.1) as a means of storing information and simplifying communication about nature (Hyndman 1984a). Frog and Lizard are encoded on criteria of distinctiveness and not those of residualness, nor has binary opposition played any recognizable part in the encoding process. Data from other New Guinea peoples (Dwyer and Hyndman 1983) suggest Frog may be regularly encoded this way. Thus the encoding sequence Brown (1979, 1981) has devised for zoological life–form taxa may not fully depict the situation for peoples in New Guinea.

The set of cultural rules, conventions and determinants encoded in Wopkaimin plant and animal life–forms transforms information about the environment into practices which effect ecological relations and production. They possess a folk model of the environment as well as for

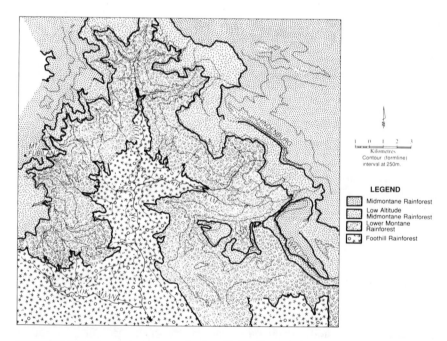

FIGURE 2.5 Vegetation zones in the Ok Tedi headwaters.

TABLE 2.1 Wopkaimin Animal Life–Forms and Their Appropriation

Life–form	Generics	Actor	Search and Kill Mode[a]
Awon 'birds, bats and sugar glider'	260	men women	A, S B, S
Nuk 'game mammals'	40	men women	A, B, C, S, T, A–d, B, S
Maian 'dogs'	2	men	B
Bia 'cassowaries'	2	men	A, B, C, S, T
Kong 'pigs'	2	men women	A, B, C, S, T Domestic pig custodians
Kul 'frogs'	54	women	S
Takam 'fish'	10	women	T
Atim 'lizards'	22	women	A, S
Feimkan 'snakes'	12	women	B

[a]Terminology from Bulmer (1968).

A	Ambush	C	Chase
A–d	Ambush–drive	S	Stalking
B	Besetting	T	Trapping

behavior directed towards the environment. Wopkaimin ethno–ecology determines the scale, intensity and frequency of appropriation of particular species and guides varying mixtures of ecologically–integrated, sustained–yield production activities that have had minimal, not negligible, impact on natural resources.

Food production in Wopkaimin kinship relations of production does not utilize all resources available. Like most rain forest peoples they approach their complex ecosystem through biotopes, because "sanctional behavior and breadth of perception reduce the utilization of natural resources to a small number of possible choices" (Nietschmann 1973:110). Living plant and animal resources are available to the Wopkaimin through numerous biotopes they perceive in their environment. Biotopes are not only etic descriptive categories utilized by human ecologists (Hardesty 1977:109, 111–112), among the Wopkaimin (Hyndman 1982a), and other indigenous peoples in New Guinea, they are common emic categories having cognitive and behavioral consequences (Bowers 1968; Clarke 1971; Dornstreich 1973). There is a very steep biotope gradient through the Wopkaimin ancestral rain forests (Figure 2.6). For a complete analysis with Wopkaimin and Western scientific names of the associated plant and animal resources see Hyndman (1982a).

Biotope 1, Ok Tedi River (Wok Teil)

The Ok Tedi River is a corruption of the Wopkaimin term *wok teil* but the former is now generally used. Fish are the important food source obtained from Biotope 1, the Ok Tedi River. Six species are taken by the Wopkaimin, the most important is the largest catfish (*dol*), which occurs at elevations of up to 1000 m until the Ok Tedi becomes too shallow and the current too rapid. The number and size of fish species are related to conditions in the Ok Tedi and its tributaries. Catfish are taken from deep pools when the river's flow and particulate load are at a minimum. Riverbank frogs and reptiles are additional resources.

Biotope 2, Sago Groves (Wom Yon)

The Wopkaimin plant small groves (*wom yon*) of 10 to 12 *sago* palms in the Foothill Rain Forest between 500 and 1000 m, which is the upper altitudinal distribution of sago in New Guinea. They distinguish nine varieties, a range similar to the ten recognized by the Sanio–Hiowe (Townsend 1969:19) elsewhere in the Mid–altitude fringe. Sago starch is the most important food resource, but breadfruit and fruit–bearing *Pandanus* are occasionally planted as well. Quantities of frogs and wood–boring larvae are also taken from the sago groves.

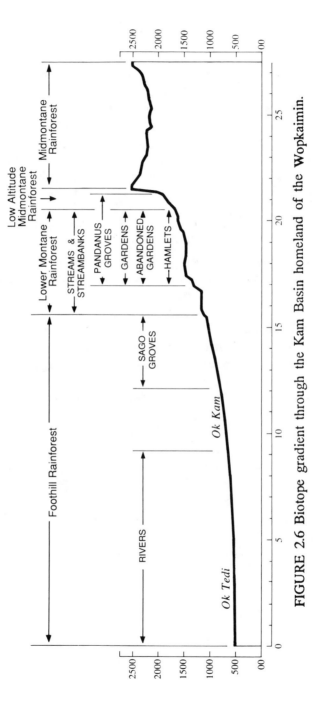

FIGURE 2.6 Biotope gradient through the Kam Basin homeland of the Wopkaimin.

Biotope 3, Foothill Rain Forest (Gip Sak)

Foothill Rain Forest (*gip sak*) is the most ecologically complex environmental zone within the Wopkaimin homeland. A significant number of food and raw material plants are found here. The larger game birds are numerous only in Lowland and Foothill Rain Forests in New Guinea (Bulmer 1968:305), but relatively smaller doves, honey-eaters, and lorikeets are more frequently taken. The Wopkaimin are skillful bird hunters, they do not range haphazardly in search of game birds but concentrate their efforts on certain feeding plants. By stalking between feeding plants and using decoy calls, a prospective ambush site is chosen. Combining stalking and ambush is a common bird-hunting strategy in the Mid-altitude fringe (Bulmer 1968:309; Majnep and Bulmer 1977:41-44).

Of the terrestrial fauna, only the cassowary and the wild pig grow as large as humans and are the only animals capable of maiming or killing a Wopkaimin hunter. Stalking, ambushing, trapping, besetting, and chasing are strategies used in hunting terrestrial game. Hunters use detailed knowledge of animal behavior to locate and constrain the animals' opportunity to escape, but frequently there is a chase after an escaped or wounded quarry, often with the aid of dogs. Wallabies, in particular, are often hunted by means of the ambush-drive.

Canopy layers of the Foothill Rain Forest are densely intertwined with epiphytes and lianas, which produce complex ecological niches for arboreal animals (Harrison 1962; Richards 1966). Successful arboreal game animal hunting requires expert skill in interpreting tracks, droppings, and food remnants and the use of stalking, ambush, besetting, and trapping. All this is a male activity, whereas females collect small mammals, frogs, reptiles, and insects. There is an important functional relationship between Biotopes 1, 2 and 3. Diversified hunting, fishing, and collecting activities are contingent upon processing sago, which provides the starch staple for sustained resource appropriation below 1000 m.

Biotope 4, Streams and Streambanks (Wok Katep)

The streams (*wok katep*) of the Kam Basin homeland of the Wopkaimin are an important resource for frogs and fish, especially the small Rough-Scaled Loters (*bom*). Food resources from the streams are exclusively appropriated by women. Fish and streambank frogs are typically collected on overnight trips. From their temporary shelters (*kulam*) women fish in the late afternoon by probing under sodden logs and boulders in shallow stream waters. After nightfall, torches of splintered *Pandanus* prop roots are lit and the streambanks are combed for frogs.

Biotope 5, Lower Montane Rain Forest (Fakkam Sak)

The Lower Montane Rain Forest (*fakkam sak*) is dominated by giant oaks (*Castanopsis acuminatissima*), the acorns are consumed raw or cooked and they may have been an important subsistence resource in preagricultural New Guinea (Bulmer and Bulmer 1964:147). Many other fruits, nuts, palms, lianas and gingers are seasonally great favorites. *Asplenium*, a spontaneously occurring epiphyte, is burned to produce an ash which is used as a salt, especially for pork. Bark raincloaks (*yuusuum*) are fashioned from fig trees and worn by women and girls. They are used as protection from heavy rains and they are regularly traded to the Tifalmin for tobacco.

Feral pigs and cassowaries only occasionally range into *fakkam sak*, the Lower Montane Rain Forest. Different arboreal possums occur in this biotope but the game mammal (*nuk*) most frequently taken by men in the Kam Basin is the cuscus possum *kitam* (*Phalanger sericeus*).

Biotope 6, Gardens (Yon)

Gardens (*yon*) are the most anthropogenically induced biotope in the Kam Basin. The Wopkaimin have taro (*yaman, Colocasia esculenta*), as their staple crop and it plays a very important role in the ritual life of all Mountain Ok peoples (Barth 1975; Morren 1986; Wheatcroft 1975). The Wopkaimin and other Mountain Ok of the Mid–altitude fringe practise a taro monoculture and sweet potato is absent or marginal (Morren and Hyndman 1987), while the Sibilmin (Reynders 1964), Oksapmin (Perey 1973) and Bimin (Bayliss–Smith 1985) in the Highland core separate sweet potato from taro gardens and sweet potato is the staple.

Garden plots under slash and mulch cultivation are not rapidly opened to sunlight. Women slash undergrowth and men cut away lianas, epiphytes and moss from the trees to a height of three meters. When a plot of approximately 800 m^2 has been cleared over a few mornings' work, women use dibble sticks to plant taro stalks and men start the process of tree defoliation by ringing or scorching. Aggregate gardens slowly expand to around two ha over several weeks of slashing, defoliating and planting. As the trees gradually die and lose their leaves

Plate 2.2 Wopkaimin taro garden in the Kam Basin (photo courtesy of the author).

the taro matures and forms an interlocking leaf canopy protecting the soil from direct sun and rain.

The Wopkaimin prefer aggregate to individual gardens, a pattern also followed by the Baktamanmin (Barth 1975:30). In the Kam Basin between 1974 and 1975, approximately 7.5 ha were under cultivation; 88 percent of which was represented by three aggregate gardens located on the Ok Talel, Ok Utamkan and the Ok Kam (Figure 2.7). Land under cultivation averages 0.11 ha per person, which falls within the 0.08–0.12 ha per person average for Melanesian rain forest peoples (Barrau 1958:25). This contrasts with the Highland core, where Bimin mixed sweet potato–taro gardens average 0.056 ha per person (Bayliss–Smith 1985:112).

Taro occupies about 75 percent of garden space and is planted about 1.5 m apart to equal about 6700 per ha. Gardens are not fenced as feral pigs are primarily confined to the Foothill Rain Forest. Men and women weed the garden together about four months after the taro has sprouted. Cucumbers are first harvested at this time and leafy greens follow as the garden is opened to sunlight. After 12 months *taro* becomes available and is harvested over the next six months. Bananas and sugarcane ripen during the last of 18–24 month productive life of the garden.

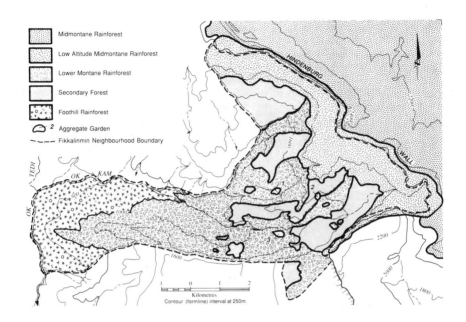

Midmontane Rainforest

Low Altitude Midmontane Rainforest

Lower Montane Rainforest

Secondary Forest

Foothill Rainforest

2 **Aggregate Garden**

Fikkalinmin Neighbourhood Boundary

FIGURE 2.7 Gardens and vegetation zones in the Kam Basin, 1975.

Garden production is approximately 81 percent from taro and, in descending order of importance, leafy greens (7 percent), pumpkin and cucurbit (3 percent each), sago and other tubers (2 percent each) and bananas and sugar cane (1 percent each). The Wopkaimin high flexibility–low risk taro monoculture is buffered by heavy rainfall, a low–seasonality climate and the presence and exploitation of a wide variety of alternative wild and domesticated foods.

Biotope 7, Hamlets in Use (Abip)

Wopkaimin hamlets (*abip*) contain on average some 40 residents, but people are continually dispersing to other living sites, such as frog–collecting shelters (*kulam*), and garden, hunting, fishing, and sago–processing shelters (*nukam*).

Hamlets represent substantial time investments, since each house requires between 600 and 900 work–hours to build (Morren 1974:151–

52). Stilts, posts, ridgepole and rafters are constructed from a variety of hardwood trees. *Pandanus galorei* from Biotope 5 is essential to house construction; prop roots are split as roof lathing, wider lathes are tied with cordage to support poles for walls and floors and walls are lined in the flattened outer rind. Thatching is always in fronds carried in from the sago groves. Houses have floor–level clay hearths that are suspended in a cradle framework below the floor. Firewood is dried in storage racks above the hearth. Little cooking is done outdoors because of the heavy rain. At dawn and dusk taro is baked in the suspended hearths and smoke floats through the glistening pitch black thatching to imperceptibly merge into thick layers of low–hanging stratus cloud.

The Wopkaimin devote considerable attention to dooryard plantings as a source of emergency rations. Food crops are never fenced because domestic pigs are not raised in the hamlets but they are butchered, cooked, and consumed there. The common practice among the Mountain Ok is to foster their pigs communally in bush houses, with the woman who fosters the pig providing all its food and care (Barth 1975:35). In the Kam Basin the Wopkaimin outnumber their pigs by 2:1.

Dogs are owned by, and constantly associated with, men in the hamlets. Some are so small, scruffy, emaciated and weak that they serve more as pets than as economic assets, but a few are outstanding hunting dogs. Since Mountain Ok dogs breed in captivity and give birth in the presence of their owners (Barth 1975:37), it is common for a half–starved mother to bring prey back to her pup, whereupon the women of the household capture her catch (Morren 1974:289). Such captured prey is termed *maiangam* and is classified as an edible food for females. Domestic dog flesh is not consumed by the Wopkaimin but wild dog is considered edible for senior initiated men. In male initiation rites, a domestic dog is killed and its penis and intestines fed to the initiated boys (Barth 1975:64).

Biotope 8, Pandanus Groves (Kaiepyon, Salyon)

Fruit *Pandanus conoideus* (*kaiepyon*) and nut *P. julianettii* (*salyon*) are the most important trees planted and maintained by the Wopkaimin (Hyndman 1984a). Although never planted in the same grove, both species are included in Biotope 8 because their internal environment is similar, regardless of their elevational locality in the Kam Basin. *Fruit Pandanus* groves occur from 700–1300 m, whereas nut *Pandanus* groves occur from 1500–2000 m.

Fruit *Pandanus* groves are one of the most durable anthropogenically induced biotopes in the Wopkaimin cultural appropriation of nature. They occur in varying ages in a way structurally similar to taro gardens and secondary regrowth. Some 12 varietals are mixed planted 5–10/100 m^2 in small unfenced groves, the work of planting, maintaining and harvesting is exclusively for adult men. The single most important resource from these groves is the seasonally (December–March) available red, oily sauce obtained from the waxy mesocarp and pericarp between the hard, inedible seeds, which is a rich source of vegetable fat (Clarke 1971:37).

Nut *Pandanus* is mixed planted in 18 varietals in groves of 5–10/100 m^2 and the work is also the exclusive work of adult men. The important resource from these groves is the large nut cluster, which ripens between March and April every other year. The cephalium reaches five kg and is comprised of hundreds of finger–sized nuts with thin drupe shells that can be cracked with the teeth. The kernel (endosperm) and the yellowish pulp (mesocarp) at the base of the drupe shell are eaten raw and some kernels are roasted.

PLATE 2.3 Preparation of *Pandanus* sauce to eat with baked taro (photo courtesy of the author).

Biotope 9, Abandoned Gardens and Hamlets (Binop)

Biotope 9, stages of secondary regrowth (*binop*) of abandoned gardens, are biotic communities in the Kam Basin in which the Wopkaimin move about daily. A spontaneously diverse habitat is created by horticulturally induced disturbance. When gardening, trees are pollarded or retarded with hot coals in the knowledge that many will rejuvenate, especially figs. Cucurbitaceae, tree ferns, leafy greens and fleshy grasses are wild plants that form an integrated food–procurement subsystem (*taton*), which is common throughout the Mid–altitude fringe (Dornstreich 1973:132).

Many tropical rain forest hunter–horticulturalists plant gardens to attract game animals (Holmberg 1969:69; Hughes 1970:9; Dornstreich 1973:136; Morren 1974; Linares 1976). The Wopkaimin proscribe hunting in their taro gardens but hunt extensively within *binop* patches scattered through the Kam Basin. Many of the fruit and flower birds attracted to Biotope 9 are the same as those in the Lower Montane Rain Forest but as they are concentrated closer to the hamlets they are hunted more frequently.

Men spend about half their work–hours hunting and many game mammals are attracted to habitats created by the manipulation of domesticated plants. A large part of the non–domesticated resources used by the Wopkaimin are 'tamed' by manipulation of the habitat. Moreover, this manipulation permits plant and animal recovery through fallow rotation of hunting zones.

Gardening manipulates the habitat of tree ferns, ferns, shrubs and herbs and encourages regrowth of these plants that are highly desirable food for both people and mammals. These ecological relationships are given ethnobiological recognition in the term *taton* that generically glosses these plants as edible. In the term *nuknuk* (*nuk* is life–form for mammals) for *Cyathea* because it is a favorite food of game mammals. In the term *dubolmanawil* (*dubol* is the tree kangaroo, *Dendrolagus dorianus*) for the *Cyclosorus* fern because it is food and both the plant and the animal grow coiled tails. Gardening and fallowing also promotes regrowth of flowering *Schefflera* trees for obtaining birds (Hyndman and Frodin 1980) and of *Piper* (*kwiamban*) for obtaining the game mammal *kwiam* (*Phalanger gymnotis*), which sits (*ban*) on the branches.

Biotope 9 is not overlooked by Wopkaimin children. Girls and boys often spend several hours a day playing in abandoned gardens. Part of this playtime is devoted to collecting frogs and skinks. Boys often use toy bows and arrows to hunt skinks. Two colonizing skinks are given special attention by adult women, who create litter mounds (*atim moon*) as breeding colonies for the skinks and then collect them and their eggs.

Biotope 10, Low Altitude Midmontane Rain Forest (Ilein Sak)

Adults find limited usefulness for Biotope 10, the low altitude Midmontane Rain Forest (*ilein sak*) and children almost never spend any time there. Little grows on the trees except moss. The huge *aian Pandanus* is a useful resource, its nuts are occasionally eaten and its fronds are used to thatch hunting shelters. Three hunting shelters are located near waterfalls of the main Karkil and Kam headwaters below the Hindenburg Wall. Bird ambush blinds are erected close to these hunting shelters. Although some of the game birds have crossed boundaries from lower elevations, the valuable Splendid Astrapia Bird of Paradise first occurs in Biotope 10. Arboreal possums change and give way to the ringtail possum *kaian* (*Pseudocheirus cupreus*), which is the second most frequently taken game mammal. When women shelter overnight for frog collecting they will occasionally extend their collecting range into *ilein sak*.

Biotope 11, Midmontane Rain Forest (Atinaang Sak)

Biotope 11, the Midmontane Rain Forest (*atinaang sak*) is an undulating plateau above the Hindenburg Wall. Different species of nut *Pandanus* are the principal raw material and food plant resource of *atinaang sak*. Wild nut *Pandanus* is well known within this elevational range elsewhere in New Guinea (Powell 1976:132) but *Pandanus iwen* is apparently unique to *atinaang sak* and has been identified by its Wopkaimin name (Stone 1984). They ripen every other year between March and April and are an important seasonal food (Hyndman 1984b). Many are transported back to the Kam Basin and hunters find them a valuable food when hunting in Biotope 11.

The well–used trade route between the Wopkaimin and the Tifalmin has three main hunting shelters: Kafarom, near the rim of the Hindenburg Wall; Finimterr, near Mt. Fugilil; and Arikarikterr, near the Bahrman Mountains. Additional hunting shelters are distributed east and west of the trading route. Game bird hunting is not as seriously pursued as in the Kam Basin but ambush blinds are erected when seeking the black plumes of the Splendid Astrapia. The Dwarf Cassowary is the largest game animal in Biotope 11 and Rand and Gilliard (1967:25) report its occurrence in other Midmontane Rain Forests in New Guinea. The possum *kaian* extends its range into Biotope 11 but the most frequently killed game animal is *norim* (*Phalanger carmelitae*). The fruit bat (*Aproteles bulmerae*), thought until recently to be extinct, roosts in Luplupwintem Cave (Hyndman and Menzies 1980).

3

Abipkagup: A Kinship Mode of Production

Gender Relations in a Great–Man Society

There are only about 700 Wopkaimin and, with only 0.90 people per km², they have one of the lowest population densities of the Mountain Ok. Descent groups within relatively autonomous parish units are not very important, especially among the Wopkaimin and other western Mountain Ok. The Wopkaimin have cognatic, named descent groups (*kinumit*) with overlapping membership. Interpersonal behavior is organized in a kinship idiom. Cognatic social systems are also found among the Tifalmin, Urapmin and Telefolmin to the north of the Wopkaimin in the Sepik Source Basin (Figure 1.2) (Wheatcroft 1975:94; Jorgensen 1976:1).

Among the Wopkaimin descent is reckoned through males and females and terminologically the system goes back two, or rarely three, generations. The three main *kinumits* distributed in the Kam Basin are the Fikkalinmin, Wanansengiunmin and Wimurapmin (Figure 1.4) and each one maintains its own myth of origin place associated with a waterfall or sink hole. With parish endogamy and patrilocal residence commonly practised, the prohibition of incest is extended bilaterally and the exogamous unit becomes the close group of bilateral kin based on nuclear family and sibling relationships. Neighborhood coresidence is the important principle that guides the distribution of resources and land. Hamlets and gardens are located within neighborhood boundaries, whereas access to rain forest resources is a right of parish membership.

Nuclear families are only independent in taro production and do not function as distribution and consumption units in Wopkaimin kinship relations of production. Married couples not only share limited realms of

41

production but practice residential and commensal separation in the hamlets. Each hamlet consists of a men's house and a number of women's houses distributed around a central ceremonial plaza. The men's house is used for men's eating, sleeping and ceremonies. The Fikkalinmin maintain the *Amokam* cult house in Bakonabip. The supreme Wopkaimin cult house, the *Futmanam*, is maintained by the Wanansengiunmin in Bultem. Ceremonies (*bans*) conducted in the *Futmanam* align all Wopkaimin parishes.

The Wopkaimin believe their way of life was founded by the 'great mother' ancestress Afek who built their most sacred cult house, the *Futmanam* after she built the *Telefolip*. The *Futmanam*, permanently located in their Kam Basin homeland in Bultem, integrates the Wopkaimin into a male initiatory cult where youths are housed and transformed into men. Great mother Afek nurtures her Wopkaimin children, in return for their maintenance of the sacred relics and performance of rituals and animal sacrifices to the ancestors inside the *Futmanam* and the men's houses. The Afek male cult excludes women and male domination pervades Wopkaimin kinship relations of production. There is minimal circulation of rights on social labor outside the kinumit-based neighborhoods and hamlet sharing (*abipkagup*) is mediated through the Afek cult, the men's house and a pervasive separation between the sexes.

One of the most common ideas about women in the New Guinea Highlands is a belief in their inherent polluting nature (Langness 1976; Buchbinder and Rappaport 1976; Gelber 1986). Pollution notions express a general view of social order (Douglas 1969), which among the Wopkaimin justifies sexual inequality and autonomy of men from women. Residential segregation of the sexes is premised on women's polluting nature. Women must go into seclusion for the duration of their period and the fear of women's capacity to endanger men is reflected in the residential pattern, common across New Guinea (Fairthorn 1975), of men living together in the men's house while women are relegated to the non-male sections of the hamlet. The ideology of female pollutedness mediates the cultural use of residential space among all Mountain Ok peoples.

In the vertical plane of the Wopkaimin purity–pollution continuum, the sky represents purity and the ground the other extreme of pollution. Within the cultural construction of hamlet space women's houses are constructed low to the ground and placed around the central plaza in a semi–circle domain of females and children only reluctantly entered by

PLATE 3.1 The supreme Wopkaimin cult house, the *Futmanam*, located in Bultem hamlet, 1981 (photo courtesy of the author).

the men. The placement of menstrual huts on the ground at the hamlet outskirts demarcates women's greater state of pollution during menses. Men's and cult houses are erected on the highest poles and thus safely above ground pollution (see Barth 1975:20).

In the Highland big–men societies east of the Mountain Ok, explanations for male domination over women have tended to portray men as transactors (Feil 1984; Strathern 1971) exploiting the surplus value of women's labor to further their own economic and political purposes (Shapiro 1988). In big–men societies oscillating male inequality between givers and receivers takes place. Among the Tombema Enga, Feil (1984:158) shifts the blame from the exploiters to the exploited by arguing that women are in fact the source of gender inequality manifested in unequal exchange between male *tee* partners. By assuming that women's subordination varies inversely with the social value of their labor, Feil (1984) fails to distinguish between use and exchange–value of pigs, whereas Modjeska (1982) and Jorgensen (1991) show that, in big–men societies, women work harder while receiving proportionally less of the value they create.

Critical political economy approaches seen in the writings of Godelier (1986) and others (A. Strathern 1982; Modjeska 1982; Josephides 1985; Jorgensen 1991) locate gender inequality in the totality of kinship relations of production operating in New Guinean societies. Making production the center of analysis challenged the applicability of Sahlins' (1963) big–man model throughout the Melanesia. Godelier's (1986) work demonstrated that there is different kinds of inequality between men and between the sexes to consider. In this regard, the Wopkaimin, like the Baruya (Godelier 1986), have a great–man rather than a big–man society. Pigs, while valued, are not used to reproduce prestige hierarchies. Instead, Wopkaimin and other Mountain Ok become great–men through prominence in hunting, gardening, *abipkagup* sharing, warfare and custodial care of sacred objects and knowledge (Jorgensen 1991).

Division of labor in the appropriation of nature, kinship relations, *abipkagup* sharing, male initiation and conflict all involve inequitable relations between men and women. Division of labor itself, however, does not lead to male domination but presupposes the existence of a system of inequality based on gender (Josephides 1985:112). Wopkaimin women can use land and own tools for gardening and gathering but they cannot own weapons for hunting or armed conflict, thus like the Baruya (Godelier 1986:29) they are denied the means of destruction. In the production of kinship relations, important for social reproduction, Wopkaimin women occupy a subordinate position and men exchange women among themselves and between *kinumit* groups by the criteria that one woman is only equal to one woman in exchange. Women cannot direct the flow of *abipkagup* sharing, especially the distribution of meat which is the most esteemed resource. Wopkaimin women are excluded from owning and using sacred objects, so like the Baruya (Godelier 1986:29) they are excluded from the material supernatural means of controlling the reproduction of strength and social life.

Wopkaimin men do not themselves cease being direct producers, they themselves continue to produce the material means of existence. Analysis then of inequality must be "rooted in the analysis of the social whole" (Josephides 1985:104). Gender relations in Wopkaimin kinship relations of production are presented in the entirety of production, distribution and consumption.

Gender in Production

Seven systems of food production integrate with the resources of 11 recognized biotopes in Wopkaimin kinship relations of production.

Gardening

Shifting cultivation based around a taro monoculture is the mainstay of Wopkaimin food production. Gardens are established between 1200 and 1750 m in secondary forest that has been fallowed for 25–30 years and plantings are also made around the hamlets. Three aggregate gardens in the Kam Basin (Figure 2.7) were visited in 1975 during periods of slashing, tree killing, planting, weeding, and harvesting to measure and record time expenditures. The Wopkaimin work an average 1600 hours per ha under their system of shifting cultivation. Travel accounts for some seven percent of gardening time. Some gardens are over two hours away from hamlets because secondary forest in the Kam Basin is widely distributed.

The domestic unit of production is the nuclear family and married couples work as gardening partners. However, gardening and hunting are a focus of the Afek cult and male productivity emphasises their exclusive responsibility for certain labor and crops. Men are responsible for tree killing by ringing and root scorching. Coals are carried from the taro hearth of the men's house, and only men tend to the fires which must be located outside the margins of the garden. Furthermore, certain taro cultivars, as well as yams, bananas and sugarcane are only planted and tended by men. Considering variations in family size, women's responsibilities of pig raising, and men's labor and cropping responsibilities and commitment to other production, especially hunting, individual gardeners work between 635 and 950 hours per year.

Sago and Pandanus Groves

All Wopkaimin tree crops except bananas are planted in groves (Biotopes 2,8). Sago is common to the Lowlands (Lea 1972; Ohtsuka 1977a, 1977b), fruit *Pandanus*, breadfruit and banana are common to the Mid–altitude fringe (Barrau 1958:53–54, 55–60) and nut *Pandanus* is common to the Highlands (Bowers 1968; Waddell 1972).

Groves of tree crops are owned, planted and tended exclusively by men. These tree crops and the special male garden crops are treated by the

Wopkaimin, and other Mountain Ok, by an elaborate system of food taboos as though they were game (Jorgensen 1991:265). Tree crops and garden produce most restricted are red in color and thus associated with blood and hunting and consequently forbidden to women.

Sago is culturally valued, greatly esteemed as a food and is considered a staple food second only to taro. A sago palm produces maximum starch content when it flowers around the fifteenth year of growth. The manufacture of sago starch is a straining process, which is remarkably similar across the Mid–altitude fringe (Townsend 1969:26–33; Dornstreich 1973:208–211, 331–334). The sexual division of labor in sago manufacture involves men and women in (1) traveling to the sago grove, (2) felling and splitting, (3) pulverizing, and (4) constructing the straining apparatus; and involves women in (5) washing, and (6) transporting of finished starch. Starch collected in a special net bag in the initial straining process is reserved exclusively for consumption in the men's house.

The Wopkaimin wash about 15.6 kg of sago per hour. They take about 15 work hours to produce around 28.5 kg of edible starch. Raw sago is not channeled to pigs, nor are palms felled to encourage sago grub colonization. Sago introduces flexibility to Wopkaimin subsistence because it provides reliable bulk food to sustain movement into the Foothill Rain Forest for gathering, hunting, fishing, and collecting.

There is no comparable sexual division of labor or technological complexity in *Pandanus* silviculture. Fruit *Pandanus* is red and certain cultivars are only eaten by old men. It is harvested yearly, but nut *Pandanus* yields only every other year. Location of *Pandanus* groves, intensity of labor inputs, and yields are influenced by distance from the hamlet. Elsewhere in the Mid–altitude fringe, Clarke (1971:139, 174) estimates that Maring men work 45 minutes on each fruit *Pandanus* per year. Wopkaimin silviculture techniques are similar to those of the Maring, but they maintain fewer *Pandanus*; about 10 fruit and 10 nut pandans per male owner. Each Wopkaimin man works about 15 hours per year in their *Pandanus* groves and another 25 hours per year on their sago groves.

Gathering

Gathering is a system for acquiring wild plant foods and is a supplementary food production undertaken by women which is spread over six biotopes and 43 different species. Ferns, leafy greens, nuts, fruits,

PLATE 3.2 Wopkaimin woman washing sago near Ulatem sago grove, 1975 (photo courtesy of the author).

roots, grass stems, palm stems, vines, and fungi are the types of wild plants frequently eaten by the Wopkaimin. From June to August 1975, over 3,000 kg of cultivated and wild plant foods were consumed by residents of Bakonabip hamlet. Wild plants amounted to 69 kg and equaled 2 percent by weight of all plant food. Ninety percent of gathered plant food consisted of edible ferns and leafy greens. Elsewhere in the Mid–altitude fringe, Gadio women (Dornstreich 1973:227–230) work 165 hours to gather 375 kg of edible ferns and leafy greens. These wild plants are easily obtained and they involve little diversion in time or distance from a woman's normal day's gardening. Average gathering time spent over the year by each Wopkaimin woman is about 120 hours. Gathering is important to subsistence because it (1) requires no special technology, (2) has high food value, (3) complements a carbohydrate–based diet, and (4) reduces subsistence risk because the exploited resources occur at known places at known times (Nietschmann 1973:152).

Pig Raising

Domestic pigs contribute more importantly to Wopkaimin ritual than diet, but as with other Mountain Ok, they do not play a major role in reproduction of social groups (Jorgensen 1991:261). They are considered absolutely essential sacrificial animals for initiation and curing ceremonies which are always performed in hamlets. Domestic pigs are wild, semidomestic, and domestic during different parts of their life cycle, a pattern quite common across the Mid–altitude fringe (Dornstreich 1973:236). The neighborhood pig population is increased through piglet capture, purchase, and trade and through the uncertainties of sow breeding associated with newborn mortality and feral boar availability.

The Wopkaimin pattern of mobility and settlement dispersion is not compatible with the pattern of food and care required in pig raising. The problem is resolved by fostering pigs to women in a system of communal management in residentially separate people and pig houses kept away from the main residential hamlets. The demands of bedding, food, and care of pigs fall exclusively to women.

PLATE 3.3 Wopkaimin men butchering a domestic pig in front of the Bakonabip men's house and *Amokam* cult house, 1975 (photo courtesy of the author).

Wopkaimin families foster out one or two domestic pigs and while valued, there are only about 0.5 maintained per person. All fodder comes from taro gardens, and each pig consumes an amount equivalent to the daily human ration. About 90–125 women's work hours per year, 14 percent of gardening time, is channeled to domestic pigs.

Hunting

The core of Wopkaimin male life revolves around hunting, which is spread over six biotopes and 130 species. Meat has tremendous cultural value and is necessary for sacrificial provisioning in the Afek cult and in *abipkagup* sharing. Men's hunting surpasses women's pig raising in emotional and social importance and nutritional significance. Hunting outproduces women's pork production, it is their major means of obtaining meat, and by New Guinea standards they are very successful at it.

The younger men are more mobile for hunting but every adult male hunts because it has such positive emotional and social value, and there is no other productive activity that yields such a large quantity of meat in such a short period of time. The same hunting equipment complex is used wherever the men hunt. Black palm bows are traded from the Ningerum

PLATE 3.4 A Wopkaimin hunter carrying his dog at the edge of Bakonabip hamlet, 1975 (photo courtesy of the author).

people on their southern border. The bow is strung with shaved rattan. Arrows are fashioned from cane grass. Projectile points made from bamboo are used in hunting feral pigs; those made from palm wood are used in hunting game mammals. Multipronged and blunted projectile points are used in hunting birds and in fishing. Other hunting equipment includes the ax, a braided tree–climbing ring (*makar*), and the hunting dog.

The dog is important to hunting returns and is as culturally important to men as the domestic pig is to women; another common pattern across the Mid–altitude fringe (Clarke 1971:89). The favored hunting strategy is to use the dog while stalking, besetting, and chasing. Men hunt alone and form loosely structured partnerships of up to five–six hunters centered around the presence of an acknowledged skillful hunting dog and his owner. The two most time–consuming hunting activities are putting distance between hamlet and hunter and stalking. Every hunter integrates his knowledge of game animal biotope preference, feeding habits, and topographic features to guide his stalking activity. The Wopkaimin possess accurate ecological and animal behavioral knowledge necessary for successful and intensive rain forest hunting.

From June to August 1975 in the Kam Basin (Figure 1.4), Wopkaimin men hunted from Finimterr and Bleilimal in Midmontane Rain Forest (Biotope 11), Bansikin in Lower Montane Rain Forest (Biotope 5) and Ulatem in Foothill Rain Forest (Biotope 1). Four hundred hours of hunting returned 68 game animals weighing 188 kg for 5.9 hours per animal, 2.13 hours per kg and 0.47 kg per hour (Table 3.1).

Elsewhere in the Mid–altitude fringe, although the Etolo (600–1200 m on the southern slopes of Mt. Haliago) and the Kundagai (1200–2800 m on the northern slopes of the Bismarck Mountains) spend less hunting hours per game animal, their returns for their effort do not exceed the Wopkaimin (Table 3.2). Moreover, evidence from the Rofaifo (900–2200 m) demonstrates that hunting productivity in the more densely populated Eastern Highlands is very poor compared with the Mid–altitude fringe (Table 3.2).

The Wopkaimin direct their hunting efforts primarily at four animals that offer the least production risk in terms of cultural meat preferences and recognition of habits and biotopes. Two large terrestrial game animals, the feral pig (27%) and cassowary (29%), took 18 percent of the hunting time and required an average round–trip distance of over 16 km. Two arboreal game mammals *kitam, Phalanger sericeus* (8%) and *kaian,*

TABLE 3.1 Productivity from 400 Hours of Wopkaimin Hunting

Location	Hunters No.	Total Hours	Prey No.	Returns Kg	Hours Per Prey	Hours Per Kg	Kg per Hours
Biotope 11	5	188	43	39.5	4.4	4.8	0.21
Biotope 12	4	54.5	9	12.2	6.1	4.5	0.22
Biotope 5	5	88.5	12	26.6	7.4	3.3	0.30
Biotope 1	4	70	4	109.5	17.5	0.6	1.56
Total		401	68	188	5.9	2.13	0.47

TABLE 3.2 Hunting Productivity in the New Guinea Highlands and Mid-Altitude Fringe

Location People	Hunters No.	Total Hours	Prey No.	Returns Kg	Hours Per Prey	Hours Per Kg	Kg per Hours
M/a fringe Wopkaimin		401	68	188	5.9	2.13	0.47
M/a fringe Etolo[a]		2899.6	592	1004.4	4.9	2.89	0.35
M/a fringe Kundagai[b]		90	23	14.4	3.9	6.26	0.16
Highlands Rofaifo[a]		497	37	19.8	13.4	25.1	0.04

[a]Source: Dwyer (1983)
[b]Source: Healey (1988).

Pseudocheirus cupreus (11%), took 82 percent of the hunting time and required an average round trip distance of five km.

The costs and returns of Wopkaimin hunting compare favorably with other peoples in the Mid–altitude fringe and Highlands (Table 3.3). Comparisons are based on food values for game animals from Dornstreich

TABLE 3.3 Costs and Returns of Hunting in the New Guinea Mid–Altitude Fringe and Highlands

Location People	Hunting Hours	Edible wt g per hr	Protein g per hr	Protein g/person/ day	Energy Benefit/ Cost
M/a fringe Wopkaimin	401	232.0	49.5	12.4	2.09
M/a fringe Etolo[a]	2899	212.6	33.6	3.3	1.34
M/a fringe Gadio[a]	245	884.9	119.3	9.2	13.25
Highlands Rofaifo[a]	497	23.6	3.7	0.2	0.2

[a]Source: Dwyer (1983).

(1973) and a mean energy expenditure average of 3.98 kcal per minute (Norgan *et al.* 1974:341–43). Four hundred hours of Wopkaimin hunting returns 232 edible g per hour, 49.5 g of protein per hour, 12.4 g of protein per person/per day for an energy benefit cost of 2.09. Returns from Etolo hunting are close to the Wopkaimin in edible weight and protein per hour and *Pseudocheirus cupreus* (43%) and *Phalanger sericeus* (*vestitus*) (22%) similarly dominate the catch (Dwyer 1983:155). Wopkaimin exceed Etolo in protein g/person/day and energy cost/benefit because the Etolo only hunt mammals, whereas 27 percent of the Wopkaimin catch is feral pig which returns well over twice the calories per 100 g. The Gadio live in Foothill Rain Forest from 300–1000 m and their captures were made up of 33 feral pigs, 30 cuscus (*Phalanger gymnotis*) and two bandicoots (Dornstreich 1973:322–32). Living with abundant wild pig, the Gadio hunt less for greater returns from hunting than is possible in higher altitudes of the Mid–altitude fringe. Hunting is poor in the densely settled Highlands and Rofaifo hunting has a negative energy benefit/cost. By dispersing their hunting over biotopes 1, 5 and 11, the Wopkaimin have better returns than is possible in just the Midmontane Rain Forest (Rofaifo) or Lower Montane Rain Forest (Etolo). Extrapolating from the 400–hour sample, Wopkaimin men hunt about

500 work hours per year for an approximate yearly catch return of around 160 kg of game animals.

Fishing

There is a clear sexual division of labor in Wopkaimin fishing. Women are primarily involved because men are prohibited from catching and consuming fish during initiation ceremonies. Fully initiated men rarely eat fish, and cult house leaders (*awem kinum*) observe a complete food taboo on fish.

Hand probing and erecting small stone weirs in streams (Biotope 4) are two fishing techniques used by women. Almost all women's fishing is focused on the Rough–scaled Loter found in Lower Montane Rain Forest streams, and on the Spotted Mountain and Dusky Mountain Goby found in Foothill Rain Forest streams. Hand probing and small stone weirs are integrated women's fishing techniques appropriate to catching these small fish weighing less than 100 g. Previously men fished with poison, basket traps (*warap*) made from the climbing palm and fish spears. Today they still spear fish but prefer to use steel hooks and monofilament line. Men fish for the large catfish found in the Ok Tedi and its tributaries below 650 m.

Fishing is associated with temporary settlement shifts to alternate living sites. On two fishing trips to Biotope 1 from June to August 1975, 100 work hours returned 20 kg of fish for five hours per kg and 0.2 kg per hour, which is similar to returns from hunting. However, fishing only returns 87 edible g per hour and 11.1 g of protein per hour. Even assuming fishing is about half as strenuous as hunting, the energy benefit/cost is only 0.5, which indicates fishing is less efficient for returns compared to hunting. Extrapolating from the 100–hour sample, each man works about 70 hours per year in fishing and each woman works about 150 hours per year in fishing for an approximate return of 3.8 kg per hour.

Collecting

Collecting refers to the acquisition of small animals as food. The large python and the agamid lizard are the only animals collected by men. These larger animals are generally cooked, shared and consumed at the hamlet. Collecting small animals such as frogs, lizards and skinks, snakes, insects, and mammals is food production of women and children. It spans

8 biotopes and 79 species. Collecting is reliable and regularly followed in conjunction with gardening and gathering. When obtained in small quantities, these collected animals are consumed away from hamlets.

Certain collecting techniques return sufficient quantities of small animals to justify transporting them back to hamlets. Women's combined fishing and frogging trips regularly return the highest yield of small animals and they are important for women and children because they are the only wild animal foods specifically channeled to them in kinship relations of production that otherwise disadvantages them in the pattern of meat distribution. On the basis of several comparative observations, women spend about 50 work hours per year collecting, about half the time spent on gathering. The return from one hour of collecting averages 300 kcal for every 100 kcal expended. Collecting is marginally efficient, but as a system of acquiring quality protein, it does have the advantages of no waste, abundance, reliability, and occasional avoidance of sharing (see Dornstreich 1973:271).

Although men and women work roughly the same number of hours per year to produce about the same weight of food return per year, men produce less than half the kcal produced by women (Table 3.4). Men work about 1,245 hours to produce about 724 kg of food per year and women work about 1,400 hours to produce about 866 kg of food per year (Table 3.4). Elsewhere in New Guinea, the Wopkaimin compare to 1,150 work hours for the Bomagai–Angoiang gardener (Clarke 1971:174) and to 1,356–1,539 work hours for the Lowland Oriomo Papuans (Ohtsuka 1977a:255; 1977b:472). However, relatively equal work–hours for weight of food return between the sexes actually obscures gender differences in food production among the Wopkaimin.

Foods are not nutritionally equal, therefore, the relative importance of gender relations can be calculated in relationship to male and female domains of food production. Men are less committed to shifting cultivation than are the women and therefore, produce only about 2850 kcal per day (Table 3.4). Moreover, planted groves and hunting are male only domains of food production. Nutritionally women produce nearly 6400 kcal per day, which represents over two thirds of the daily energy used by the Wopkaimin. The bulk of nutrient returns are provided by women's plant food production (Table 3.4). Shifting cultivation is most significant because it provides the greatest percentages of all nutrients except proteins and fats. Women's work contributes more to the Wopkaimin staple food taro (*Colocasia esculenta*), which provides

66 percent of all calories. Taro is a high–calorie food and is eaten in large quantities every day. It has more protein than any other New Guinea staple food (Oomen 1971).

TABLE 3.4 Gender Differences in Wopkaimin Food Production

Subsistence Subsystem	Work/ h Inputs	Men kg Yield	Kcal Yield	Work/ h Inputs	Women kg Yield	Kcal Yield
Gardening	635	470	503,000	950	700	749,000
Silviculture	40	80	260,000	40	80	260,000
Gathering				120	11	4,200
Pig raising				90– 135	40	1,080,000
Hunting	500	160	162,500			
Fishing	70	14	115,200	150	30	230,400
Collecting				50	5	3,120
Total (yearly mean)	1,245	724	1,040,700	1,400	866	2,326,720
Total (daily mean)	3.4	2.0	2,850	3.6	2.4	6,375

Gathering is a good source of iron, vitamin A, and vitamin C. Leafy greens are seven percent by weight of all foodstuffs produced. Wopkaimin women gather tender upper shoots of these plants which contain the highest protein content (Rogers and Miner 1963; Terra 1964; Whiting and Morton 1966; Stanley and Lewis 1969). Leafy greens and edible ferns are also quite good providers of vitamin A, vitamin C, thiamine, riboflavin, and niacin. New Guineans generally receive adequate thiamine, carotene, calcium, iron, vitamin C, and potassium in their diet (Oomen 1971:16–17).

Animals contribute eight percent by weight of foods eaten by the Wopkaimin, which is very high by New Guinea standards. Highland diets consist almost entirely of plants (Sinnett 1977:70) and Lowland coastal diets, even with fish available, are reportedly only 2.2 percent animal food by weight (Norgan and Durnin 1974:323). Only the Mid–altitude fringe Gadio (5%) and Sanio–Hiowe (8%) are reported to consume about as much weight in animals as do the Wopkaimin (Dornstreich 1973:366; Townsend 1969:62). About 46 percent of men's yearly food production is directed to procuring animals, compared to only 12 percent of women's work directed to procuring animals.

Production of animal food provides 95 percent of the fats and half of the protein for the Wopkaimin. Women's pig raising contributes the bulk of dietary fat. Men's hunting provides over 23 percent of total dietary protein and hunting is the greatest contributor of protein from animal food production. Women's collecting is negligible in overall dietary terms except for protein and phosphorus. Likewise, fishing is nutritionally insignificant except for protein and calcium.

Fat is the nutrient most lacking in New Guinean diets (Oomen 1971:16–17). Fat makes food more palatable, and it enables the body to use other nutrients. Vitamins A, D, E, and K are fat soluble and require the presence of fat for their complete utilization. Whiting and Morton (1966:10) indicate that diets dependent upon leafy greens require at least seven percent of dietary calories from fat in order for vitamin A to be fully utilized. Since the Wopkaimin derive only two percent of their dietary calories from fat, they may not be fully absorbing the large quantity of vitamin A they regularly eat. Fat is generally limiting to the Wopkaimin. Women's work in pig raising contributes 87 percent of fat. Men's hunting of birds and game animals contributes another 8 percent of fats and *Pandanus* silviculture the remaining five percent.

Gender in Distribution

Consumption Taxa

The fundamental difference between natural discontinuities and those that reflect culturally imposed discontinuities is reflected in Wopkaimin distinctions between life–form and consumption taxa. Plant and animal life–forms are classified according to natural discontinuities and the manner in which they are appropriated. Consumption taxa classify plants and animals according to the system of taboos, restrictions and preferences based on gender (Table 3.5).

TABLE 3.5 Wopkaimin Consumption Taxa and Their Appropriation

Taxa	Associated Behavior
wanim (dim)	Vertebrate animal 'meat' which is unrestricted
falei (dim)	Vertebrate animal 'meat' which is restricted
falei (kil)	Less desirable animal or plant 'flesh' which is restricted
awem	Any food restricted because of taboo

Jorgensen (1991:265) has insightfully noted the relationship of game to food taboo systems among the Mountain Ok, whereby taboos derived from hunting form part of a set which forbids women to come in contact with blood and by association red plants. The Wopkaimin make a distinction between potential foodstuffs that are denied to everyone because of taboo (*awem*) and those that are simply restricted (*falei*) for some individuals and not for others. There are far more foods that are simply restricted (*falei*) as compared to being tabooed. Only a few animals are unrestricted (*wanin*) for everyone. By contrast, most cultivated foods are generally free from allocation restrictions.

All edible plants and animals are categorized as flesh (*kil*) foods or meat (*dim*) foods. Meat occupies the most prominent place in the scale of preferences and plays a significant role in everyday life. The desire for meat is preeminent in dietary preferences among the Wopkaimin and other Mountain Ok Mid–altitude fringe peoples (Morren 1986) and in many indigenous, subsistence–oriented peoples (Woodburn 1968, Nietschmann 1973). The Tasbapauni Miskito of eastern Nicaragua, according to Nietschmann (1973:108) "do not consider all animal flesh as belonging to the same generic classification 'meat'. A subtle distinction is made between animals which are regarded as having *real* meat, and lesser animals which have second quality meat." On the basis of taste and texture the Wopkaimin make a similar distinction between animals that have meat (*dim*) such as cassowaries, pigs and marsupials, and animals that have only flesh (*kil*) such as fish, frogs, snakes and lizards. All plant foods are classified as having flesh (*kil*).

When Wopkaimin life–form and consumption taxa are combined (Table 3.6), the *awem* category consists of a total of eight animals forbidden to everyone, but this constitutes a total ban on a few rare species. The remaining correlations of life–form and consumption taxa relate to ideology and hunting extractive efficiency and ecological availability. The Wopkaimin also use consumption taxa to index ritual status by the avoidance of certain foods, as do the Baktamanmin (Barth

TABLE 3.6 Wopkaimin Life–Form and Consumption Taxa Correlated by Number of Generics

Life–form	Generics	wanim dim	falei dim	falei kil	awem
Awon	260[a]	140 (22)	120 (14)		
Nuk	40[b]	2	36 (15)	2	
Maian	2		1		1
Bia	2		2		
Kong	2	1	1		
Kul	54			53	1
Takam	10			20	
Atim	22	1		20	1
Feimkan	12		1	8	3
Totals	405	144 (26)	161 (34)	91	8

[a](36) regularly eaten
[b](17) regularly eaten.

1975:165) and other Mountain Ok. Men are subject to far more dietary restrictions than women and children. Of the 168 principal Wopkaimin foods, 64 are restricted to men in the prime of life, 19 to women and eight to children. These 91 restricted (*falei*) foods indicate that the Wopkaimin carry a heavy load of status, age and sex avoidances. The system of food taboos, restrictions and preferences discriminates sharply between plant and animal foods: 87 of the 91 restricted foods are animals. Animals and meat are overriding concerns of the Wopkaimin and they restrict access to nearly the entire range of local fauna.

Barth (1975:165-66) alludes to the gender basis of Baktamanmin food distribution and how it revolves around social distinctions drawn on the basis of age-sex groups but incorrectly assumes that distribution does not monopolize privilege for men. To the extent the Wopkaimin do not obey their own norms, inequalities in distribution based on gender distinctions would be diminished. However, as observed in 1975 there was no distinction among the Wopkaimin between norms and behavior because they regularly followed the gender basis of distribution. Small game animals, reptiles and invertebrates are denied to adult males and they outnumber adult male foods. They are fairly regularly consumed, but they are nutritionally less significant animal foods compared to the feral pigs and cassowaries which are exclusively for adult male consumption. Furthermore, many large game mammals are denied to women, especially those that are pregnant or lactating.

The regular supply of game during 1975 to the Wopkaimin was 5.5 times as frequently available to men as to women (Table 3.7). Avoidances based on gender are preeminent in the distinctions made between meat and flesh bearing animals. As men acquire adulthood and ritual status they stop eating the flesh bearing animals of females and childhood. Gender is such a fundamental distinction in the allocation of these animals that less than 30 percent of the largest, most regularly esteemed and hunted game animals are allowed to women of childbearing age.

The consumption taxa unrestricted meat (*wanin dim*) stresses the importance of bird hunting by adult men and this includes bats which also belong to the life-form *awon* (Table 3.7). From June to August 1975 bird hunting returned 3.8 kg and bats 6.63 kg, for a total of 10.43 kg (Table 3.7). The highest esteemed consumption taxa *wanin dim* accounts for only 7 percent of the wild animals consumed by the Wopkaimin but it is a significant amount considering that the most frequently occuring *awon* animals are all small.

The consumption taxa restricted meat (*falei dim*) is the next lowest esteemed, and the emphasis is on large terrestrial and arboreal game animals hunting by adult men (Table 3.7). Large terrestrial game animals include the life-forms *bia* (cassowaries) and *samin* (feral pig). Affiliating *bia* and *samin* to the less esteemed *falei dim* consumption taxa reduces the chance of overpredation. Wopkaimin cassowary hunting returned 38.20 kg

TABLE 3.7 Wild Animal Returns Correlated by Life–Form and Consumption Taxa

| Life–form | Generics | Consumption Taxa (Weight Kg) | | | |
		wanim dim	falei dim	falei kil	awem
Awon	yawok	2.0			
	kasup	1.0			
	kawatokin	0.2			
	kalkol	0.3			
	kulkulbagel	0.3			
	slul	6.63			
Nuk	galwem		0.2		
	botok		0.6		
	frim		1.8		
	abilim		0.06		
	takinok		0.2		
	sanok		0.77		
	kaian		14.51		
	dawam		1.02		
	sarip		5.45		
	norim		5.7		
	kwiam		4.1		
	nareim		4.63		
	kitam		11.24		
Bia	bia		38.20		
Kong	samin		36.25		
Kul	gireit			6.48	
	atem				
	talin				
	nawhe				
	sawep				
	krum				
	sawan				
	bagok				
Takam	dol			6.23	
	bom			1.92	
Atim	gunong			0.43	
	brik				
	taneimkan				
	gauun				
	wokleiup				
Feimkan	gungfeimkan			0.25	
		3.8	131.36	15.31	
Total kg					150.47

and feral pig hunting returned 36.25 kg, which represents 48 percent of the total (Table 3.7). Small arboreal game animals (*nuk*) are all placed in the *falei* consumption taxa. *Nuk* hunting returned 50.28 kg; the most frequently taken are the ringtail (*kaian*) 29 percent, and the cuscus (*kitam*) 22 percent (Table 3.7).

The least desirable consumption taxa is restricted flesh food (*falei kil*), which is behaviorally associated with fishing and collecting by women. The life–forms associated with *falei kil* are fish (*takam*), snakes (*feimkan*), frogs (*kul*) and lizards (*atim*). Fishing emphasises catfish and loters, which returned 6.23 kg and 1.92 kg respectively (Table 3.7). The overwhelming contribution from collecting is frogs (*kul*), but their return from collecting of 6.96 kg was only four percent of the total weight of all wild animals (Table 3.7). Placing life–forms *takam*, *feimkan*, *kul* and *atim* in *falei kil* relates to their low animal biomass and sparse animal distribution. The taboo category (*awem*) negatively weighs against a few animals for which low effort is expended on collecting.

Hunting and collecting are spread widely over the range of locally occuring animals. Consumption taxa is divided into degrees of situational restrictions (see Barth 1975:167–168). Addition of a preference scale for foods, the *dim* and *kil* classification, further enhances gender sensitivity. Gender distinctions in the distribution of hunting effort is regulated through the system of consumption taxa, while life–form taxa stores the information required for men's efficient investment of their effort.

Abipkagup Sharing

In the Highlands big–man societies women's production is appropriated and deployed in a male–controlled system of circulation. This contrasts with the great–men societies of the Mountain Ok where concern is with the constitution of an exclusively masculine realm of production (Jorgensen 1991:264) and there are no formal prestations between socially defined categories of person (Gardner 1990). However, there is a pervasive, informal sharing of goods and services between individuals within the same and different hamlets. Around the time of preparing food in the late afternoon children move between women's houses and men return to the mens' house carrying cooked taro and leaf–bundles of other food. Such informal transaction of staple food and everyday objects occurs widely across New Guinea village life (Gardner 1990). Wopkaimin men also trade on an ad hoc basis with Ningerum men for black–palm bows and with Tifalmin men for tobacco. But distribution of valuables,

62

goods and services is not characterized by trade networks with enduring partnerships and formal exchange is absent.

Certain kinds of sharing among the Mountain Ok achieve a more public, formal grounding (Gardner 1990) and these kinds of interpersonal relationships are known to the Wopkaimin as *abipkagup*. Each kinumit descent group has a man addressed and referred to as *kamokim*. Their leadership status is achieved through the nodal position they play in *abipkagup* sharing. Wopkaimin leaders, like their Mountain Ok counterparts (Gardner 1990), are constrained within the limits imposed upon all individuals and share the most important goods and services to the extent they can procure and provide them.

PLATE 3.5 The Wopkaimin leader (*kamokim*) and ritual specialist (*awem kinum*) Gesoch carrying embers from the Bakonabip men's house to his garden in 1975 (photo courtesy of the author).

The Wopkaimin *kamokim*, like the Miyanmin *kamok* (Gardner 1990), stand out by virtue of the volume of *abipkagup* sharing transactions and the relative influence of those with whom they form their closest links. The *kamokim* in the Kam Basin, where the Wopkaimin *Futmanam* cult house is located, is also the leader of the male cult (*awem kinum*). Leaders exert influence because they addressed immediate concerns of guidance in gardening, provisioning of taro fertility and performance of male initiation. The men's cult focusses not only on male initiation and warfare but also on gardening and cult rituals are considered as work which casts men as benefactors of all sectors of society (Jorgensen 1991).

Feeding of male visitors is a conspicuous feature of *abipkagup* sharing, especially of meat shared from the men's house. There is little surplus relative to immediate need, which enhances the key position of the men's house in *abipkagup* sharing. *Kamokim* leaders are pivotal in the sharing of meat, especially hunted game distributed through the men's house. Meat is the supreme valuable among the Wopkaimin. It is not circulated but shared amongst fewer or greater men or the wider community.

Meat is shared in *abipkagup* sharing but meat and other goods and services only have use–value, they are not alienated for their exchange value. Thus, there is neither institutionalized circulation of wealth nor individuals differentiated by their control of the circulation of wealth (Gardner 1990). Masculinity is fundamentally defined in terms of production and differs profoundly from big–men societies where men are transactors and women are producers (Jorgensen 1991).

Gender in Consumption

Men/Women and Diet

Game and pigs only have use–value for consumption, as they do not have exchange–value they do not function in the creation of social value. The central importance of game distributed through the men's house in *abipkagup* sharing accentuates gender differences, monopolizes male privilege and creates a nutritionally superior diet for adult men. Some age–sex groups are better nourished than others elsewhere in the New Guinea Highlands (Venkatachalam 1962:11; Hipsley and Kirk 1965:8; Sorenson and Gajdusek 1969:304–07) and the Mid–altitude fringe (Rappaport 1968:79–80; Townsend 1969:61, 69; Clarke 1971:24–25; Dornstreich 1973:403–412).

It is not just that women and children eat different types of food from men, the allocation of the game (Table 3.7) through *abipkagup* sharing results in a significantly different nutrient intake between men and women (Table 3.8). Nutrient requirements of the Wopkaimin (Ulijaszek, Hyndman and Lourie 1987) are based on the weights and heights taken by the PNG Institute of Medical Research (IMR) in their 1975 Wopkaimin health survey. Every nutrient responsive to animal food intake, which only excludes vitamins A and C, is significantly different between men and women. Animal size and amount affect the allocation of nutrients, and although collected animals are regularly consumed away from the hamlets, gender–based distribution continues to affect the nutritional pay–off for settlement shifts and mobility (see Dornstreich 1973:406–07).

During sago working at Ulatem (Figure 1.4) women significantly improved upon their hamlet–based diet. In four days, 57 kg of sago, 7.2 kg of ferns, 1.5 kg of fish, 1.6 kg of frogs and 0.5 kg of larvae were consumed at Ulatem. The average daily intake of 3722 kcal was 50 percent higher than normal. Sago boosted caloric intake, but since it contains few other nutrients, all of the small animals consumed did not adequately compensate to boost per day nutrient intake above normal.

After the first four days of sago working, several women and children shifted from Ulatem to hunt and fish. Two brothers, their sister and their families moved for four days to Tambik (Figure 1.4). They harvested *Xanthosoma* taro, *aibika* leaves and *Sechium edule* fruits and leaves from an abandoned garden. Together with gathered wild yam and ferns, their average daily plant food intake was 1202 kcal. Hunting, fishing and collecting returns were very successful, including a cassowary (17 kg); many birds (2.9 kg); a cuscus (5.5 kg); fish (6.8 kg); and frogs (140 g).

Daily animal food intake for women averaged 320 kcal; the intake for men averaged 2080 kcal. Women averaged a daily intake of 76.6 g of protein and 18 g of fat per day; the daily average for men was 325.8 g of protein and 118.5 g of fat per day. By leaving Ulatem the women traded off a superabundance of calories for a protein intake 47 percent higher than normal. Gender–based differences in consumption is reflected in nutrient returns for men that averaged 30 percent higher for calories, 76 percent higher for proteins and 48 percent higher for fats. Diet patterns at Ulatem and Tambik reveal that mobile women away from their residential hamlets raise their calorie and protein intake levels above normal, but not proportionately as high as for men. Gender in

TABLE 3.8 Gender Differences in Wopkaimin Nutrient Returns, 1975

Nutrient	Men	SD	%>[a]	Women	SD	%>[a]
Calories	2476 (1361[c])	2267	40	1963[b] (1345[c])	1583	32
Protein g	84 (32[c])	130	49	41[d] (28.5[c])	36	57
Fat g	67 (3[c])	162	22	21[b] (3[c])	83	04
Vitamin A I.U.	7922	12955	64	7922	12955	64
Vitamin B1 mg	2.4 (1[c])	2.4	74	1.9[b] (1[c])	1.5	72
Vitamin B2 mg	2.1 (0.6[c])	4.7	45	0.9^2 (0.6[c])	0.7	43
Niacin mg	24.5 (11[c])	32	45	17.3[b] (11[c])	18	43
Vitamin C mg	213	183	87	213	183	87
Calcium mg	864 (549[c])	719	64	848 (527[c])	692	57
Iron mg	34 (19[c])	31	85	30[b] (19[c])	27	83

[a]Percentage of occurrence in excess of high nutrient requirement
[b]$p < 0.05$
[c]Median values within 25th 75th percentile
[d]$p < 0.01$.

consumption continues to operate in mobility and private eating to allocate meat inequitably.

Wopkaimin women have a nutritionally inferior diet to that of adult men. Adult men receive adequate calories, proteins, fats, vitamins and minerals; their diet actually exceeds high value requirements for six out of ten nutrients (Table 3.8). The diet of adult women is inadequate by comparison. They are nutritionally deficient in fats and vitamin B2 and have only a marginally adequate calorie intake (Table 3.8). Men have more meat in their diet than women; by eating more animals they more than double their average daily protein intake over that of women, which makes it the most significantly different nutrient between men and women (Table 3.8). Men regularly consume more calories, fats, vitamin B2 and niacin than women and the intake of these nutrients, including the portion derived from animals, is significantly different (Table 3.8). The implication is that women irregularly receive adequate calories and fats to sustain their level of production.

Men/Women and Health

The PNG IMR (Table 3.9) and the World Health Organization (WHO) (North Fly Clinico-Epidemiological Pilot Study [NFCEPS] 1979a) made health assessments of the Wopkaimin in the 1970s. According to these surveys, the Wopkaimin enjoyed a reasonable standard of health and, as expected, their major health abnormality was infectious disease (Taukuro *et al.* 1980). Neither dental caries, skin diseases nor chronic respiratory disease was common among the Wopkaimin (NFCEPS 1979a:8). Intestinal protozoa *Enterobius* and *Trichuris* were also very rare but *Ascaris* was present in Atemkit residents (Taukuro *et al.* 1980). Hookworm, probably *Necator americanus*, infected 84 percent of the Atemkit residents (NFCEPS 1979b).

The principal cause of ill-health is malaria (Taukuro *et al.* 1980:80). Endemicity of malaria is derived from considering the prevalence and degree of enlarged spleen (splenomegaly). From the Ningerum foothills into the Wopkaimin mountains splenomegaly is 62 percent. Enlarged spleen and liver (hepatomegaly) is statistically significant (Taukuro *et al.* 1980:84). Repeated bouts of malaria and other factors are involved in the pathogenesis of hepatomegaly.

Malaria is hyperendemic in the lower elevational ranges of the Wopkaimin homeland. The Wopkaimin undergo repeated bouts of malaria when they temporarily shift settlements to shelters below 1000 m in elevation like Ulatem and Tambik for hunting, fishing and processing sago. Here they succumb to malaria attacks and return to their higher altitude hamlets around 1500 m to escape the zone of hyperendemic malaria. According to the WHO (Taukuro *et al.* 1980:82) "there is frequent movement to and sojourn in areas of higher endemicity by the adults."

The work of Buchbinder (1973) and Venkatachalam (1962) indicates that protein deficiency is an important factor contributing to the pathogenesis of hepatomegaly and the WHO indicates that malnutrition might be incriminated in the case of the Wopkaimin as well (Taukuro *et al.* 1980:84).

The most significant gender differences in health among the Wopkaimin occurs in adulthood (Tables 3.9A and 3.9B). Anemia is quite common with generally slight and symptomless depression of hemoglobin levels (Taukuro *et al.* 1980:84). Hemoglobin levels are significantly different between adult men and women in the 20–24 age group (Table 3.9B). Although malaria is hyperendemic and hookworm is common, it is more than an uncomplicated malarial anemia and the WHO found that insufficient intake of iron may be a contributory cause. This is particularly so in the women because their Mean Corpuscular Hemoglobin Concentration (MCHC), the amount of hemoglobin per red blood cell, is significantly lower than in the men (Taukuro *et al.* 1980:84; Table 3.9B).

The WHO report a striking lack of elderly people older than their mid–forties (NFCEPS 1979a), especially among the women. Wopkaimin weight, height and skinfold declines with increasing age (Table 3.9A) and decreasing body weight with advancing age has been reported for a number of New Guinea peoples (Hipsley and Clements 1947; Whyte 1958; Venkatachalam 1962; Jansen 1963; Hipsley and Kirk 1965; Vines 1970). Skinfold and mean triceps thickness measure subcutaneous fat in the body, which in PNG is normally low. Fat is the most limiting nutrient in the Wopkaimin diet, especially for women who consume significantly less than men (Table 3.8). Advanced age stunting in height and weight is significantly greater in women (Table 3.9A) and this may be a factor contributing to their increased death rate in middle–age. Women's diet (Table 3.8) and health (Tables 3.9A and 3.9B) profile is significantly different from that of the men. The most significant differences in diet and health occur at the onset of adulthood when the interrelationship of gender and diet creates a negative feedback nutritional problem among the Wopkaimin, which is widespread in New Guinea (Hipsley and Kirk 1965:8), whereby continuous energy demand and irregular caloric intake produces women who experience gradually deteriorating energy storage status as they grow older.

The theme in gender relations in great–men societies is the creation of an autonomous male sphere which excludes and owes nothing to women (Jorgensen 1991:266). Lindenbaum (1984) suggests this leads to two different strategies of male domination. In big–men societies exchanges of wealth emphasize mystification of women's powers of men's

TABLE 3.9A Gender Differences in Aspects of Wopkaimin Health, 1975

Age	Sex	Height	Weight	Skinfold
40>	M	1565	47.3	4.4
	F	1457[a]	41.0[b]	4.6
25–40	M	1535	49.4	4.8
	F	1487[b]	44.4[b]	6.2[a]
20–24	M	1526	49.8	4.7
	F	1489	45.2	7.0[b]
15–19	M	1535	45.0	4.3
	F	1420	47.0	11.1[b]
10–14	M	1308	27.0	6.9
	F	1364	31.4	7.3
5–9	M	1077	22.0	6.1
	F	1196[b]	21.0	6.0
2–4	M	947	12.1	5.9
	F	797[b]	8.6[b]	6.1
1–2	M	802	6.6	5.6
	F	743	6.6	5.1

[a] $p < 0.01$
[b] $p < 0.05$

production, whereas in great–men societies the central place of cults obscure women's powers of reproduction. In those with ritualized homosexuality, semen in conception theory is analogous to that played by wealth in shells and pigs in big–men societies.

No form of ritual homosexuality is practised among the Wopkaimin, nor reported among other Mountain Ok (Jorgensen 1991:267). Elaborate male initiation sequences among the Wopkaimin, and other Mountain Ok (Barth 1975; Poole 1982), begin in adolescence and do not terminate until men are 20–24 years of age. Over a decade duration young men completely alter their gender and ritual status through staged initiations (Poole 1981). What is important is not the circulation of male substance but the insulation of a male realm distinct from that of women (Jorgensen 1991:268) during which time men gradually acquire the dietary changes

TABLE 3.9B Gender Differences in Aspects of Wopkaimin Health, 1975

Age	Sex	Hackett	Hemo.	MCHC	PCV
40>	M	0.6	11.5	29.6	38.1
	F	0.1	11.1	30.9*	35.9
25–40	M	1.1	11.7	30.7	37.8
	F	1.1	11.1	30.5	36.2
20–24	M	0.7	11.9	31.7	37.4
	F	1.4	10.7*	30.4*	35.3
15–19	M	0.8	12.0	30.3	39.8
	F	1.0	11.2	30.3	37.0
10–14	M	1.3	10.9	30.1	36.0
	F	1.6	11.0	29.8	36.6
5–9	M	1.3	10.8	30.9	35.1
	F	1.0	11.3	30.1	37.6
2–4	M	1.3	9.8	29.5	33.2
	F	2.0	9.4	30.8	29.0
1–2	M	0.8	8.4	27.9	33.0
	F	1.0	10.4	29.6	35.0

*$p < 0.05$.

necessary to attaining their superior adult diet and health status. Gender differences ecologically and socially adjust the Wopkaimin to their environment by limiting population size through women's gradually deteriorating diet and health.

Jorgensen (1991:269) importantly observed that the seemingly endless proliferation of taboos and secrecy among the Mountain Ok serves to impose divisions between the sexes. Men construct through exclusion their exclusive domain, the logic being one of separation, closure and boundaries: all so different from public transactions in big–men societies where the system of circulation binds the sexes together while placing them unequally within it. The Wopkaimin, and other Mountain Ok (Jorgensen 1991:270), elaborate a distinct sphere of autonomous masculine work and ritual that seeks power not over but apart from women.

4

A Sacred Mountain of Gold: The Creation of a Mining Resource Frontier

Colonial Intrusion to the Other Side of the Frontier

Austen (1923) provides a detailed account of the first colonial intrusion into the Wopkaimin homeland. It was not until 1920 that Austen, a colonial Papua administrative officer, suspected there was any human occupation along the Alice and Ok Tedi Rivers above the D'Albertis Junction. Based on statements from interpreters and his first examination of the Dutch Schetskaart van Nieuw Guinee (Star Mountains) map published in 1919 (Austen 1923:336–7), he led an exploration patrol of the lower Ok Tedi River up to 600 m between 12 January and 5 April 1922. According to the location and elevation indicated on his sketch map, Austen (1923:339) probably crossed into the Wopkaimin Migalsim parish (Figure 1.3). His ethnographic discussion of peoples encountered during the northern part of the patrol is descriptive of the Wopkaimin:

> The tribes on both sides of the Tedi quite openly admitted the practice of eating human flesh, but they state it is only an enemy that is killed in war that is eaten ...
>
> The natives on both banks of the Tedi and among the Star Mountains as far as I traveled, had the same type of garden, usually on the slope of a hill. The cultivation seems very primitive. The dense timber on the hillside and down at the bottom is chopped and allowed to rot in the ground where it has fallen. It is never burnt off, for we passed through many gardens in our travels that were in various stages of cultivation. It may be that originally their gardens were made only where the whole village lived, and the fallen

trees acted as a defence. Now, however, gardens are made on other hills away from the village as well as round the village itself. Or again, it may be that the people have found that the decayed leaves from the fallen timber form a better manure than ash. None of the gardens were fenced ...

The numbers from one to five are counted in the finger of the left hand, beginning with the little finger. Six to ten are shown by marking various parts of the body. I do not think they count further ...

Friends meeting after an interval hook fingers by placing the first finger of the right hand of one in between the first and second fingers of the right hand of the other. Then the fingers are pulled sharply apart, making a clicking sound (Austen 1923:344-6).

Together, Austen's brief observations above are not enough to confirm he met the Wopkaimin. However, they were certainly encountered by Austen on his second patrol late in 1922 and his map places him in the Wopkaimin Iralim parish (Figure 1.3) (Austen 1923:339):

On October 16 I left Wukpit with eight Native Police and eighteen of my carriers. We proceeded along the Tedi in canoe–rafts as far as it was possible to fight against the current. After leaving the rafts we walked overland to the Star Mountains and reached within a few miles of the source of the Tedi river ...

Owing to the lack of instruments, no observations could be made to find the height reached in the Star Mountains, but at one point I was able with the help of a Dutch map, to resect position, and I do not consider I ascended at any time more than 5000 feet above sea level ...

Among the Star Mountains many small villages were seen on razor–backed ridge tops, near to one another as the crow flies; but the precipitous country made it difficult to travel quickly from one village to another ...

The Woram [Aekyom] seem to extend as far north as the lower spurs of the Star Mountains, but I was unable to obtain any further information as to the name of those living among the mountains to the north of the Ok Tedi. Of a dozen fully grown men from the northern Woram the majority measured not more than 5 feet, some of them going as low as 4 feet 8 inches ...

Among the mountains to the north of the Ok Tedi, the few I saw appeared to equal the smaller Woram ...

In the villages of the lower Tedi on both sides, the natives were only as dark as our Northern Division police, and occasionally much lighter. Further north on the western side were more and more of the lighter people, until among the Star Mountains they predominated. The hair was generally woolly and very dark brown, but several men in the Star Mountains had hair rusty brown ...

The further north one goes the less sago is seen, and in the Star Mountains, out of what looked to be three fine trees, we got only one kerosene tinful of very poor sago. The mountain people seem to live on sweet potatoes, the red variety of pandanus, bananas, and a variety of uncultivated nuts and roots from the bush. The pandanus is cultivated in large quantities, and as far as I could ascertain is cooked in lengths of bamboo ...

The further north we proceeded, the fewer iron axes were seen, until when we reached our most northerly point the natives, though they had heard of knives and axes, apparently had never used them. Bamboo knives and flint chips take the place of European or Malay–made knives ...

The bark of the Wun tree was used to stupefy fish, and small stacks of it were seen near many small creeks, even on the upper Tedi. Fish–traps made by fencing the mouth of a creek were also seen in these higher altitudes, but more of the conical–shaped fish–traps were noticed among the Woram. Fish arrows of six prongs were seen even in the mountain villages near the source of the Tedi ...

The people of the western upper Tedi ... grow more sweet potatoes and taro than the lower Tedi people ... But though the mountain people have these in large gardens, there seems only enough for their own use, and even a small party like mine could not depend on the village for even two days' food, without leaving the villagers short ...

Where the high mountains begin, the main tracks follow the creeks as much as possible, but wherever the water becomes deep, the track continues up over scarped cliffs and down again to the shingle, the carriers had a most arduous time climbing precipices. Once or twice I tried to avoid them by going further inland, but decided that the native tracks were the best after all (Austen 1923:346–9).

Austen's appearance in the Wopkaimin homeland is one of the earliest colonial intrusions among the Mountain Ok peoples. According to Craig (1969:18), the German–Dutch expedition led by Leonhard Schultze–Jena penetrated the northern Atbalmin (Figure 1.2) homeland in 1910 during their search for the source of the Sepik River. Later in 1914 the German colonial explorer Thurnwald reached the Sepik Source Basin and met the Telefolmin and Feramin (Wheatcroft 1975:42). Although Austen established an initial Australian colonial presence among the Mountain Ok only a few years later, the Wopkaimin did not see *tabasep* (Europeans) again for 30 years, as Australian colonization shifted from the southern Mountain Ok back to the Sepik Source Basin.

Champion (1966) crossed New Guinea in 1927. The Hindenburg Wall was such an obstacle his first attempt was unsuccessful. Late in 1927 accompanied by Karius, they completed a south to north crossing of New Guinea for the Australian colonial administration. They passed through the Engkaiakmin hamlet of Bolivip well to the east of the Wopkaimin (Figure 1.2).

Gold prospectors crossed the Hindenburg Wall 10 years later. Kienzle and Campbell (1937) followed Champion's route and they, too, did not encounter the Wopkaimin. In the Sepik Source Basin they cleared an airstrip on Telefolmin land. They (Campbell 1938) did not find gold and only made limited ethnographic observations about the Mountain Ok.

Black and Taylor conducted a large Australian colonial patrol out of Mt. Hagen to the Mountain Ok (Black 1970). Craig (1969:27) traces the movements of the patrol through the Telefolmin homeland and Morren (1974:45–7) documents their encounter with the Miyanmin. They did not pass through the southern Mountain Ok region.

Attempting to escape the Japanese during World War II, Thurston (Champion 1966:214) led seven Europeans and 80 carriers successfully through Mountain Ok territory, this time from north to south. Later during the war American soldiers landed at the Telefolmin airstrip. With the aid of a small bulldozer dropped in by glider, they expanded the airstrip to 1000 m in 1945 (Craig 1969:31).

Colonial intrusion for the Mountain Ok people of central New Guinea really started after the war when Champion (1966:212) opened the first Australian patrol post in 1948 in the Sepik Source Basin near the *Telefolip*, the Telefolmin's most sacred cult house and the region's foremost focus of cultural identity (Figure 1.2). The Australian Baptist Missionary Society arrived shortly after in 1950. Initial resistance against colonial invaders was expressed in 1953. Attacking and killing of Australian patrol officers and indigenous policemen organized by the ritual leaders of the *Telefolip* led to 10 years' imprisonment of 33 Telefolmin men (Quinlaven 1954). The Telefolmin were retaliating against intolerable sexual offenses against their women and they still do not feel justice has been done, especially since 33 of their men went to prison (Craig 1990). The Telefolmin reprisal was viewed as a grave setback by the colonial administration, therefore "despite the relatively early start of patrolling from Telefolmin, the whole area did not proceed beyond the consolidation phase until around 1960" (Jackson 1975:11–13).

Nolan, on patrol from Telefolmin, was the next to pass through the Iralim parish but he did not contact the Wopkaimin. Both the Kent and Jacobs 1954 patrol out of Kiunga and the Bottrill and Pople patrol out of

Telefolmin likewise passed through Wopkaimin territory without encountering any people. The Wopkaimin were well aware of Australian retribution against the Telefolmin and refrained from attacking Patrol Officer Booth from Telefolmin, who in 1957 met them in their Kam Basin homeland (Booth 1957). Everyone but an old man and his two children ran from Tumgunabip when Booth arrived. He killed the old man's pig to feed his patrol and by late afternoon 70 Wopkaimin had congregated in Tumgunabip. How narrowly Booth missed disaster befalling himself and his patrol over the pig killing is documented in the following account collected in the Bakonabip men's house in July 1975:

> Back when the kiap (patrol officer) first came to the Kam Basin we were fighting the Kamfaiwolmin. We have many *wasi sung* (war stories) that tell how we drove the Kamfaiwolmin out of the Kam Basin to Lake Sokilmik. When the kiap first arrived at Tumgunabip everyone fled except our *kamokim* (leader). The kiap was accompanied by policemen, carriers, and a Telefolmin interpreter. The interpreter told the *kamokim* we had to build a rest house in Tumgunabip because the kiaps would need a place to sleep on their future patrols. Then the policemen demanded that the *kamokim* kill his pig and arrange for other food to be brought to Tumgunabip. They killed the *kamokim's* hunting dog to demonstrate their guns. The *kamokim* was frightened and angry and reluctantly gave away his pig for some soap, matches, salt and cloth. Women brought taro while the men fully armed themselves and secretly surrounded Tumgunabip. One brave man joined the *kamokim* but they were unsuccessful in negotiating for some steel knives for the food they presented to the kiap. Although the men felt they had been treated unfairly, they in the end, hid their weapons and peacefully returned to Tumgunabip because they were afraid that if they attacked the patrol, the government would retaliate against them as harshly they had against the Telefolmin four years earlier.

Pacification of the Wopkaimin was the foremost objective of the colonial administration. Several law and order and census patrols followed out of Telefolmin. Aisbett (1958a), the next to come south, censused few Wopkaimin. He correctly assumed the Kamfaiwolmin were refugees between their Wopkaimin and Faiwolmin enemies and noted they feared attack from the Wopkaimin of Migalsim parish. Aisbett (1958a) described (1) the persistence of cloud, fog and rain; (2) the abundance of food; (3) the importance of hunting pigs, cassowaries, possums and wallabies; and (4) the prevalence of huge gardens cleared by the much prized, round-headed steel ax of Dutch origin.

On a return patrol in October 1958 Aisbett (1958b) was the first colonial officer to enter Bultem and he correctly assumed it must be the largest Wopkaimin hamlet with its cult house (*Futmanam*), men's house and eight women's residential houses. In April 1959 Fenton (1959) took the first census in Migalsimabip but only counted 20 Wopkaimin. The Kamfaiwolmin also complained to Fenton that they feared a raid from the Migalsim parish. According to the Wopkaimin, they had every reason to fear reprisal, because unknown to the colonial administration they had killed several Migalsim men since imposition of colonial law and order. The Migalsim parish felt their numbers were too reduced to counterattack and that the other Wopkaimin parishes may not join them for fear of the administration.

Tierney (1960) attempted another Wopkaimin census in June 1960, but in 12 days he only counted 58 people. He then returned in January 1961 via Tifalmin and down the Hindenburg Wall (Tierney 1961) and accounted for 225 Wopkaimin in the Iralim parish. He described this as the best patrol to date to the Wopkaimin, but after nine patrols only the Migalsim and Iralim parishes had been encountered and the Fitiktaman, Beinglim and Kavorbang parishes (Figure 1.3) remained unknown to the colonial administration.

The Fitzer (1963) patrol out of Kiunga in 1963 took 124 days of "geographic hell for foot travelers" to reach the Beinglim and Kavorbang parishes. Contrary to popular misconception (Jackson 1982:43), the Fitzer patrol of 1963 was not the first to the Wopkaimin, but only the first finally to reach the parishes west of the Ok Tedi. The 50 Wopkaimin seen in the Beinglim parish in February 1963 were described as "extremely kindly and helpful." Fitzer (1963) estimated he had encountered no more than 250 during the patrol. Because of the "indescribable roughness, the weathered limestone and the confused ridges", Fitzer (1963) had "no hesitation in stating that there was no possibility of establishing a patrol post on the Papuan side of the Star Mountains."

The 1 Pacific Island Regiment (PIR) was the next patrol from Telefolmin into the southern Mountain Ok region in 1963. In August 1963 they reached the Iralim parish seven days out of Telefolmin (PIR 1963). Residents of Tumgunabip were reportedly nervous at the first entry of the colonial army into the Kam Basin, but Migalsimabip residents supposedly welcomed more army patrols because they and the Kamfaiwolmin still feared one another (PIR 1963).

Australian colonizers by this time decided they should have a greater presence and more administration among the southern Mountain Ok. Fitzer had already dismissed the Wopkaimin Beinglim and Kavorbang parishes for locating a patrol post and a site was chosen instead on the upper Fly River. Hoad (1964) established the Olsobip Patrol Post on Fegolmin land and in June 1964 led the first patrol from Olsobip to Wopkaimin territory. Hoad (1964) remembers the Kam Basin hamlet of Bakonabip "as the most pleasant village I have yet seen", but he was considerably less optimistic about a Western capitalist economic future for the area, stating that "the Wopkaimin are so far removed and devoid of resources that they simply have no potential for development". After Hoad's trip in November, Patrol Commander Nelson (1964) led another army patrol through the Wopkaimin Migalsim and Iralim parishes and to Lake Sokilmik in Kamfaiwolmin territory.

Over a year went by without a colonial presence among the Wopkaimin until Patrol Commander Bell (1966) led an army patrol from Ningerum to the Wopkaimin in 1966. He included accurate impressions of vegetation, streams and hamlet plans and locations along the Ok Mani and Ok Tedi Rivers. Soon after in 1966, Strempel (1966) led another army patrol from Telefolmin to the Iralim parish. Residents of Ningningabip were described as "friendly but reserved, very superstitious, they believe that drinking from certain creeks one will bring heavy rain, certain wild birds and certain areas are 'sacred' at certain times of the year," which to Strempel (1966) indicated that after 10 years of contact the Wopkaimin were still living "traditional" lives.

In June 1966 Dent's (1966) patrol established the first colonial administration village constable system among the Wopkaimin, but he ruled out an aid post for Tumgunabip because of its extreme isolation from Olsobip Patrol Post. Luhrs (1966) attempted but failed to bring the colonial administration for the second time to the Beinglim and Kavorbang parishes later in 1966. Earlier Wopkaimin enthusiasm for colonial patrols had dampened. There were only 10 village constables among all the southern Mountain Ok and there were still no Melanesian Tok Pisin speakers among the Wopkaimin.

In August 1966, Young (1966) succeeded in bringing the Wopkaimin residents of the Beinglim and Kavorbang parishes into the Olsobip Patrol Post census division and in December 1 PIR (1966) passed through the Migalsim parish. Cleared tracks and a rest house awaited Young's (1966) arrival in Kavorabip and he indicated that he spent nine days with the friendly residents of Kavorabip and Gigabip. Young (1966) came to have more profound impact on the Wopkaimin than any previous colonial administrative or army patrol. As he was "enduring the bitterly cold weather at night, early morning and late afternoon" and was "struggling over sheer ridges, mountain peaks, waterfalls, landslip scars and pounding rivers" below the Benkwin Bluff, he made ethnographic observations but more importantly he recorded that the streams seemed to contain copper deposits!

After more than four decades, the Australian colonial presence was very marginal among the Wopkaimin. Leo Austen entered Wopkaimin territory in 1922 but then three decades went by without further colonial intrusion. Only a handful of colonial administrative and army patrols had passed through the Wopkaimin homeland and the people were still inadequately censused when Young's suspicion of copper deposits in the region was reported. The Wopkaimin continued kinship relations of production and were still effectively on the other side of a slowly advancing colonial frontier.

Kennecott: Invasion of a Sacred Mountain

Based on Young's routine patrol report, the American transnational Kennecott took out prospecting authorities No. 28 and 35 P on Wopkaimin land with the Australian colonial Department of Lands in 1967. McGregor's (1968) patrol of January 1968 informed the Wopkaimin and the Kamfaiwolmin for the first time that Kennecott prospectors would be arriving on their land to prospect for mineral wealth, which was considered to be owned by the state. McGregor (1968) confused indigenous people's identities with their most important hamlet names and misnamed the landowners as 'Bultems' (Wopkaimin) and 'Wangbins' (Kamfaiwolmin). According to McGregor (1968) everyone enthusiastically awaited the Kennecott prospectors and Kennecott had treated the people quite fairly.

Prior intrusion of the Australian colonial state had only slightly impacted on Wopkaimin kinship relations of production, and they were certainly not prepared for the Kennecott invasion and their first incorporation into the world capitalist system. By dividing the Ok Tedi mining project into an economic base and a derivative sociopolitical and ideological superstructure (see Godoy 1985), the economic base of mining was established in 1968 when Kennecott opened their major base camp at Tabubil and started prospecting in the Wopkaimin ancestral rain forests. Later in 1968, Patrol Officer Eggleton (1968) observed that Western clothing, tobacco, steel axes and knives and Melanesian Pidgin English had spread rapidly among the Wopkaimin, as well as influenza which had killed five to six percent of the people.

Missionary influence in the southern Mountain Ok region was entirely dispersed east of the Wopkaimin among the Summer Institute of Linguistics (SIL) in the Fegolmin hamlet of Laubip, the Baptists around the Olsobip Patrol Post and the Montford Catholic Mission at the Enkaiakmin hamlet of Bolivip. Kennecott never permitted white missionaries to use their airstrip at Tabubil and thus prevented them access to the Wopkaimin.

Sustained onslaught to Wopkaimin place and culture started with Kennecott test drilling on Mt Fubilan (Figure 1.4) in 1969, the location now commonly referred to as the "Pot of Gold" (Jackson 1982). To the Wopkaimin, Fubilan is a sacred mountain sitting on top of the land of the dead (Jorgensen 1990). To the exploration geologists, it was a 2200 m peak situated on the extremely rugged and unstable Star and Hindenburg Mountains that received over 1100 cm of rainfall every year, making it the wettest place recorded anywhere in New Guinea. Exploration between 1969 and 1971 costing A$13 million determined that an extremely ambitious engineering project could convert Mt Fubilan's 137 million tonnes of 0.88 percent copper ore containing 0.66 grams per tonne of gold into a profitable mining project (Pintz 1984:33).

Eggleton (1969) patrolled through Wopkaimin and Kamfaiwolmin hamlets in 1969 to inform the people that the colonial administration had assigned them to a new Star Mountains Census Division out of Ningerum and he remained on a semipermanent basis in Kennecott's Tabubil base camp. He reported (Eggleton 1969) that landowners did not comprehend how the state was to assume resource owner rights and Kennecott was to assume resource developer rights, while they themselves would receive only A$563 in occupation fees.

The next year Richards (1970), while assessing the Star Mountains Census Division for local government, found the Wopkaimin did not appreciate that although PNG had a self-governing House of Assembly, it still remained an Australian colony. Richards (1970) felt that if lumped with the Ningerum, the Wopkaimin would be a minority with little in common with the majority. Kennecott was operating a full drilling program on Mt Fubilan with a staff of 45 Europeans and 500 PNG nationals mostly from the Southern Highlands, with only a few able-bodied Wopkaimin men.

By 1971 Kennecott had financed the first aid post and first primary school with room and board in Tabubil for workers and other Wopkaimin and the Kamfaiwolmin. In 1972 Brillante (1972) again patrolled to lecture about House of Assembly elections but the Wopkaimin were apparently incapable of interpreting photographs for voting purposes. The Ningerum Local Government Council was first opened in November 1971, but none of the Wopkaimin or any other southern Mountain Ok attended.

In his later patrol from Ningerum in 1972, McGrath (1972) acknowledged that the Wopkaimin and Kamfaiwolmin had never had a qualified medical patrol and that many deaths had occurred in 1971, which he attributed to whooping cough. McGrath (1972) backed resettling the Wopkaimin, advocating the frequently voiced colonial administration line that (1) isolated hamlets wasted patrol time; (2) goods, services, health and education were at Tabubil; (3) Tabubil offered the sole source of cash income; (4) moving would uplift the standard of living; and (5) present garden sites higher in the mountains were no good because they only grew taro that took a year to mature. McGrath (1972) condemned the Wopkaimin to a "bare subsistence level" of existence as long as they continued kinship relations of production in their ancestral rain forests. To the colonial state, the mere possibility of cash income generated by Kennecott prospecting ushered in prospects of capitalist relations of production equated unchallengingly with a superior standard of living.

The Kamfaiwolmin were to relocate on their own land east of Tabubil. Wopkaimin parishes were to variously relocate on portions of their land closest to Tabubil. Migalsim parish was to go to Wokdonkan near the confluence of the Ok Tedi and Ok Mani. Beinglim and Kavorbang parishes, considered the most isolated, were to go to the Ok Mani one day's walk west of Tabubil. The Iralim parish had land across the Ok Tedi from Tabubil and north at the Woktemwanin sago groves. Resettlement was contingent on Kennecott mining and expanding their facilities at Tabubil but this never happened.

By 1971 Kennecott was negotiating a mining agreement with the Australian colonial government. As Kennecott continued negotiations, Parker (1972) conducted another Local Government survey in the Star Mountains Census Division in 1972. Parker (1972:7) proposed a Bultem

Ward, a Gigabip and Kavorabip Ward and a Wangbin and Migalsimabip Ward and stated that "at its meeting of 4 September, 1972 the [Ningerum] Council resolved that three wards of the above composition be added to the council and that the Council Constitution be accordingly amended."

It had taken over a year for the three proposed new Council Wards to elect their first Councilor. Upon my arrival in Tabubil in December 1973 the Councilor was leaving for his first Council meeting in Ningerum. Negotiations between Kennecott and the Australian colonial administration were still under way. Of the earlier total of some 550 Kennecott prospecting personnel, only three Europeans under Field Manager Charlie Cole and about a dozen southern Mountain Ok laborers remained at Tabubil. The prospecting operation on Mt Fubilan was drastically reduced and Kennecott had totally discontinued its operation among the Tifalmin (Wheatcroft 1975:61). Except for a few laborers at Tabubil, all the Wopkaimin were home practising kinship relations of production in their ancestral rain forests.

Kennecott never mined the pot of gold. Having their copper mines in Chile nationalized by the Allende government frightened Kennecott into abandoning the Ok Tedi project shortly before independence in PNG in September 1975. From the beginning tax and arbitration provisions (Jackson 1982:40–72; Pintz 1984:32–49), rather than environmental or landowner protection, were the national government's primary concern. Kennecott refused to accept demands from the new PNG government for 50 percent of mining profits. Following prolonged deadlocks at the negotiating table, Kennecott's prospecting authority was withdrawn on 12 March 1975 (Jackson 1982:66; Townsend 1988:107) and the state established its own Ok Tedi Development Company.

Ok Tedi Mining Limited: Mining a Sacred Mountain

Although Austen formally encountered the Wopkaimin as far back as the 1920s, by the 1960s they essentially remained on the other side of the colonial frontier. With independence in 1975, government services were drastically reduced to the Wopkaimin and throughout remote PNG. Ransley (1975) conducted the last colonial administrative patrol in May–June 1975 during the period of self–government. He was the first and last patrol officer that censused in every parish and he counted 694 Wopkaimin. Since independence the Wopkaimin have never been patrolled by the administration. Neither the colonial nor the national government ever really intruded on the Wopkaimin kinship mode of production. It was only in the 1970s with mineral prospecting on their land that the Wopkaimin experienced their first invasion of the world capitalist system. However, Kennecott's brief boom and bust impact on the Wopkaimin left their kinship mode of production intact.

The PNG national government signed the Ok Tedi Agreement with Dampier Mining Company in March 1976, a year after the failed Kennecott negotiations. It was only an agreement to investigate the possibility of mining, but did specify in detail what conditions would apply if mining proceeded. Before the end of 1979 the 'Big Australian' mining transnational Broken Hill Proprietary Co. Ltd. (BHP) had replaced the American mining transnational Kennecott and it was to provide:

> further geological work and mapping, hydrological studies of the Ok Tedi and Fly Rivers, metallurgical investigations, feasibility studies on a locally-based copper smelter, a financial and marketing analysis, studies of the projects water supply, the design of an airstrip and mining town, calculations of workforce requirements, design of labor training schemes, studies of local business potential and environmental impact studies (Pintz 1984:62–81).

While political ties, national strategic concerns over long-term mineral supply and desires for transnational diversification were significant (Pintz 1984:61), it was the soaring gold prices that peaked in late 1979–early 1980 that finally prompted creation of the transnational Ok Tedi Mining Limited (OTML) consortium in 1981 to develop the project.

The eventual involvement of BHP has been viewed as a national duty to Australia (Pintz 1984:55) and as a loss of political independence to PNG (Jackson 1982:87). Unlike Kennecott, BHP from the beginning focused on the gold capping of Mt Fubilan and insisted on consortium partners. Kupferexplorationsgesellschaft (KE) and Standard Oil of Indiana (AMOCO) were eventually attracted by the PNG government. The KE investment group was prompted by German dependency on outside mineral supplies and the German government extended substantial indirect support to the KE group (Pintz 1984:59). The involvement of AMOCO reflects Ray Ballmer's role as president of its minerals subsidiary in the development of the mine on Bougainville. BHP and America's Amoco both have a 30 percent share, but the BHP mining transnational operates the consortium. The German industrial conglomerate KE took a 20 percent share as did the PNG government (Pintz 1984:14).

Once construction started on the Ok Tedi project in 1981, OTML became a much greater influence on the Wopkaimin than the colonial or national government had ever been because they were incorporated into the expanding mining frontier of the world capitalist system. Previously the Wopkaimin had been on the other side of the frontier practising kinship relations of production based on a sustained yield of living resources from their ancestral rain forests. The economic base of the mining project, by contrast, was based on the extraction of non-renewable, inorganic resources considered to be owned by the state. With the development of the Ok Tedi project, gold and copper mining became the major force in the economy and by 1982 PNG produced 18,000 kg of gold and 170,000 tonnes of copper, each were two percent of the world total (Howard 1988:9–10).

Involved as he was in representing the national government in the PNG–BHP agreement, Pintz (1984:63) acknowledged that his team of lawyers, planners and financial analysts were not particularly equipped to deal with technical questions. Nor, as eventuated, were they qualified to deal effectively with socio–ecological impact dimensions of the project. The state's negotiators were public servants working at the First Assistant Secretary level, the core of the Ok Tedi Management Committee consisted of the departments of Minerals and Energy, Finance, Justice and the National Planning Office. None had landowners or the environment as a primary departmental responsibility.

To manage and co–ordinate the state's interest, particularly in environmental protection, the Mineral Resources Development Company (MRDC) was created in 1981 with the intention that it would co–ordinate and manage departments and operate at the secretarial level. However, by 1983 MRDC was reorganized to function only as a division within Minerals and Energy (Townsend 1988:110).

Pintz (1984:69) found that the PNG bureaucracy was so thinly stretched that they simply could not cope with the massive fieldwork needed to acquire and lease land. All of the social policy studies concerning environment, township development, training and localization and business development were rejected by the national government. The sum of Kina 150,000 specified for the environmental impact studies was ludicrously inadequate Jackson (1982:85–86). According to the state "when assessing any environment plans the N.E.C. [PNG Cabinet] will bear strongly in mind the particular importance of rivers and waterways to the life of the people of the Western Province" (Pintz 1984:77). The national government actually commissioned their own environmental investigation in 1979 which raised substantial questions about the effects of dumping wastes and mine effluents into the Ok Tedi River and the cost was four times the consortium's program. The candid observation from Pintz (1984:70–81) was that "there is little positive to be said about either the government's or the consortium's treatment of social issues other than to note that eventually differences were reconciled without resort to arbitration."

Nonetheless, environmental concerns created an advisarial relationship between the two groups. To the national government resource usage meant types and grades of ore and environmental impact meant sediment and effluent studies, and reticence of the consortium to spend environmental funds reinforced an image of ecologically abusive mining transnationals (Pintz 1984:90–1). With PNG functioning as project shareholder and resource owner, landowners and environment were left considerably underrepresented. In January 1981 the national government undertook "a limited support commitment (i.e., guarantee or completion undertaking) for Stages II and III and a minimum equity contribution for Stage I in return for a relatively high figure for initially committed finance (e.g., US$650 million)" (Pintz 1984:119). This was considered a favorable position for the state vis-a-vis other shareholders, but not, as almost happened, if only the gold cap was removed and the copper ore was left unmined.

The construction transnational Bechtel was chosen as the contractor to build the infrastructure for the Ok Tedi project and they were based in Tabubil and Melbourne. The OTML management was based primarily in Port Moresby and began dealing directly with the Secretary of Finance, Secretary of Minerals and Energy and other government ministers and by 1983 MRDC had been completely bypassed as the point of contact as designated in 1981 (Townsend 1988:110). Thus, rarely did MRDC brief ministers or appear before the National Executive Council and this effectively removed technical considerations from the decision–making process (Townsend 1988:111).

Devolution of decision making to provincial governments was an immediate domestic political issue in post–independent PNG. However, the Western, or Fly River, provincial government was not considered administratively competent to handle decentralization of the Ok Tedi project. For assigning certain management and policy functions back to the central government, the Fly River Province received an initial grant of US$0.75 million and an annual budgetary supplement of US$1.5 million each year until 1987, when replaced by normal royalty receipts (Pintz 1984:127). Financial returns to the province from the mining project are meagre.

From the beginning of Ok Tedi, "the government could conceive and execute analytical studies and negotiate sophisticated investor agreements but lacked the capacity to follow through on broad social recommendations in the field" (Pintz 1984:142). They considered their commissioned socio–economic impact study (Jackson *et al* 1980) to be erratic, emotional and polemic (Pintz 1984:142), which was a cover–up for their administrative incompetence to act on it.

A broadly defined surrogate administration was created for the Ok Tedi region. It took on land acquisition and established a policy of recognizing traditional clan boundary delineation practices rather than using surveyed boundaries. Customary land uses were to be recognized and continued hunting access to leased areas was permitted until needed for mining. An ecological buffer zone planned around Tabubil was intended primarily for the eventual control of squatters.

The PNG government and OTML anticipated that with their compensation payments of about one Kina per person per day, the Wopkaimin would undergo a transition from 'traditional' to 'modern' (Pintz 1984:130). The PNG government and OTML erroneously equated the Wopkaimin desire for cash as a desire for the transition to modernity. Not surprisingly, Barth and Wikan (1982:8) found that there "is a tendency both among expatriates in Bechtel/MKI and the senior government personnel in Port Moresby to see the question as one of how far the population has moved towards effective participation in Ok Tedi developments."

The Wopkaimin are perceived as traditional primitives. In land policy discussions the government assumed "the situation was somewhat confusing to the average person, but well nigh impossible to explain to a traditional landowner in the Star Mountains" (Pintz 1984:129). It was incredible to Jackson (1982:18) that "so isolated were many of the groups who constitute the Min people of the Star Mountains, that Barth could talk of the 183 Baktaman he studied as a 'nation' who sustain through their own activities, a whole culture and world of their own." The OTML promotional book *Ok Tedi 24:00* repeatedly made insensitive mockery of Wopkaimin 'primitivism'. Appearing naked except for penis gourd and ceremonial headdress, a Wopkaimin community relations employee of

OTML repeatedly undressed for contrived poses contrasting primitive villagers with civilized, high–tech sophisticated workers (e.g. Browne 1983:88).

To the PNG government and OTML the transition from primitivism to modernity is a foregone conclusion that inevitably involves psychological trauma. When Wopkaimin leaders were taken by the government to the Panguna mining project on Bougainville so they could assess a large open cut mining operation, they were assumed to have gained nothing from the experience due to their primitivism:

> More needs to be learnt about the peoples' attitude to large volumes of non-flowing water. Obviously, the Wopkaimin people are accustomed to flowing water. Their rivers are quite large, fast flowing and can rise to terrifying heights displaying tremendous force. On the other hand, Lake Wangbin is a 'spirit place'--people are reluctant to fish or swim in it, let alone drink from it. Most of those on the recent tour were reluctant to go anywhere near the sea. Because of their knowledge of the very might of their streams in full flood, it is probably inconceivable that man can 'banisim' (close off) a river. Even so, when these people relate damming to closing off, it is difficult to believe other than that in a full flood the river is going to back right up, especially when one has no concept of spillways and constant flow–through of penstocks and turbines on down the lower river... It is obvious that the older men, now back home, cannot believe that all they saw was real and happening. It was, and is more so now, just a dream. If it was mostly real, some aspects were not, they feel. The Moresby crowds, they believe arrive from the sea each morning and return there each night whilst the large trucks at the Panguna mine are driven by the same type of spirit (Pintz 1984:24).

In discussions with the Wopkaimin *kamokim* and *awem kinum* leader about his Bougainville mine visit, he did not relate a story of incomprehensible spirit power. It was meeting the Nasioi land owners in Bougainville and their hosting a welcoming ceremony with baked pork that impressed him. Continuity of a sharing etiquette and kinship relations of production in the midst of the European's capitalist relations of production was the enduring memory, not an unreal dream as misconstrued by the government.

Resource expropriation in New Guinea has spatial as well as temporal aspects. Resources are being transported from the past of their "primitive" locations to the present of an industrial, capitalist economy. The temporal conception of movement has always served to legitimize the colonial and transnational enterprise (Fabian 1983:95). The passage from savagery to civilization has long ideologically served to justify resource expropriation for Western markets. New Guinea gold and copper become commodities when they are possessed, removed from their resource context and placed into the history of Western commerce (Wolf 1982).

A system of production that had long worked is being replaced by a system that does not. On the Ok Tedi mining frontier it has become a clash between indigenous nation and state and between kinship and capitalist relations of production. By structurally equating rational with modern, the persistence of the Wopkaimin as a distinct people with their kinship relations of production within the expanding capitalist mining frontier has been misrepresented as irrational and improbable.

5

Peoples of the OK Tedi and Fly Rivers:
A Socio–Ecological Region under Threat

Commoditization of Natural Resources in Papua New Guinea

Being in a mining resource frontier at the periphery of the world
capitalist system, PNG produces for the world market and imports to
supply the home market. The Australian colonial administration laid the
groundwork for the production of commodities for export and promoted
the use of natural resources to finance 'economic development':

> The exploitation of natural resources would be handed over to foreign
> companies, who would bring in capital and technology. All that the country
> had to do was give concessions, skim off a portion of the revenues from the
> production and export raw materials, and then employ the available resources
> for national development (Kreye and Castell 1990:17).

PNG has since followed a typical mining trajectory where the state
takes the subsoil minerals while being vague about indemnifying
indigenous peoples against resulting ecological devastations (Godoy
1985:208). Clause 29.13 of the 1976 Ok Tedi agreement states:

> regard ... shall be had to the limited present use of the area, to the need for
> its development, to the State's desire for the project to proceed, and to the
> effect the project must 'necessarily' have on the environment.

According to Jackson (1982:86) the "implication was clear: environment
was not considered to be as important a consideration as the need to raise

capital for the national exchequer. Such a clause also raised many other questions: who determined that the Star Mountains needed developing? Who says that mining will develop it? Who, of anyone, can say what environmental costs are 'necessary'?"

Peoples of the Fly River Socio–Ecological Region

Mining requirements for capital, labor and food for workers as well as the physical output of its operation integrates surrounding regions into a single socio–ecological sphere (Godoy 1985:207). From the beginning of production the Ok Tedi project has been nothing short of an environmental disaster. Weak environmental protection plans coupled with a long series of ecological disasters starting in 1984 have endangered natural resources sustaining over 40,000 indigenous peoples of the Ok Tedi and Fly Rivers. Within this socio–ecological region (Figure 5.1), the Ok Tedi––Upper Fly consists of 700 Wopkaimin Mountain Ok peoples, 3000 Ningerum and 2,200 Yonggom Lowland Ok peoples and 6000 Aekyom (Awin–Pa) peoples. Indigenous peoples of the Middle Fly speak Marind languages, including 2000 Boazi and 1,500 Zimakani. South of the Strickland confluence are 1000 Suki, 3300 Waruna and 7000 Gogodala peoples. On the Lower Fly are 200 Lewada, 170 Balamula, 280 Tirio and 23,000 Kiwai Trans Fly peoples (Voorhoeve 1975).

Since production in the mid–1980s pollution from suspended sediments and heavy metals in the Ok Tedi has been 10,000 percent greater than American Environmental Protection Agency standards (AMDEL 1984:42). Pollution threatens subsistence staples like fish, crustaceans, turtles and crocodiles from the river and gardens and sago palms growing along the riverbanks and backswamps. By 1989 it became clear that continued sediment and chemical discharge from the mining project threatened pollution and massive loss of aquatic life down the entire Fly River socio–ecological region.

"Excellent Environmental Protection"
for the Ok Tedi and Its Peoples

At first the state considered it was not politically feasible to permit the Ok Tedi project to repeat the scale of pollution that occurred with the

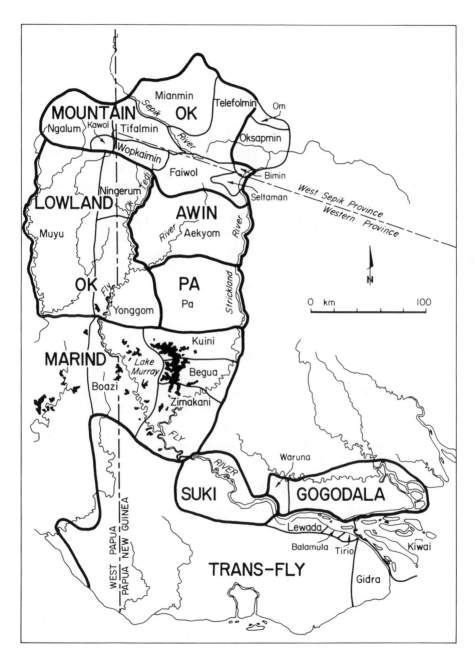

FIGURE 5.1 Peoples of the Fly River socio–ecological region.

earlier Panguna gold and copper mine on Bougainville. Therefore, they negotiated in the 1976 Agreement for a permanent tailings dam on the Ok Ma to prevent mining wastes, sediments, and chemicals from entering the Fly River (Hyndman 1987:27). The Ok Tedi project is exempted from the Environmental Protection Act of 1978 because the 1982 *Ok Tedi Environmental Study* (OTES) is considered more environmentally appropriate. The fifth volume of the OTES outlines the ethnoecology and resource utilization of the indigenous peoples impacted by the project (Hyndman 1982b; Pernetta and Hyndman 1982; Frodin and Hyndman 1982).

The original intention of the mining agreement was for no significant impact on the greater Ok Tedi River and the Fly River was to remain undamaged (Townsend 1988:117). However, the state's definition of "excellent environmental protection" (*Pacific Islands Monthly* 1984:29) meant that the Ok Mani River near the mine would be contaminated for human consumption for two decades and that aquatic life from the Ok Tedi would be contaminated downstream to Ningerum (Pintz 1984:93). They decided for the Wopkaimin and other indigenous peoples of the Ok Tedi region (Figure 5.2) that their natural resources were to become national resources. The OTES predicted some 200 million tonnes of sediments would enter the Fly River system from waste dumps and dissolved copper would increase up to 200 parts per billion (ppb) at Ningerum over 100 km below the mine, the state had earlier insisted upon 50 ppb of peak soluble copper at Ningerum (Chambers 1985:181–2). As circumstances unfolded, the state renegotiated the project six times to sustain mining production, thereby cancelling the environmental protection envisioned in the original OTES.

From the beginning the Ok Tedi project was built on the 'fast track' approach where the engineer and construction company were the same. OTML's intention was to keep the state out of technical review and this effectively eliminated a second evaluation which typically occurs in large mining projects (Townsend 1988:114). PNG made ineffective use of the two MRDC staff that were hired. The first stage of construction started in mid–1981 without the state setting up an adequate managing team, which effectively eliminated a second project review process.

PNG authorized start of construction in August 1981. After little more than a year in November 1982, the state was informed that the project was eight months behind schedule. By early 1983 construction on the Ok Menga hydroelectric facility was terminated due to the movement of a

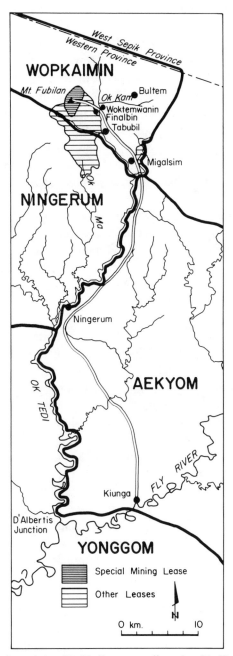

FIGURE 5.2 Peoples of the Ok Tedi surrounding the Ok Tedi mine.

massive block of land, but not before OTML had spent over US$89 million dollars on the failed project. Late in 1983, without adequate geological or design preparation, construction was rapidly undertaken on the Ok Ma tailings dam (Townsend 1988:114). As Bechtel incurred major schedule delays and cost overrides, OTML presented the state with an 'Accelerated Gold Production Scheme' (AGPS) in October–November 1983. Initially the request was rejected by then Prime Minister Somare, who issued a stern reprimand stating that "it is important that developers understand the strong view that government has on environmental protection. They must also understand that the government expects developers to adhere to agreements" (*Pacific Islands Monthly* 1984:29).

From the beginning OTML was required to report to the state at six-month intervals their accumulated and analyzed data on heavy metals and sediment levels down the Ok Tedi and the first report period started from July–December 1982. This was a period of severe drought in the middle Fly River that dried up Lake Bosset and other preferred water holes forcing the Boazi to camp on the Fly River and take their drinking water from the river. Bechtel was constructing the access road between Kiunga and Mt Fubilan as well as the mine and town site infrastructure, which put massive amounts of heavy metals into the river system. This went unreported for over a year and the state learned that heavy metal pollution would be a serious problem only after the approval of the AGPS (Townsend 1988:116).

In January 1984 a 50 million tonne, one kilometer long landslide on the Ok Ma essentially destroyed all prospects of a permanent tailings dam as a limitation to pollution problems. PNG had ignored the MRDC recommendation to spend US$50,000 to get technical advise on the proposed tailings dam. In the end the state's 20 percent share of the OTML expenditure on the aborted Ok Ma and Ok Menga dams cost US$30 million and left the project without hydroelectric power or environmental protection planned from the tailings dam. According to Townsend (1988:114) the "decision to terminate construction of the Ok Ma Dam and the National Executive Council's decision to approve the Interim Tailings Scheme was done with no technical input from the State. The whole exercise was handled in the administrative and political arena." Essentially, the landslide destruction of the Ok Ma tailings dam site eliminated the state's chances of meaningful protection of the Fly River socio–ecological region (Townsend 1988:114).

"Impossible to Build a Safe Dam":
Pollution Below the D'Albertis Junction

Gold and copper are extracted from Mt Fubilan and the mining plan involves a three–stage process that started in 1984. Gold was removed from the top of the mountain for the first five years using a carbon–in–pulp cyanide leach treatment. Gold production ceased in 1989 with the leveling of the summit and gold is now obtained only as a by–product of copper smelting using standard sulphide flotation techniques. Gold and copper is expected to continue until 2005 by which time the mountain will be transformed into a 1200 m deep mining pit.

PLATE 5.1 Mt. Fubilan in 1984 at the start of removing gold from the top of the mountain (photo courtesy of the author).

After the Ok Ma landslide Irwin Newman, a former General Manager of OTML, stated that "it will be impossible to build a safe dam in the area" (*Pacific Islands Monthly* 1984:31), thus forcing PNG to reconsider the OTML's AGPS proposal. PNG accepted the scheme knowing it involved releasing undesirably larger quantities of sediment, tailings and chemical wastes into the Ok Tedi River. Quite independent of impacts from cyanide (4–700 ppb), suspended sediments (50–800 mg/l) and other metals (lead 4–140 ppb; zinc 3–8 ppb; cadmium 0.12–0.2 ppb), it introduced vastly excessive concentrations of copper (2400–4400 ppb) over the stipulated peak concentrations of up to 230 ppb into the river system (Chambers 1985:182). According to the state's own independent report these levels are "10,000%, two orders of magnitude, over reasonable criteria; 7500% over predictions for the original tailings dam; and 650% over the maximum total from all sources predicted in the original environmental study and rejected by the State as excessively high" (AMDEL 1984:42). By assuming a resource owner and a 20 percent shareholder role in the Ok Tedi project, the state is compromised in protecting the health, well being and resources of the Wopkaimin and other indigenous peoples of the Fly River socio–ecological region.

A few months after the Ok Ma landslide disaster, a barge transporting OTML chemicals overturned 15 km north–east of Umuda Island in the Fly River estuary in June 1984, losing 2700 60–liter drums of cyanide, the single largest loss of the world's most dangerous poison, and several stainless steel containers of hydrogen peroxide. Only 117 cyanide drums were ever recovered because OTML dropped the operation and dismantled the barge once they discovered that the lost stainless steel hydrogen peroxide tanks were not economically salvageable (Townsend 1988:116). On 3 July 1984 over 500 protesters marched on the Western Province offices of the then Premier Aitawai outraged over the decision to terminate the recovery operation with thousands of cyanide drums left in the river.

On 4 July 1984 Mr Pusal, then Minerals and Energy Minister, temporarily shut down the Ok Tedi project because of a second cyanide spill, this time at the headwaters of the river system connected with the AGPS operation. A by–pass valve opened for two hours and 12 minutes on 19 June 1984 released 1000 cubic meters of highly concentrated cyanide waste into the Ok Tedi River, a spill about which OTML was silent for two weeks until dead fish, prawns, turtles, and crocodiles started floating downstream of the mine as far south as Ningerum (*Post Courier*

19, 20 June, 4 July 1984; *Times of Papua New Guinea* 5 July 1984). In their six-monthly report covering this period, OTML acknowledged their Degussa hydrogen peroxide detoxification system failed but remained completely silent about their declaring as unsalvagable thousands of drums of cyanide at the mouth of the Fly River and they concluded that the "magnitude of environmental impact was not great during this period and the fishing resources of the Lower Ok Tedi were generally unaffected" (OTML 1985:25). In one critical incident after another OTML failed to release information or take action which clearly placed environmental protection as a low priority of the Ok Tedi project.

Since the start of the project, OTML's strategy was to undermine the state's position on environmental protection by keeping the state's technical staff as far away as possible from meaningful discussion, by removing the limit of 60 million tonnes for the southern waste dumps and by proposing the AGPS operation after the Ok Ma landslide (Townsend 1988:114). OTML and the state agreed that Ok Tedi's mobile landscape would never sustain an economical or safe tailings dam but the price has meant that unacceptable quantities of sediment, tailings, and chemical wastes are routinely discharged into the headwaters of the river system, including cyanide and heavy metals with concentrations of 2400–4400 ppb of copper (Chambers 1985:182). OTML argued they should use cyclones to split off the course fraction of tailings for waste dump storage because the course particles are damaging to fish gills. The state's concern over cyanide and chemicals on aquatic life was dismissed with "fish exhibit avoidance behavior" (Townsend 1988:115). In OTML's consideration fish migrate to side streams to avoid high levels of particulate pollution and since chemicals remain confined to the main river channel the fish are not harmed. PNG responded that "if the fish are in the side streams to avoid the fines why should the project spend money to remove the course particles from the tailings?" but they were never answered (Townsend 1988:115). Five months after the start of the AGPS operation, OTML assessed that it would have "moderate to severe biological impact on the Lower Ok Tedi and a minor impact on the Fly River" (OTML 1984). During the period between 1985 and 1990 when 30,000 tonnes was processed daily, OTML predicted the Lower Ok Tedi River fishery would be reduced from good to between poor and extremely poor (Townsend 1988:117).

The Ok Tedi project was irreversibly changed with the adoption of the AGPS operation. Pollution was no longer confined to the Wopkaimin,

Ningerum and Aekyom peoples of the upper Ok Tedi River part of the socio–ecological region. As the impact of large volumes of sediment and high levels of particulate copper destroyed the Lower Ok Tedi River it was the Yonggom who began to suffer the greatest ecological impact from the Ok Tedi project. There are over 18,000 Yonggom landowners between the Kao River in West Papua and the Ok Tedi (Figures 5.1 and 5.2), which makes then one of the largest interior lowland indigenous peoples of New Guinea (Kirsch in press).

Mine sediments are deposited on Yonggom land along the Lower Ok Tedi forming 5–10 m–wide stretches of knee–deep mud and when the river overflows the banks the waste sediment destroys fertile garden land that once could be grown almost continuously along the edge of the river (Kirsch in press). Few fish now live in the Lower Ok Tedi and heavy rains upstream cause mine sediment to wash into the streams feeding the Ok Tedi threatening prawns, lobsters and bivalves (Kirsch in press). Regularly flooded rain forests are dying as the Ok Tedi River raised 2–3 m from mining sedimentation with 1–2 g particulate copper per kg of sediment. The freshly ground sand from mining produced sharp–edged particles which injured fish gills and made fish susceptible to infectious agents. Turbidity 100 times higher than before mining did not permit enough light for plant growth, which reduced river biomass production to zero (Keyre and Castell 1990:44–45).

Protein provided by aquatic resources was unable to be replaced in the Yonggom diet and the intimate association between myth, belief and environment was broken (Kirsch in press). It is impossible to drink from the river, nor can the Yonggom swim, bathe or wash clothes in it. An integral part of the Yonggom homeland has been ecologically sacrificed for continuation of the Ok Tedi project, yet neither PNG nor OTML takes any responsibility for compensation to the Yonggom (Kirsch in press). By not compensating the Yonggom, OTML avoided setting a precedent for any payments to affected peoples throughout the socio–ecological region.

In January 1985 the state refused to renew the OTML AGPS operation, not because of pollution but for contractual failure to develop a long–term copper mine. Because of low world prices in copper, OTML did not want to proceed to stage two of the project once they had stripped the more valuable gold resource from the top of Mt Fubilan by 1985. Amoco wanted to leave the consortium and PNG shut down the project over the gold versus copper issue with a deadline of June 1985. The state continued negotiating with OTML to meet their contractual obligations while considering an offer from China to form a joint venture, but they eventually permitted OTML to resume full operations in April 1985 (Hyndman 1987:29).

In May 1985 the project again moved ahead through A$288 million provided by a group of banks headed by Bank of America (Howard 1988:105). Two Amoco second-hand copper rolling and grinding mills from the United States were relocated to Tabubil and a 170 km long copper slurry pipeline was constructed from Mt Fubilan to Kiunga. Under the sixth supplemental agreement, the second stage of mining commenced in September 1986 to process 30,000 tonnes of gold and 70,000 tonnes of copper per day. Unbelievably, the Ok Tedi project went ahead without a permanent tailings dam, hydroelectric scheme or ocean port, thus making a complete mockery of the 1982 OTES. The then Minerals and Energy Minister John Kaputin somehow found the optimism to thank Roy Shipes, another former OTML General Manager, for his "magic leadership" (*Times of Papua New Guinea* 19 September 1986), which propelled PNG into gold dependency and locked the peoples of the Fly River socio-ecological region into pollution and resource degradation.

During the course of the 1980s an impressive infrastructure of roads, town, pipeline, river port and power station were slowly created for the needs of OTML and its employees. Limited use is granted to residents of the socio-ecological region or the provincial government. The state advanced US$50 million for road construction and met, or cofinanced, other infrastructural running costs (Keyre and Castell 1990:29-31). Tabubil is a totally artificial town not built for a long life and other infrastructure will no longer be required or maintained once mining is finished. Moreover, the crucial dam and retention basin for tailings for environmental protection have never been constructed.

Production in 1989 reached 441,796 tonnes of copper concentrate with a content of 135,000 tonnes of copper, 15.8 tonnes of gold and 30 tonnes of silver (Kreye and Castell 1991:22) and by the first six months of 1990 over 246,000 tonnes of copper concentrate was produced (*Post Courier* 11 October 1990). Waste rock from the leached gold capping is dumped into three creek headwaters flowing into the Ok Tedi and stronger waste rock is used to transform the Ok Gilor Valley into a waste dump. Copper concentrated in the mountain mining town of Tabubil is trucked and piped over 150 km down a newly constructed all-weather road to Kiunga (Figure 5.2) and then transported by barge to the mouth of the Fly River where it is transferred to ocean vessels for delivery to copper refineries in Germany, Japan and Korea. KE has been responsible for marketing the concentrate since 1988 (Kreye and Castell 1991:21).

Mine processing rates increased with stage three in 1991 and, without a tailings dam:

> Currently some 70,000 tonnes of ore are mined daily and processed into copper concentrate. The waste rock and tailings from the production of the concentrate (c. 98% of the ore), totalling 150,000 tonnes a day, are either discharged directly into the Ok Tedi (tailings) or dumped and washed into the river by the rain (waste rock). A large portion of this sedimentary load is carried via the Ok Tedi into the Fly River. According to the company, the Ok Tedi and Fly River systems have to carry an additional load of 70 million tonnes a year at full production, more than 1,000 million tonnes over the life of the mine (Keyre and Castell 1990:33).

OTML (1984) predicted that "excessive concentrations of suspended solids will decimate the fish populations of the Lower Ok Tedi" and that below the D'Albertis Junction to the Middle Fly there would be reduced numbers of fish species and individuals. OTML suggested that peoples of the Fly River socio–ecological region should be compensated for expenses incurred in motor boating to back swamps for subsistence fishing (Townsend 1988:118). This ignored that river water feeds into the back swamps and lakes and that during drought people regularly relocate to the banks of the Fly River.

"Environment or Economy": Sacrificing the Longest River in New Guinea

As outrage mounted from peoples throughout the Fly River socio-ecological region over increased river pollution, the PNG government was forced to contract Applied Geology Associates of New Zealand to independently reassess the environmental impact of the Ok Tedi project. The national government bypassed 1 January and 1 April 1989 deadlines for declaring Acceptable Particulate Levels (APL), but then Prime Minister Rabbie Namaliu stated emphatically that "we cannot and will not allow the wholesale destruction of aquatic life in the Fly River" (*Post Courier*, 6 April 1989).

The national government had to make a choice between total discharge into the Ok Tedi or closure of the mine and by the end of July 1989 they were making an "environment or economy" (*Post Courier*, 25 July 1989) decision for the peoples of the Fly River socio–ecological region. In their environmental sample from the bridge south of Tabubil, Kreye and Castell (1990:43) discovered that:

> The copper content here is c. 1000 times higher than before mining began; the iron, manganese, zinc and lead content is c. 200 times greater; the arsenic content and the turbidity c. 100 times greater. These are shocking figures and represent industrial effluents on a scale not permitted in any river in the western world.

According to the Applied Geology Associates report, the pollution from continued production with total discharge would be staggering with an:

> 80% fish kill to the Middle Fly in the immediate term between 1990–1993 and a 60% fish kill for the life of the mine. The severe effect (60%) would continue down to the delta as well as into the Gulf of Papua and possibly the Torres Strait (*Post Courier*, 27 July 1989).

Beyond the Fly estuary, salt water samples collected by Keyre and Castell (1990:51) had "a lead content c. 400 times greater, cadmium c. 200 times greater, and zinc c. 100 times greater than concentrations found in open ocean waters. There is already evidence of heavy metal contamination of prawns" (*New Scientist*, 18 November 1989, p.19).

With production under total discharge affecting international pollution control commitments and severely jeopardizing domestic prawn, lobster and barramundi fisheries, concern mounted in Australia and the Great Barrier Reef Marine Park Authority initiated the 'Sustained Development for the Traditional Inhabitants of the Torres Strait Region Conference' in November 1990. Indigenous peoples of the Fly River socio–ecological region and the Torres Strait attended along with OTML staff and academics and government personnel from Australia and PNG. Australia initiated a Torres Strait Baseline Study and PNG intended to undertake a comprehensive social and environmental assessment of the Middle–Lower Fly socio–ecological region.

In my (Hyndman 1991a) discussion of the Fly River socio–ecological region I presented findings from the Applied Geology Associates report, to which OTML responded that information reported in newspapers should not be discussed in a scientific conference, while not offering any of their own scientific findings. It was Busse (1991) who presented crucial OTML six-monthly public domain data that had been routinely provided to the PNG government (Table 5.1).

The OTML environmental and management program typically minimizes the dangers their mining operation poses to the Fly River socio-ecological region. The Sixth Supplemental Agreement Environmental Study and Supplementary Investigations established an Acceptable Particulate Level (APL) of 940 mg/l (Eagle and Higgins 1991). The state is simply informed by OTML that ever renegotiated APL compliance standards are being met and that environmental damage from their mining is temporary and unavoidable. After their expensive, decade-long monitoring program OTML is seemingly still unable to acknowledge the extent of pollution attributable to mining:

> Because of the geographical extent of the Fly system and the natural variabilities that occur, however, uncertainty remains surrounding any interpretation of system characteristics and responses to the mining operation (Eagle and Higgins 1991:54).

Nonetheless, OTML is at pains to confirm the innocuousness of their operation and recently concluded that:

> Increases in suspended sediment concentrations as a result of mine discharges will cause a decrease in fisheries resources in the middle Fly; these resources will, however, continue to exceed the demand placed on them by users, principally artisinal fishermen, although increased effort may be needed to achieve present catches (Eagle and Higgins 1991:56).

OTML assumed that the subsistence fishery of the Fly River socio-ecological region took only 10 percent of the fish, which should not be jeopardized by the 90 percent fish-loss decimated by their operation. This was a rather optimistic conclusion considering that OTML actually expected an even greater fish loss in the Fly River than was cautioned by the Applied Geology Associates report (Tables 5.1A and 5.1B) and that ecologists have doubts that fisheries can recover from as little as a 30 percent fish-loss.

The PNG national government was concerned that in closing the mine they would lose 4000 jobs, reduce the rate of the state's economic growth and hamper their international image. Shortly before the third APL deadline of 30 July 1989, Namaliu declared that it "must be put back by a couple of months" (*Post Courier*, 23 July 1989).

TABLE 5.1A   OTML Estimated Fisheries Loss for the Fly River

	Fly River Locations							
	Kiambit				Obo			
	Fish Catch				Fish Catch			
			Loss %				Loss %	
	ss	pCu	ss	pCu	ss	pCu	ss	pCu
Background	110	45	0	0	103	45	0	0
Current Mine Plan								
1990	758	1236	54	88	531	1150	17	88
1991	803	905	57	77	612	1202	18	78
1992	805	715	57	69	647	879	18	69
1993	803	875	57	77	649	693	18	77
1994	842	581	59	61	647	850	18	60
1995	842	581	59	61	677	564	18	60
1996	784	562	56	61	677	564	17	60

'ss' refers to the level of suspended sediment.
'pCu' refers to the level of particulate copper.
'fish catch loss' refers to the predicted percentage reduction in fish catch
   for the predicted levels of suspended sediment and particulate coper.

Source: Busse (1991).

The further two month extension met with sustained political pressure from Western Province MPs and then Premier Norbert Makmop for a permanent tailings dam, which, however, would have little effect on the fish kill unless waste rock was also retained (*Post Courier*, 27 July 1989). Parry Zeipi, MP for South Fly and current Minister for Environment and Conservation, warned the government that "if it is not careful in its dealings on the Ok Tedi environmental situation, another potential Bougainville scenario is brewing" (*Post Courier*, 27 July 1989). During

TABLE 5.1B OTML Estimated Fisheries Loss for the Fly River

			Fly River Locations			
		Ogwa			*Delta*	
		Fish Catch				
			Loss %		*ss*	*pCu*
	ss	*pCu*	*ss*	*pCu*		
Background	430	45	0	0	430	42
Current Mine Plan						
1990	665	524	22	57	665	149
1991	681	401	23	46	681	174
1992	682	321	23	32	682	184
1993	681	388	23	44	681	201
1994	695	270	24	33	695	201
1995	695	270	24	33	695	200
1996	674	253	23	33	674	195

'ss' refers to the level of suspended sediment.
'pCu' refers to the level of particulate copper.
'fish catch loss' refers to the predicted percentage reduction in fish catch
  for the predicted levels of suspended sediment and particulate coper.

Source: Busse (1991).

the extension period OTML declared a K8.1 million loss for the first half
of 1989 compared to a K39.9 million gain the same period in 1988 and
blamed the loss on the failure of the ore delivery system. Production was
shut down on 24 August 1989 when a major landslide buried a bulldozer
and operator. The national government presented a special development
package to the landowners based on renegotiations of the Bougainville
and Porgera mining projects. In addition to increased social services for
landowners, they and the Western Province government were offered

one-half of the state's 20 percent share in the Ok Tedi mine (*Post Courier*, 25 August 1989).

Finally on the 29th September 1989 Jim Yer Waim, former Environment and Conservation Minister, announced "we decided in favor of the people" (*Post Courier*, 29 September 1989). OTML was to avoid the estimated cost of K380 million for a permanent tailings dam and continued mining with total discharge of wastes in exchange for offering compensation money to the peoples of the Fly River socio-ecological region. An Ok Tedi Fly River Development Trust Fund of K2.5 million was to be created out of a levy paid to the national government for each tonne of ore processed and waste mined. According to then Minister Waim, the state wanted to offset potential loss of fish with fish ponds, chicken farms and piggeries as alternative sources of protein.

By 1989 the total sum the state derived from OTML taxes, royalties, import duties and rent was only K19 million. Of the US$1.4 billion invested in Ok Tedi to 1989, 20 percent was raised in equity capital, 54 percent through loans and the remaining 26 percent from gold production earnings (Kreye and Castell 1991:24). Foreign shareholders contributed an outlay of K240 million but the national government had to raise K60 million to acquire the state's share in Ok Tedi, a sum which was denied to other development projects (Kreye and Castell 1991:24). OTML distributed no profits to shareholders during the initial gold mining phase and promised none before 1992. The state was not to receive income from its shares in the mine until 1992. The declared years of profit since 1984 have been used by the state for investment or debt-service (Kreye and Castell 1991:25).

Jackson (1982:177) anticipated the state would take dividend payments of K470 million over the 25 year duration of the mining project. Such dividend returns are unlikely to be attained since many years of unrecorded profits have already gone by and the bulk of declared profits leaves the country. It now appears that the state will accrue only K820 million over the full life of the mine (Kreye and Castell 1991:26), less than one-third of the US$2,900 million originally expected (Jackson 1982:148-9). Moreover, public expenditure in the 1990 budget reveals that mining revenues received by the state were too insignificant to finance national development projects (Kreye and Castell 1991:27).

The decision "in favor of the people" is one of political expediency that jeopardized the livelihood, welfare and health of the 40,000 people in the Fly River socio-ecological region. On 19 January 1990 over

2000 landowners responded to continued mining production with total discharge by blocking all access roads and closing the mine. The Workers' Union and the Ok Tedi National Staff Association of OTML supported landowner protest for better economic compensation, and a large student demonstration at the University of Papua New Guinea against the ecocide decision had already been held in support of peoples of the Fly River socio–ecological region.

Obvious concerns regarding damage to the socio–ecological region from the Ok Tedi project were heard in a case before the second International Water Tribunal in February 1992 held in The Netherlands. An independent international jury heard the case of water mismanagement and aquatic pollution and found the Ok Tedi project guilty of disrupting the socio–ecological regions fragile ecosystem and the PNG national government was criticized for encouraging it. They concluded their findings with the following summary:

The mine has no satisfactory system for disposal of residual;

that OTML has discharged large quantities of tailings and waste water, and dumped tonnes of waste rock and overburden in the headwaters of the Ok Tedi River;

waste disposal has led to the aggredation of the river bed, and consequential flooding of gardens and plantations. and disrupted the river ecosystem and subsequent fishing and boat transportation;

OTML should not use foreign revenue to influence the government to make exceptions regarding the law, environment and people;

OTML's foreign shareholders should ensure that the company's environmental standards are comparable to the ones enforced in their own countries;

this is a good example of the need for establishing liability of the shareholding foreign companies for damage caused;

that the environmental monitoring should be administered by a state institution not associated with OTML;

that the externalised costs of the development project grossly exceed the benefits, and consequently OTML should be phased out; and

OTML should prepare an assessment of long–term effects (social and environmental) of its operations after the closure. The government could consider establishing legally binding provisions for OTML to avoid long–term environmental damage (*The Times of Papua New Guinea*, 27 February 1992).

Particulate pollution and heavy metals in the Fly River are not only derived from tailings alone, a substantial amount comes from Ok Tedi's stable Northern waste dumps and the unstable Southern waste dumps (Townsend 1988:117). The settling out of residual tailings particles and pollution from the dumps will continue long after Ok Tedi mining operations have ceased. Not only has OTML done as little as possible to protect the environment because it reduces profit, but the Ok Tedi mine will impact upon the Fly River socio–ecological region long after the project stops. The state has not taken in enough current revenue return from Ok Tedi to meet even daily food needs of the peoples of the socio-ecological region should their systems of subsistence break down as a consequence of mining.

In December 1992 the Australian Conservation Foundation (ACF) conducted an environmental investigation of OTML. A comprehensive report on the Ok Tedi investigation from ACF appeared at the end of 1993 and was extracted in their magazine *Habitat* in November 1993. According to ACF, the environmental regulation of the mine is based on monitoring compliance under a narrow range of standards established on the basis of OTML's own research which is insufficient to ensure the ecological viability of the Fly River socioecological region (*Habitat* vol. 21, 1993:43). In the view of ACF, the prime goal of the OTML environmental management program has been to set Acceptable Particulate Levels to facilitate the realisation of the mining schedule, rather than ecological and social responsibility (*Habitat* vol. 21, 1993:43).

The absence of informed community participation and scale of ecological destruction resulted in villagers of the Fly River socioecological region taking out a Australian$4 billion compensation claim against BHP in May 1994 (*The Australian* 4 May 1994:37). The claim, the largest in Australian legal history and lodged in the Victorian Supreme Court, sought Australian$2 billion in compensation damage and Australian$2 billion in exemplary damages, and included a mandatory injunction that would force BHP and its partners to build a tailings dam (*The Australian* 4 May 1994:37). BHP indicated that the mine operated in compliance with PNG laws and that capital commitment to a tailings dam and a successful compensation claim would close the mine (*The Australian* 4 May 1994:37).

6

Changing Relations of Production
in the Wopkaimin Roadside Villages:
"For Ne'er the Twain Shall Meet"

Vulgar Fringe of the Mining Resource Frontier

Capitalist relations of production represented by OTML have always been uncritically regarded by the Australian colonial administration and the PNG national government as the standard of modernity and a goal for the Wopkaimin and other peoples of the Fly River socio-ecological region (Figure 5.1). From the outset of the Ok Tedi project Barth and Wikan (1982:8-9) countered that "a construction camp, or a mining operation, in fact, provides no model or blueprint for the social and cultural institutions of a whole population. What is demonstrated in Tabubil cannot be exemplary for settlement patterns, social life, family organization, or even major sectors of household economies."

Tabubil, the operational and residential center of the Ok Tedi project, is a highly stratified township with a few family houses provided for the wealthy, mostly expatriate, elite employees. The thousands of single male, mostly outsider PNG nationals, are housed in crowded dormitory accommodation. Colonial invasion started with single male patrol officers followed by single male prospectors. Today there are still very few women represented in the mining enclave of Tabubil. The nearly all-male Ok Tedi mining operation exaggerates the importance of male technical-productive activities over other values. This local mining fringe of the world capitalist system has become the only image and model of new relations of production for the Wopkaimin. Community schooling, instruction from outsiders in training centers and employment experience at the mine have not provided the organization and lifeways necessary for the Wopkaimin to transfer to capitalist relations of production. The vulgar fringe of the mining frontier ushered in a clash between kinship and capitalist relations of production and thereby posed a threat to Wopkaimin social and cultural reproduction.

PLATE 6.1 Tabubil in 1985. The highly stratified operational and residential center of the Ok Tedi project provides a few family homes for the wealthy, mostly expatriate, elite employees (photo courtesy of the author).

Roadside Villages: Transformation of Productive Relations

The majority of the Wopkaimin initially lived away from the Kennecott prospectors in the late 1960s and maintained kinship relations of production and subsistence autonomy in their ancestral rain forests. When the Kennecott prospectors invaded, the Wopkaimin surrendered small portions of communally-owned land in expectation of receiving money for the first time. About a dozen Wopkaimin workers and their families lived for several years in Tabubil until 1981 when the OTML consortium was created to start the project. The transnational construction giant Bechtel was contracted to convert the entire Tabubil plateau into an instant township to house over 5000 outsiders. As white executives and their families moved in, all Wopkaimin workers with their families were forced out of Tabubil.

Employment rather than lease payments was initially perceived as the main source of benefits to be derived from the mining project (Barth and Wikan 1982:24). Schooling and job-training to enhance skills and experience for personal participation in the mining project capitalist relations of production were, therefore valued. They perceived promised wage earning, education and health facilities as beneficial but they had no clear idea of the land requirements of the Ok Tedi project or of the substantial socio-ecological impact it was to have on their way of life.

By the time of stage one gold production almost all Wopkaimin had relocated from their ancestral rain forest hamlets to Woktemwanin and Finalbin (Figure 5.2), locations previously used as temporary base camps for sago processing and hunting and fishing expeditions. First expanded into small hamlets and then into new roadside villages, Finalbin and Woktemwanin became extremely congested by Wopkaimin standards and by 1985 they each accommodated over 350 residents. Although residents were predominantly Wopkaimin, other Mountain Ok from the Sepik Source Basin had moved in as well. Non-Wopkaimin were permitted to reside in the roadside villages but not to hunt or garden, so the migrants were totally dependent on trade store commodities for subsistence.

Traditional houses were oval in shape with a central hearth and were constructed of *Pandanus* with sago leaf thatching. Houses in the roadside villages were a bricolage of packing crates salvaged from the Tabubil rubbish tip. They were erected in a rectangular shape with several interior rooms, and doors were fitted with tradestore Chinese padlocks. Cooking over wood fire was external to the house, usually on cut-down 60 liter metal drums located on the verandah. These "monuments to the petty accumulation of cash and commodities by individuals and households" (Polier 1990) have also sprung up among the Fegolmin and elsewhere in the socio-ecological region financed from wage labor at the mine.

PLATE 6.2 White executives and their families moved into Tabubil in 1985 and these "no trespassing" signs were posted as the Wopkaimin were forced out of the township (photo courtesy of the author).

Melanesian kinship relations of production typically involved an elaborate gender–based division of labor and access to land guaranteed by the operation of some combination of locality, residence, descent, ego–oriented kinship or gift exchange (Wesley–Smith 1989; Strathern 1982). Social class was conspicuously absent in Wopkaimin kinship relations of production. Land was used for production and symbolic purposes. Membership in cognatic descent groups (*kinumits*) were the essential basis for claiming use rights to land. There was no sense of rights to alienate or lease land and each kinumit was linked to certain tracts of ancestral rain forest. Community membership formed the basis for production and embraced the right to build houses and hamlets and fostered an awareness of shared rights for all within the homeland.

Purchase or compensation for usufruct to Wopkaimin land was not extended to non–Wopkaimin in the roadside villages, and was granted without precedent for OTML operations. However, their ancestral rain forests were also endowed with a sacred geography and certain sites were associated with recurrent ritual activity. It was also recognized that mythical significance could be bestowed on the same cultural landscape by different and competing Mountain Ok peoples and this formed the basis for permitting non–Wopkaimin to reside in the roadside villages.

Men and women maintained highly distinctive lives socially and spatially under Wopkaimin kinship relations of production. Men monopolized public life and formal religious activity but women participated in decision making on matters other than the secret male cult. There was little difference in authority in the family unit of production and husband and wife normally made decisions by consensus. However, gender so permeated relations of production, distribution and consumption

PLATE 6.3 Houses in Woktemwanin in 1985 were a bricolage of packing crates salvaged from the Tabubil rubbish tip (photo courtesy of the author).

that men and women could exercise similar sanctions of withdrawing into temporary self–sufficiency and isolation. Wopkaimin social and cultural reproduction emphasized distinctive gender–based spheres of production with a roughly equal possibility of men and women to influence one another. Gender relations altered dramatically in the roadside villages. Wopkaimin roadside villagers used the term 'corners' to refer to the aggregate of disparate neighborhoods formed around their previous residential and descent group affiliations. Established patterns of domesticity and sociality were significantly modified. Nuclear families resided together in co–resident commensality. Men did not have a men's house in which to congregate at the expense of conjugal ties, but they tended to maintain bedrooms separate from the wife and children. With household sovereignty in consumption, food was no longer segregated by gender and food prohibitions were abandoned. This reversed male–directed sharing of meat from the men's house, a pattern which had previously denied household autonomy and separated the sexes.

Kennecott and the Ok Tedi Development Company initiated free room and board co–educational schooling for the Wopkaimin, but this ended under OTML. The Wopkaimin community school was destroyed when Tabubil was converted into a mining town and for a long time there was only an exclusive international school catering to expatriate staff. Eventually, a co–educational community school was built on the fringe of Tabubil without free room and board. Schooling from the first grade was in English, which is totally alien to the children and relating the curriculum to their routine life experiences was unresolved (Barth and Wikan 1982:29). Initial positive attitudes towards schooling and training were a poor measure of the depth of internalizing the Western world view and capitalist relations of production.

Coffee, cattle and *bisnis* (Melanesian Tok Pisin for economic ventures leading to involvement with the cash economy in virtually any capacity other than as wage earner) have extensively monetized kinship modes of production across the Highlands. These activities were absent among the Wopkaimin and other Mountain Ok peoples in the socio–ecological region. The previous lack of cash–earning activities relegated the Wopkaimin to a peripheral, unskilled wage–earner role in the Ok Tedi project. Over half of the Wopkaimin men worked at the mine during the Bechtel construction phase of the project (Jackson and Ilave 1983:26) because they wanted to participate fully in the new capitalist mode of production. The job of preference was heavy machine operator or big truck driver, but only a few men attained the qualifications.

The overt emergence of nuclear families appeared modern and was encouraged by the state and OTML. What seemed like loss of gender distinction with co-residence in family dwellings actually did little initially to further equality between the sexes. Such co-residence without a men's house precluded male cult activities but it introduced a sharp discontinuity between mothers and daughters who were formally very close and created a loss of one of the wife's counterweights to her husband's influence (Barth and Wikan 1982:15). A pattern of great-man-based gender relations (see Godelier 1986; Jorgensen 1991) continued with a separate realm of male production in the roadside villages. Only men were wage earners and they were far more exposed to capitalist relations of production. Initially, women's work virtually disappeared in the roadside villages because of non-participation in capitalist relations of production and the abandonment of subsistence gardening. This led to a reduction of women's social status and a stronger identification and dependence of wives on husbands.

Each corner in the roadside villages had a trade store and rice and tinned meat and fish became dietary staples and commodities to be sold rather than shared reciprocally, even among neighborhood residents. The process of household nucleation and privatization of consumption in capitalist relations of production swept through the roadside villages. In the 1970s the Wopkaimin were entirely subsistence-oriented and dietarily self-sufficient. By the 1980s the Wopkaimin had become increasingly dependent on a diet with fewer and fewer subsistence resources; especially of the staple *Colocasia* taro.

The ancient Wopkaimin taro monoculture (Morren and Hyndman 1987) all but disappeared during the Bechtel construction phase of the mining project. By the time OTML started gold mining operations in 1984 wage earning opportunities for the Wopkaimin men had dropped-off drastically. The women again turned to agricultural production. Subsistence gardening shifted from the Lower Montane Rain Forest heartland of *Colocasia* taro cultivation in the Kam Basin to the lower altitude Foothill Rain Forest located near the roadside villages. Woktemwanin residents extensively cleared portions of Foothill Rain Forest around the confluence of the Ok Kam and Ok Tedi Rivers (Figure 5.2) and enlarged Bombakan hunting shelter into a full-sized hamlet.

The new gardens were planted to sweet potato, banana and *Xanthosoma* taro in the cultivation pattern of "fell the trees on top of the crop" as

PLATE 6.4 1985 new "fell the trees on top of the crop" gardens near Woktemwanin were planted to *Xanthosoma* taro, sweet potato and bananas (photo courtesy of the author).

described by Schieffelin (1975) for post–colonial Papuan Plateau peoples. Men felled the trees but the new sweet potato gardens were planted, maintained and harvested by women. They yielded in about half the time of the high altitude *Colocasia* taro gardens but were exhausted after a single harvest, which placed pressure on Foothill Rain Forest near the roadside villages. As *Colocasia* taro dropped out of the Wopkaimin diet, sweet potato (*Ipomoea batatas*) became the new subsistence staple, while store–bought and imported Western foods continued to be the main sources of energy and protein for those families with income from wage earning (Ulijaszek, Hyndman and Lourie 1987).

By the time OTML started gold mining operations the Wopkaimin had shifted to roadside villages with women in subsistence gardening and men participating as wage laborers in a transnational economic enclave. Gender distinctions in labor continued to be rather strict with men selling their labor for a wage and women taking on a greater share of subsistence production, a pattern which spread among the southern Mountain Ok of the socio–ecological region. However, unlike the Fegolmin (Polier 1990), Wopkaimin women were not smallscale commodity producers. Women did not produce market vegetables for sale to OTML, nor did they sell portions of their garden production at the Saturday Tabubil market. Rather, it was the Wopkaimin who purchased the subsistence crops and fresh pork sold by the Ningerum and other southern Mountain Ok producers at the Tabubil market.

Dialectics of Articulation and Crisis

In kinship relations of production daily reciprocities between husband and wife were powerfully symbolized in the imagery of men's hunted game from the ancestral rain forests for women's harvested and baked taro. This in turn was mirrored in male sacrifice of game to the ancestors in return for taro fertility. With capitalist relations of production in the roadside villages, the gender imagery of game for taro was replaced with sweet potato produced by women and tinned meat or fish purchased by men.

A significant feature of distribution and consumption in kinship relations of production was the limited degree to which rate of production and form of consumption were linked (Barth and Wikan 1982:36). The ecological basis and means of production created a subsistence economy without storage. Taro, slaughtered domestic pigs and hunted game all had to be consumed quickly. There were no saving and accumulation, only programming the relations of producing, harvesting and sharing. Sharing based on the men's house directed the allocation of meat and insured extensive redistribution because of the obligations of gender and taboo present in every act of consumption.

Capital accumulation and management had no precedent in kinship relations of production. During the early Bechtel construction phase, capitalist relations of production in the roadside villages were characterized by plenty on the cash side and shortage on the supply side (Barth and Wikan 1982:37). In Tabubil Wopkaimin wage earners were not permitted to purchase in the town commissary, which was restricted to executive (mostly white) employees. Instead the Wopkaimin had to confine their purchases to an inferior and irregular supply of goods from the town tradestore. Opportunities for purchase were scarce and the only new prestige commodity available to the Wopkaimin was beer. Wages were used for family consumption of rice and tinned fish or meat and for male consumption of beer.

Wopkaimin wage earners worked long, difficult 60 hour work weeks and it was years before they were granted annual leave enjoyed by outside PNG nationals and expatriates. With beer the only new luxury to buy and little time to exercise the option of consuming extras, accumulated money tended to be hoarded in pass–book savings. When OTML finally started operations a large general merchandise and food store was opened to anyone with money wanting to make purchases. Ironically, by this time far fewer Wopkaimin were employed and women were actively involved in subsistence production again.

Wopkaimin *bisnis* in the roadside villages was virtually absent, and earning a wage remained the preferred participation in the new capitalist relations of production. The process of proletarianization initiated by the Bechtel construction phase was far from complete by the time gold mining started in the mid–1980s. A few men opened tradestores and fewer still black–marketed the sale of beer and sold the services of prostitutes, but they lacked prestige in the eyes of the community. Certain corners based around previous residence and descent affiliations formed the basis of limited male *bisnis* groups in the roadside villages. They used accumulated wages and compensation money for the purchase of 4–wheel drive trucks, which were offered for passenger hire to Tabubil or Kiunga. Most of the vehicles have gone off the road and are irretrievable wrecks along the steep slopes.

Wopkaimin men began economically manipulating the marriage system as a form of *bisnis*. Money entered prestations at marriage. Barth and Wikan (1982:35) noted that at the outset of the mining project in January 1982 fathers were demanding up to K300 for their daughters. By 1985 one Woktemwanin man had paid K3500 for a second Wopkaimin wife and another had paid K9000 for a wife from Central Province. Women became ranked according to inflated money prestations at marriage. Marriage manipulation as a form of *bisnis* devalued women in the eyes of their men and themselves, a situation that also occurred after mining started on Bougainville (Nash 1981). Adultery and prostitution became easier as women's sexuality was alienated from themselves and controlled by men.

A major social problem spawned in the new roadside villages was the introduction of alcohol, which had previously been absent in the Wopkaimin diet. Initially when the Tabubil commissary was open only to higher paid workers residing in company houses, Wopkaimin men focused on beer as the only new prestige commodity available to them. Gender restrictions excluded women from beer drinking. During the construction phase of the project in 1982, as the Wopkaimin first started drinking, 62 percent of men over 15 used beer compared to only 10 percent among women of the same age. By 1986 beer became institutionalized as a male domain, with an increase to 70 percent among men over 15 and a drop to only one percent among women over 15 (Lourie 1987). Aggressive drunken behavior, black–marketing, fighting and adultery associated with heavy beer drinking in the roadside villages threatened family life.

The Wopkaimin used the Melanesian Tok Pisin term *spakman* not only to refer to excessive beer drinkers but also to contrast those who moved into the new roadside villages from those who continued to reside in the former mountain hamlets. On my last visit an old friend who had already made the *spakman* transition to Woktemwanin was proud to tell me that "my older brother is a *spakman* now". He meant he was pleased to have his brother residing with him in Woktemwanin. However, it brought with it the contradictions of abandoning male cult traditions based on the culture heroine Afek and taking up drinking in the new social order. *Spakmen* are married and unmarried men under 35 years of age. Loose beers are known as *wokmafuk* (vernacular for bad drink) and cases of 24 bottles are known as 'tool boxes'. Night–long, all–male drinking sessions typically lead to vomiting and urinating in the open, fights and adultery, all in violation of established cultural norms.

The use–value of beer in the new capitalist relations of production was structurally similar to the use value of meat in the kinship relations of production. Beer and meat are both concerned with an exclusive masculine realm of production and the absence of formal prestations by socially defined categories of men. In kinship relations of production there was the nodal position of the men's house and the emergence of leaders through the volume of meat sharing. Feeding meat to male visitors was the conspicuous feature of sharing based on the men's house. Meat was the supreme valuable and was shared, not circulated. Meat had only use–value, it was not alienated for its exchange–value. Thus, masculinity was defined by production and consumption of meat, which accentuated gender differences and monopolized male privilege.

Moreover, the *spakman* acted out a kind of fantasy of himself as a white by communicating in Melanesian Tok Pisin and listening to Western cassette music, a pattern that occurred among the Nasioi when the Bougainville mining project started (Ogan 1966). Nevertheless, obvious gaps remained between the desired and the actual social situation and this generated tensions which were discharged in drunkenness and the extreme behavior associated with it.

Wopkaimin men regularly propositioned new white women they saw in Tabubil with the sexually provocative Tok Pisin phrase *fortnight o?*, which had the double meaning of 'Can you accommodate me sexually?' and 'Will you last here longer than a few days?' The prevailing white and PNG national staff attitude to indigenous women of the socio–ecological region was even worse. In 1985, most of the PNG national women clerical staff allegedly made more money at night selling sex than they made from their wages. This, and certain Wopkaimin men selling some of their women's sex, accommodated working men in Tabubil. Men working in temporary camps away from Tabubil reportedly kidnapped and raped indigenous women gardening near the road. The nickname "GBH" for the fighting that regularly broke out in the new roadside communities over adultery and rape, originated from the frequency of Grievous Bodily Harm charges heard in the new Police Station and Court in Tabubil. The few Wopkaimin men remaining in their mountain hamlets in the Kam Basin viewed becoming a *spakman* with ambivalence because they were fearful of subjecting their wives to GBH. The spakman was afraid his wife would be assaulted in the roadside villages while he was away earning wages or hunting.

Gender Differences in Changing Diet and Health

The OTES recommended social, demographic, dietary and health monitoring for Ok Tedi peoples in the OTES, especially for the Wopkaimin who were undergoing the most rapid change in the socio–ecological region (Hyndman 1982a). In 1975 Hyndman conducted a diet study and the PNG Institute of Medical Research conducted a health survey of 206 Wopkaimin (see Hyndman 1989). These 1975 studies provided the basis for nutritional comparison with dietary surveys conducted by Ulijaszek in 1984 (see Ulijaszek, Hyndman and Lourie 1987). The 1975 studies also provided the basis for health comparisons with surveys conducted by Lourie of the entire Wopkaimin population in 1982 and 1986 (see Hyndman, Ulijaszek and Lourie 1989; Lourie *et al.* 1986; Lourie 1987).

The Ok Tedi Health and Nutrition Project (OTHNP), which started in 1982, has provided a comparative assessment of changing patterns of Wopkaimin health and nutrition. In the initial period of infrastructure construction changing relations of production adjusted the Wopkaimin to new diet and health problems in the roadside villages through an exclusive masculine sphere of wage–earning. By 1986 gold mining was characterized by unemployment for the Wopkaimin men. Gender roles socially adjusted the Wopkaimin to a feminine sphere of production in subsistence gardening and a masculine sphere of production in controlling compensation money and beer.

Between workers and non–workers in the years 1975 and 1984, intakes of energy among Wopkaimin men were below those recommended, even after standardization for body weight (Table 6.1). Intakes of calcium were particularly low in 1984, as were intakes of riboflavin. Intakes of protein and niacin met the requirements, and intakes of iron and thiamine were well above the recommended levels in all three groups. Although few of the differences in nutrient intakes between the groups attained significance, they are still worthy of comment. Workers in 1984 had the highest *per capita* intake of energy, protein and fat, but the lowest intakes of calcium and iron. Men in 1975 had the lowest intakes of energy and fat, but the highest intakes of calcium and iron. There was little difference between the three groups in *per capita* intakes of thiamine, riboflavin and niacin. However, when these values are related to energy intake, the adequacy of intake decreased across the three groups. Men in 1975 had the largest values, followed by the 1984 non–workers, with the 1984 workers having the least adequate intakes (Table 6.1).

Among Wopkaimin women, the dietary pattern between 1975 and 1984 is similar to that of the men (Table 6.1). Energy intakes were low in all groups, and intakes of calcium and riboflavin were low in 1984. Intakes of iron fell within the range of values recommended by the WHO. Intakes of protein and niacin were adequate, and intakes of thiamine were well above the recommended values. 1984 workers' wives had the highest *per capita* intakes of energy, protein and fat, but the lowest intakes of iron. Women in 1975 had the lowest intakes of energy and fat, but the highest

TABLE 6.1 Gender Differences in Wopkaimin Nutrient Intake, 1984[a]

	1975	1984 Non-working	1984 Working	1975/84 Non-working	1984 Working 1984 Non-working
	(Men) (Women)	(Men) (Women)	(Men) (Women)		
Survey Intake Days	47	32	11		
Energy (kcal)	1361	1786	2238	0.2	1.4
	1345	1491	1743	0.8	1.3
Protein (g)	32.0	30.1	39.6	0.6	2.4
	28.5	27.3	35.9	0.01	3.2
Fat (g)	3.0	5.7	22.3	3.8	3.2
	3.0	13.6	16.2	18.1[b]	0.9
Calcium (mg)	549	339	330	6.3	0.4
	527	329	273	6.7[c]	0.3
Iron (mg)	19.0	18.2	13.5		
	19.0	17.3	14.7	1.3	0.2
Thiamin (mg)	1.0	1.0	1.0	4.2	0.6
	1.0	1.0	1.0	2.3	1.4
Riboflavin (mg)	0.6	0.6	0.6	0.3	0.1
	0.6	0.5	0.4	0.3	0.6
Niacin (mg)	11.0	10.0	10.0	2.5	0.1
	11.0	8.0	8.0	2.8	0.6

[a]Within 25th and 75th percentiles
[b]$p < 0.001$
[c]$p < 0.01$
Chi-square: (df = 3).

intakes of calcium and iron. As with the men, there was little difference between the three groups in *per capita* intakes of thiamine, riboflavin and niacin. When related to energy intake, the adequacy of intake again decreased, with women in 1975 having the highest intake and the 1984 workers' wives the lowest.

The proportion of dietary energy obtained from different foods and food categories can be compared between subsistence production in Bakonabip in 1975, subsistence production in Atemkit in 1984 and workers resident in the roadside village of Woktemwanin in 1984 (Table 6.2). In 1975 *Colocasia* taro was the single most important staple food, providing the greatest amount of dietary energy. In 1984 sweet potato and *Xanthosoma* taro had become equally important subsistence staples. Sweet potato and *Xanthosoma* taro had successfully replaced *Colocasia* taro as the staple and the subsistence shift to these new staples may, therefore, be responsible for an increase in the overall availability of food and in the consumption of greater quantities of food.

Pig–raising and hunting were the other most important energy sources in 1975. In 1984, pig raising and hunting in the hamlets made only a small contribution to the intake of dietary energy, with men obtaining more than women. The 1984 workers obtained only 26 percent of their dietary energy from the two staple crops, whilst 1984 workers' wives obtained 43 percent from the same sources. Imported rice was the single most important staple for the workers. For workers' wives rice was slightly behind *Xanthosoma* taro as a staple. Workers' wives obtained substantially more of their energy intake from garden foods, in general, than did the male workers. The difference is made up largely by meat, often eaten in the staff canteen by working men.

Susceptibility to infectious disease to which they have little or no immunity is being introduced to the Wopkaimin by people who immigrate to the project for work (Taukuro *et al* 1980:85). This aspect of the mining project constituted a significant health impact for the Wopkaimin who had already undergone population decline, probably due to an outbreak of influenza (Eggleton 1968; Taukuro *et al.* 1980:80). Venereal disease and alcoholism, unknown before the start of the mining project, are expected to rise sharply in prevalence (Taukuro *et al.* 1980:85).

In the changing trends in health indicators between the 1970s and 1980s (Table 6.3), the height of males up to five years of age has not increased and adult males have remained the same height since the start of mining. By comparison, the height of females up to five years of age has tended to increase but the height of adult females has likewise remained the

TABLE 6.2 Wopkaimin Energy Intake under Kinship and Capitalist Relations of Production

Food/Food Group	Bakona- bip 1975 %	Men		Women	
		Atemkit 1984 %	Woktem- wanin 1984 %	Atemkit 1984 %	Woktem- wanin 1984 %
Taro (Colocasia, Xanthosoma)	57	35	13	45	31
Sweet potato	Tr	46	13	36	12
Other starchy staples	8	3	3	5	7
Other foods	3	12	4	13	6
Rice	0	0	22	0	28
Tinned meat/fish	0	0	7	0	4
Hunting/pig raising	22	4	3	1	38
All store foods	0	Tr	64	Tr	38
All animal sources	22	4	20	1	10
All plant sources	78	96	80	99	90

same. Males and females generally became heavier since mining, with adult females increasing their weight less than adult males. Skinfold ratings for male and female children decreased since mining started, especially among adolescent females 15–19 years of age.

There has been an increase in spleen enlargement (hackett ratings) (Table 6.3) in the 1980s due to worsening malaria and tropical splenomegaly syndrome (TSS) since the start of mining (Cattani *et al.* 1983:122). *Plasmodium falciparum* went up from 66 percent in 1978 to 75.2 percent in 1982 and then down to 37.9 percent in 1986. *P. vivax*

TABLE 6.3 Gender Differences in Wopkaimin Health, 1970s–1980s

Age	Sex	Height	Weight	Hackett	Skinfold
20>					
1975	M	1542	48.5	0.8	4.6
	F	1478	43.5	0.9	5.9
1982	M	1565	53.8	1.9	4.7
	F	1477	44.1	2.4	5.8
1986	M	1566	53.2	0.8	4.8
	F	1480	47.5	1.4	6.3
15–19					
1974	M	1535	45.0	0.8	4.3
	F	1420	47.0	1.0	11.1
1982	M	1573	53.4	1.4	5.5
	F	1486	42.8	2.4	7.6
1986	M	1582	51.4	0.9	5.7
	F	1508	49.4	1.0	8.4
10–14					
1975	M	1308	27.0	1.3	6.9
	F	1364	31.4	1.6	7.3
1982	M	1408	35.5	1.7	4.7
	F	1356	32.6	2.3	5.5
1986	M	1367	32.3	1.8	4.7
	F	1384	34.5	0.7	6.5
5–9					
1975	M	1077	22.0	1.3	6.1
	F	1196	21.0	1.0	6.0
1982	M	1186	22.4	2.9	4.3
	F	1150	20.9	2.6	4.9
1986	M	1146	20.9	1.7	5.1
	F	1169	21.4	1.4	5.5
2–4					
1975	M	947	12.1	1.3	5.9
	F	797	8.6	2.0	6.1
1982	M	918	13.9	2.4	5.4
	F	941	7.9	2.2	5.3
1986	M	952	14.1	0.6	5.9
	F	936	13.9	0.7	6.4
1–2					
1975	M	802	6.6	0.8	5.6
	F	743	6.6	1.0	5.1
1982	M	723	8.5	1.0	
	F	719	7.9	0.5	
1986	M	794	9.9	0.1	6.1
	F	790	9.7	0.1	6.2

Source: Lourie (1987).

went down marginally from 18 percent in 1978 to 17.4 percent in 1982 and then up to 27.6 percent in 1986. *P. malariae* went down from 16 percent in 1978 to 7.4 percent in 1982 and then up to 34.5 percent in 1986 (Taukuro *et al.* 1980:83; Lourie 1987). The incidence of *P. falciparum* went up by nearly 10 percent with mining. By 1982 most of the Wopkaimin had moved to the roadside villages located in the Foothill Rain Forest and for the first time became permanently exposed to the *Plasmodium* parasite. TSS occurred in 79.2 percent of the adults and children over two years of age and significantly affected health because it increased susceptibility to infections (Cattani *et al.* 1983:125). The higher prevalence of *P. falciparum*, high parasite rates in children and enlarged spleens in children and adults are all indicative of changing malaria epidemiology since mining.

Wopkaimin children have undergone a body mass decline in the 1980s (Table 6.4). In the absence of known ages, weight–for–age and height–for–age assessments were impossible. Body mass findings can be expressed as the percentages of children whose weight–for–height falls into the categories below 80 percent; 80–89 percent; 90–99 percent and 100 percent and over compared to the National Center for Health Statistic (NCHS) median standards (US Department of Health, Education and Welfare 1977). Children under five whose weight–for–height is below 80 percent of the NCHS median standard are considered severely malnourished, and those between 80 and 89 percent are considered moderately malnourished. Children under five years of age have not improved in nutritional status in the years of mining between 1982 and 1986.

In 1982, of the male children living in hamlets, 11.1 percent were below 80 percent and 33.3 percent were between 80 and 89 percent of the NCHS median weight for their height (Table 6.4). This compares to 0 below 80 percent and 11.8 percent in the 80–89 percent range living in the roadside villages. By 1986 the trend reversed with no male children living in hamlets below 80 percent of the median standard and only 14.3 percent were between 80 and 89 percent. However, in the roadside villages, 5.5 percent were below 80 percent and 23.3 percent were in the range 80–89 percent.

In 1982 the female children living in the roadside villages were more malnourished than the male children (Table 6.4). In 1986, by comparison, 11.1 percent of the female children living in hamlets were below

TABLE 6.4 Body Mass Decline of Wopkaimin Children, 1982–1986

Location/Year		n	< 80%	80–89%	90–99%	100%>
Hamlets/1982	M	18	11.1	33.3	33.3	22.2
	F	22	4.5	27.3	54.5	13.6
Roadside	M	34	0	11.8	35.3	52.9
villages/1982	F	40	10.0	15.0	37.5	37.5
All children/	M	52	3.8	19.2	34.6	42.3
1982	F	62	8.1	19.4	43.5	29.0
	Both	114	6.1	19.3	39.5	35.1
Hamlets/1986	M	7	0	14.3	28.6	57.1
	F	9	11.1	33.3	33.3	22.2
Roadside	M	73	5.5	23.3	42.5	28.8
villages/1986	F	59	11.9	15.3	44.1	28.8
All children/	M	80	5.0	22.5	41.3	31.3
1986	F	68	11.8	17.6	42.6	27.9
	Both	148	8.1	20.3	41.9	29.7

Source: Lourie (1987).

80 percent of the median standard and 33.3 percent were between 80 and 89 percent. This compares to those in the roadside villages who were 11.9 percent below 89 percent of the median standard and 17.6 percent who were in the 80–89 percent range.

In the total population of children under 5 in 1982, 3.8 percent were below 80 percent and 19.2 percent were between 80 and 89 percent of the median standard (Table 6.4). This increased to 5 percent below 80 percent and 22.2 percent between 80 and 89 percent in 1986. Girls are more commonly malnourished than boys. In 1982 the lower weight–for–heights in children were most common in the hamlets, but by 1986 they were most common in the roadside villages. The nutritional status of children improved for those that had returned to the hamlets and deteriorated for those that had remained in the roadside villages.

Vaccinations for the six major communicable diseases of childhood (measles, whooping cough, tetanus, diphtheria, tuberculosis and polio–

TABLE 6.5 Changing Wopkaimin Health Patterns Under Kinship and Capitalist Relations of Production, 1982–1986

Measurement	Age–Group (Years)	1982/83 No.	1982/83 %	1986 No.	1986 %
Skin disease	Total	598	51.2	479	19.6
Leg ulcers	Total	595	15.6	485	18.4
Eye disease	Total	598	2.8	483	5.2
Ear discharge	Total	597	7.5	483	4.1
Neck lymph nodes	Total	603	21.4	484	14.7
Groin lymph nodes	Total	594	16.7	484	7.4
Heart murmurs	Total	591	14.0	476	2.7
Crepitations	Total	603	4.8	485	3.3
Dental caries	Total	585	20.7	456	19.1
Teeth (% DMF)	20>[a]	293	8.2	204	11.7
Liver enlargement	Total	590	77.0	484	16.0
Spleen enlargement	Total[b]	603	76.0	484	40.0

[a] $p < 0.01$
[b] $p < 0.001$

Source: Lourie (1987).

myelitis) were administered to most of the Wopkaimin children during the OTHNP health surveys of 1982 and 1986 (Lourie 1987). Infant mortality, most probably due to respiratory disease and malaria, was 230/1000 in 1982, but by 1986 had fallen to 139/1000. Birth intervals were still approximately five years in 1982, but had fallen to 34 months in 1986 (Taufa et al. 1986). The shorter birth intervals are associated with low birth weight and increased child morbidity and mortality.

Certain health indicators deteriorated under capitalist relations of production in the roadside villages (Table 6.5), even though aid posts were available to the Wopkaimin for the first time. Lourie's (1987) personal examination of every Wopkaimin in 1982 and 1986 revealed that skin disease, especially *Tinea imbricata*, dropped from 51 percent in 1982 to 20 percent in 1986 (Table 6.5). Between 1982 and 1986 leg ulcers in children under nine years of age more than doubled and they went up in the total population from 16 percent to 19 percent. Eye disease likewise increased markedly in children from 1982 to 1986 and its overall prevalence went up from 2.8 percent to 5.2 percent. Ear discharge dropped from 7.5 percent in 1982 to 4.1 percent in 1986. Enlarged neck lymph nodes, related to upper respiratory infections and local sepsis, was found in 21 percent of the population in 1982 and 15 percent in 1986. Enlarged groin lymph nodes, related to leg ulcers, increased in children, but reduced in the overall population from 16 percent to 6 percent. Heart murmurs, most likely related to chronic anemia, occurred in 14 percent of the population in 1982 but in only 2.7 percent in 1986; however, there are no figures to confirm a reduction in anemia. Crepitations, an indication of lower respiratory disease, underwent a fall from 5 percent to 3 percent of the population. There was little difference in the incidence of dental caries (21% v. 19%), but the overall prevalence of diseased, missing or filled (DMF) teeth in those 20 years of age and over went up from 7 percent to 11 percent.

TSS increased dramatically in 1982 as demonstrated through enlarged spleens (higher hackett ratings) (Table 6.5). By 1986 hackett ratings had fallen, as had the incidence of *Plasmodium falciparum* from 75 percent to 38 percent. The percentage of splenomegaly in the population reduced from 76.1 percent in 1982 to 39.7 percent in 1986. Spleen enlargement had dropped to 16 percent in 1986 compared to 77 percent in 1982. The reduced malaria load since 1982 has probably been due to malaria control (Lourie 1987), but malaria remains a more pervasive health problem among the Wopkaimin than it was prior to mining.

Blood pressure is a sensitive physiological indicator of stress. In all ages and sexes of the Wopkaimin there has been a highly significant rise ($p < 0.001$) in both systolic and diastolic pressure from 1982 to 1986 (Lourie 1987). In adult males aged 20 and over, the mean systolic blood pressure was 112.3 in 1982 compared to 125.3 in 1986. For adult females it was 111.2 in 1982 and 126.5 in 1986. Mean diastolic blood pressure in adult males aged 20 and over was 71.3 in 1982 and up to 80.7 in 1986. In adult females it was 70.1 in 1982 and 81.4 in 1986. Blood pressure was higher in employed than in unemployed men and was higher among those in the roadside villages compared to those who returned to their established hamlets (Lourie 1987).

Ethnicity over Class Formation:
"For Ne'er the Twain Shall Meet"

Once Bechtel constructed enough of the intended infrastructure to phase in gold processing in 1984, the Ok Tedi project became known to the Wopkaimin as the "place without work." During the height of Bechtel construction in 1982 over 60 percent of the Wopkaimin men were employed. Employment for Wopkaimin men had dropped to only 5 percent by the height of OTML's gold mining operation in 1986 (Lourie 1987). With gold processing most Wopkaimin men lost work or became dissatisfied with the role of unskilled wage earner. Enthusiasm for active participation as wage earner in the new capitalist relations of production was removed with realization that vast disparities in wealth and status separated them from the white controllers of the mining enclave.

Previously as men rose through the highest grade of initiation, they gained cultural understanding and knowledge to enable them to compete for status as great–men. Schooling and job–training did not fulfil great–man expectations. As the mining project progressed, Wopkaimin men increasingly realized that they would be relegated to insignificant roles as pupils and apprentices throughout the duration of the project. The Ok Tedi enclave required complex skills and the time never came for Wopkaimin men to wield authority and become anything else than apprentices to a succession of authoritative outsiders (Barth and Wikan 1982:32). Although females participated in schooling, they never engaged in job–training or wage earning.

The Wopkaimin continued to recognize the authority of their traditional leaders (*kamokims*). These leaders remained in the former hamlets of the ancestral homeland and followed established kinship relations of production. However, there was leadership competition in the roadside villages. A limited number of Wopkaimin men escaped the roadside villages and were allocated white helmet status with housing in Tabubil. Unskilled workers like the Wopkaimin are allocated yellow helmets. They were distrustful and suspicious of those Wopkaimin men who became white helmet workers and tended to view their class position as a contradiction in terms. One of the Wopkaimin white helmet workers exploited his status ambiguity in a bid to bridge politically the gap between the Wopkaimin and OTML. He competitively used his broker position to build personal wealth through control of the largest tradestore in Woktemwanin. However, this succeeded only in further alienating the roadside villagers who generally did not see local *bisnis* entrepreneurs as enhancing their quality of life.

Black–marketeers had limited influence as power brokers because they were seen as sustaining anti–social behavior. In Woktemwanin a sort of *bos blong spakman* emerged advocating that a proper access road, housing and local development would enhance quality of life in the roadside village. In 1985, in the community interest, black–marketeering was banned in Woktemwanin under the sentiment that "the *spakman* lives off compensation and gardens, the *bisnis*–man and black–marketeer live off everyone."

In short, once gold mining operations started there was a reversal of the proletarianization process and the roadside villages were not united by commitments and obligations to OTML and the state. As in traditional kinship relations of production, there was continuity of separate men's and women's spheres of production. Women had subsistence control of *Xanthosoma* and sweet potato gardening and this feminine sphere of production was not commoditized. The masculine sphere of production was no longer based on wage earning, but rather on control over beer and compensation money.

Land leases eventually appropriated by OTML amounted to over 18,000 ha (Pintz 1984:63). The Wopkaimin alone lost 7000 ha to the Ok Tedi project (Figure 5.2). The national government used their renegotiated arrangements for compensating Bougainvillean land owners as a precedent for the Ok Tedi project. Lease rates of about K25/ha per year were established for (1) payment of occupation fees; (2) payment for restricted access; (3) payment for cleared land; (4) payment for physically used land; (5) payment into a trust fund; and (6) payment of about K650 for each Wopkaimin per year. Because Mt Fubilan is within the Iralim Parish, Woktemwanin and Finalbin residents also received annual royalty payments between K600 to K1000 per person, depending on prevailing copper prices. This placed the non–wage income of the Woktemwanin and Finalbin three times above the national average (Pintz 1984:164) and became the source of the masculine sphere of control over beer and compensation money.

However, 'occupied land' compensation for most Wopkaimin was only around K1 per person per day with an equivalent sum placed in a trust account. Moreover, 'occupied' mining land destroyed nearly 10 percent of their homeland. This represented a substantial loss to the ecological basis of Wopkaimin subsistence production and compensation was inadequate even to substitute the daily diet with the purchase of rice and tinned fish or meat.

By 1988 squatters outnumbered the Wopkaimin, which dramatically altered the character of the roadside villages. The Wopkaimin became a demographic minority in their roadside villages. Outsider 'pasendia' (an aeronautical Melanesian Tok Pisin metaphor for the wives, children, parents and siblings visiting workers, or those seeking work) flooded into Tabubil. Northern Mountain Ok pasendia circulated in and out of Finalbin and Woktemwanin, southern Mountain Ok pasendia circulated in and out of Wangbin and Migalsim and Lowland Ok and Aekyom established themselves across the Ok Maani from Tabubil (Figure 5.2).

By the end of the 1980s one–third of the working–age men from the Fegolmin (Figure 1.2) village of Golgobip were earning a wage in Tabubil, but only a dozen worked for OTML. This social transformation involved a spatial division of labor between the Ok Tedi enclave and Golgobip and a gender division in which men sell their labor and women take on an increasing share of gardening (Polier 1990). This pattern became widespread in portions of the socio–ecological region closest to the mining project. The 1990 PNG census is predicted to reveal that the Ok Tedi enclave now has over 10,000 residents, which should be divided roughly in half between workers and pasendias. Wangbin is the largest roadside village with over 2,500 residents and Woktemwanin is next in size with between 800 and 1000 residents who are mostly non–Wopkaimin pasendia.

The dialectics of changing relations of production associated with the Ok Tedi project, as with the Panguna mining project on Bougainville, provided another example of "a general truth about Papua New Guinea: even where introduced capitalist relations of production have had the greatest effect, they have not completely eliminated those that existed before colonialism" (Wesley–Smith and Ogan 1992:261). Proletarianization initiated by the Ok Tedi project dropped away dramatically once gold and copper mining was underway. Capitalist relations of production increased inequalities between the sexes and separate feminine and masculine spheres of production were accentuated. The incipient development of social classes was complicated by ethnicity, as occurred in association with the Bougainville mining project (Hyndman 1991b; Nash and Ogan 1990; Wesley–Smith and Ogan 1992).

When Ok Tedi became the place without work and the roadside villages filled with *pasendias*, it emphasized a sense of Wopkaimin identity and they became more active in defence of their interests and ancestral domain. Bombakan grew into a major new Wopkaimin hamlet used by many families as an alternative to Woktemwanin. The Wopkaimin significantly revitalized their Afek male cult traditions and substantially abandoned Woktemwanin to *pasendias* and relocated themselves in Bombakan and elsewhere in the hamlets of their Kam Basin homeland. Articulation to capitalist relations of production remained primarily through the masculine sphere of control of compensation money. There is no commodity production in women's control of subsistence gardening. Most Wopkaimin returned, or regularly circulated back and forth, to their ancestral homeland and continued established kinship relations of production for subsistence and internal consumption of surplus.

7

Afek and *Rebaibal*:
Ideologies of Social Protest

Ideology and Resistance

The Ok Tedi project divides into an economic base and a derivative sociopolitical and ideological superstructure (Godoy 1985). The economic base of the mining enclave imposed capitalist relations of production on the Wopkaimin for the first time and a sociopolitical superstructure was derived from the clash between kinship and capitalist relations of production. Wopkaimin resistance and protest to mining was contained in the superstructure of ideology.

Studies of the superstructure of ideology among Quechua miners in Bolivia by Nash (1979) and Taussig (1980) are well-known analyses of the ideological response to mining. These ethnographies attempt to explain the effects of colonial oppression and capitalist penetration, not only on people's material and political circumstances, but also on their consciousness and construction of ideology. Taussig's post–modernist ethnography (1980) takes a literary approach to constructing Quechua ritual as fetishizing evil and mediating tensions caused by tyrannical proletarianization of people previously practicing a kinship mode of production. It ultimately is not as convincing or as politically committed as Nash's ethnography.

Nash (1979) views Quechua ritual in the tin mines as a forum for expressing worker solidarity and integrating the people into the world Capitalist System. Nash is concerned with how and when worker ideology is translated into action "whether directed toward revolutionary goals or

131

merely the maintenance of self and family" (1979:12). She is an advocate for worker solidarity and their movement for political change and examines the impact of history and specific political implications on the consciousness of the workers. When analyzing how this consciousness works as an impetus for action, she takes the position of revolutionary advocate, not objective observer. She describes a situation that is oppressive in its conditioning of the lives of the Bolivian tin miners and their search for the impetus to change that reality.

Yellow Helmets Versus White Helmets: Safety or Status?

Resource expropriation in New Guinea has spatial as well as temporal aspects. Resources are being transported from the past of their "primitive" locations to the present of an industrial, capitalist economy. The temporal conception of movement has always served to legitimize the colonial and transnational enterprise (Fabian 1983:95). The passage from savagery to civilization has long ideologically served to justify resource expropriation for Western markets. New Guinea gold and copper become commodities when they are possessed, removed from their resource context and placed into the history of Western commerce (Wolf 1982).

In the land policy discussions that were designed to possess and remove minerals from their resource context, the Wopkaimin were perceived as traditional primitives. Their previous lack of cash earning activities relegated the Wopkaimin to a peripheral, unskilled wage–earner role in the Bechtel construction phase of the Ok Tedi project. This did not prevent protest in relation to mine employment. A contentious issue was the national government's decision to allow Bechtel to employ a large number of Asian laborers, which by 1983 represented 30 percent of the manual labor budget (Howard 1988:106). The PNG Institute of Applied Social and Economic Research supported the state's position that reliance on skilled manual labor from PNG nationals would be disruptive to other areas of the economy. Mining was to fund development but not the formation of a middle class.

The Wopkaimin were certainly not supportive of the policy. In early 1983 they went on strike and OTML shut down the project and emergency airlifted out all white women and children. They were protesting against outsiders, especially Asians, taking semi–skilled employment that they perceived as being capable of performing themselves and against whites and other PNG nationals moving into Tabubil with their families as they were forced to move to the new roadside villages (Figure 1.2). The Wopkaimin returned to work after receiving higher wages but their other grievances still remain unresolved.

The death in 1984 of a construction worker from the Highlands east of the Mountain Ok region precipitated another protest strike by the Wopkaimin. The man was killed when he was thrown from his seatbeltless and doorless vehicle during a road accident. Wopkaimin workers went on strike with other PNG nationals demanding an immediate improvement in safety conditions and compensation for the dead man. For the Wopkaimin the confrontation was an occasion to express their resentment against status inequality. Their earlier complaints over safety concerns were infuriatingly dismissed by white bosses with *"yu manki tasol"*, a Melanesian Tok Pisin response implying they were only boys and not entitled to complain. Safety helmets symbolically mark status. Yellow helmets are worn by the unskilled workers like the Wopkaimin and white helmets are worn by the management, which is mostly white. During the confrontation the Wopkaimin insisted that those wearing the white helmets throw them in the mud, asserting that helmets are for safety not for status.

Work and food requirements and effluent from the Ok Tedi mining operation created a greater Fly River socio–ecological region. By 1988 people well outside the Ok Tedi socio–ecological region from the Enga and Southern Highland Provinces had settled as squatters near the mine without permission of the Wopkaimin landowners. The murder of a Telefolmin *pasendia* (a Melanesian Tok Pisin aeronautical metaphor for Mountain Ok neighbors visiting the roadside villages) by squatters early in 1988 precipitated another protest strike. Over 300 of the Wopkaimin felled trees over the mine road and again closed the project demanding that the squatters be repatriated back to their home provinces in the Highlands. They also wanted more mining jobs and contracts for providing the mine with services like vegetables and gravel to be given to local Mountain Ok peoples.

The militant Wopkaimin grievances against problems of squatters, social disturbances and pollution were suppressed by police force under orders from then Prime Minister Wingti. Leaders from the Western and North Solomons Provinces where the Ok Tedi and Panguna mining projects operated, were highly critical of the Prime Minister's actions. The former Premier of the Western Province, Norbert Makmop, stated: "Mr. Wingti seems to be trying to suppress the domestic rights of the people to air their grievances". Michael Laimo, then Member of Parliament from North Solomons, declared: "The decision demonstrated the irresponsible attitude of the national government towards the ordinary citizens of PNG who struggle to protect their environment from foreign exploitation" (quoted in Hyndman 1988).

Late in 1988 further violence erupted at the Ok Tedi mine as national workers went on strike. OTML described the strikers as "uncontrollable" after they stole 1500 cartons of beer and large quantities of spirits. Workers' demands for housing and promotions were dismissed by OTML as a law and order problem and two police mobile squads and a Defense Force squad were flown in as white families were again flown out to Port Moresby. The then Prime Minister Rabbie Namaliu ordered a board of inquiry to investigate the strike demands made by 1043 out the 1700 workers. He personally intervened to bring union and management together and took the position that management caused resentment among the workers and that the housing cost problem would be slashed by half if local enterprise was used.

The Wopkaimin again protested over the continuing pollution and squatter problem and closed the mining project early in 1990. They allowed the mine to reopen on 22 January 1990 with the warning from Biul Kirokim, President of the Star Mountains Local Government Council, that it would shut down the mine completely unless positive steps were taken to finalize their compensation demands. The landowner's counter-proposal to the national government's K2.5 million compensation package was to request that their share of the royalties be increased from 20 percent to 50 percent. They also wanted increased base payments, infrastructure payments, loan guarantees, business spin-offs, subcontracting priority and K10 million for improvement for the Tabubil road (*Post Courier*, 29 January 1990).

Personal interventions by Prime Ministers draws attention to the crucial importance of Ok Tedi royalties to the government. The motivation behind then Prime Minister Wingti's decision to use police force in 1988 to suppress Wopkaimin grievances is expressed in his statement that "investor confidence and the country's credibility would be affected deeply but at least the investors know that the government is firm" (Hyndman 1988:29). The state is committed to transnational mineral extraction projects and it appears the Ok Tedi project will continue early into the next century.

A superstructure of ideology emerged in response to colonial intrusion and capitalist penetration from the Ok Tedi project. Social protest among the Wopkaimin and other Mountain Ok peoples in the socio–ecological region became expressed in two disparate ideological movements.

Destroying the Past: The *Rebaibalists*

The Mountain Ok people believe their way of life was founded by the 'great mother' ancestress Afek. Through their male initiatory cult youths are transformed into men. Male performance of rituals, maintenance of sacred relics and sacrifice of animals insured prosperity of all. The Afek cult excludes women and elaborate prohibitions specify food production and consumption by gender.

Following the establishment of a Bible College by the Baptist mission in the Sepik Source Basin, a spectacular local evangelical movement emerged among the Telefolmin people. Many abandoned the Afek cult and replaced it with an indigenous Christian revival movement commonly referred to as *rebaibal* in Melanesian Tok Pisin.

The Baptists opened their first mission near the sacred *Telefolip* cult house in 1950, but their threat to the Afek cult did not reach a crisis point until 1974 (Frankel 1976; Jorgensen 1981). Collective ecstatic outbreaks first occurred among the Telefolmin, especially the women. Later in 1977 a Telefolmin student of the Bible College experienced ecstatic seizures at Duranmin northeast of the Sepik Source Basin triggering mass seizures, body shaking, crying, glossolalia, prophecy, healing and exorcism and the rapid spread of *rebaibal* as the first popular indigenous acceptance of Christianity.

Rebaibal completely rejected established cultural patterns but it was much more than another transformation of a traditional cult system into a distinctly Melanesian Christianity (cf. Guiart 1970). Cult houses and sacred objects were destroyed and secret knowledge was revealed. Gender roles were altered and women acquired more equal status. Food prohibitions and male control of meat shared through the Afek cult complex ended. The men's house was abandoned in favor of nuclear families working, residing and consuming together (Barr and Trompf 1983).

By the time the Ok Tedi project started, *rebaibal*, with over 3000 followers, represented the most popular indigenous acceptance of

Christianity among the northern Ok peoples (Barr 1983). It had resulted in the destruction or desecration of men's cult houses in over a dozen Telefolmin villages. In Tifalmin, the closest northern neighbors of the Wopkaimin, the important cult house in Brolemabip was burned to the ground. In the 1980s *rebaibal* spelled the end of the traditional system of regionally organized initiations centered on the Telefolmin's supremely sacred *Telefolip* cult house (Jorgensen 1990).

Rebaibal is an innovation and adjustment to culture change. Like the cargo cults of colonial and post–colonial PNG, it is a major social protest and critique of an alien cultural system. *Rebaibalists* argue there is nothing in the traditional Afek cult relevant to the problems posed by money, especially the development of the Ok Tedi project. An underlying theme of the *rebaibal* ideology is to legitimate household autonomy in opposition to community sharing in the use of cash.

Rebaibalists have remained most influential among the northern Mountain Ok, whereas Catholics have been strongest among the southern Mountain Ok. Christianity promoted men and women as equal members of the congregation in exaggerated contrast to male–centered Afek cult traditions.

Among the southern Mountain Ok, Sunday Catholic service for the Fegolmin was followed by public discussion (Barth and Wikan 1982:16). However, sermons and meetings alike were led by male catechists and only men spoke. *Rebaibalist* congregations, in contrast, incorporated solo and small group performances in their service and groups of women sang religious songs in Melanesian Tok Pisin. Women responded favorably to enhanced participation in Christian religious life, forming dependable congregations in contrast to their marginal involvement in the Afek cult. Women were particularly zealous in promulgating *rebaibal*. Indeed, participation in Christian congregations has become the dominant expression of 'modern' identity among many southern Mountain Ok women (Polier 1990).

Progressing with the Past: Cultural Reanimation Through the Afek Cult

Wopkaimin culture was characterized by individual autonomy and sensitivity to the pressures of others and to negative sanctions imposed through public opinion and their leaders are primarily ritual specialists (*awem kinum*) whose paramount concern was continuity of the Afek cult. The intense scale of information flow created a leadership crisis in the roadside villages.

There was no emergence of 'modern' leaders in the sense of manipulating and integrating traditional authority and community values with state and transnational intrusion (cf. Rodman and Counts 1983). Traditional leaders (*kamokim*) maximized information about opinions and attitudes of all persons involved and manipulated taboo to produce secrecy. Roadside village leaders needed to maximize scale, with access to wider networks, more places and more people than others (Barth and Wikan 1982:49). Although OTML wage–earning provided the networks and transportation, it greatly restricted necessary time for community interaction in the roadside villages. As wage–earning positions were lost, internal company networks shrank, while only a few remaining wage-earners continued to accumulate income and knowledge. The Wopkaimin leadership crisis was "classically the kind of situation where cultural annihilation and/or extreme reactions of rejection and defence result" (Barth and Wikan 1982:48). Defense and rejection, rather than annihilation, occurred among the Wopkaimin.

Gesock is the most important traditional Wopkaimin leader (*kamokim*). He is also the ritual specialist (*awem kinum*) in control of the *Futmanam* cult house located in the hamlet of Bultem in the Kam Basin. He was appalled after the *rebaibalists* burned down the Tifalmin cult house, and crusaded actively against their influence. In the 1980s, as the Wopkaimin established their roadside villages near the mine, Gesock ensured that they continued their commitment to the *Futmanam*. He established interpersonal networks and manipulated the flow of secret/sacred information to reaffirm his people's continued belief in the ritual legacy bequeathed to them from Afek. The Wopkaimin realized the *Telefolip* in Telefolmin had lost its pre–eminent position in the region because of the *rebaibalists*. It was Gesock who arranged and lead the traditional ceremonies focused on the *Futmanam*.

Hosting a major refurbishing ceremony of their *Futmanam* in 1981 and starting a new sequence of male initiations in 1983 provided the Wopkaimin with cultural identity as a people and legitimated their claim that the *Futmanam* remained a significant cult house in the regional system of male initiations. Every adult male temporarily left wage-earning from the mine and every boy left school to participate in the initiation ceremonies.

PLATE 7.1 Gesock, the most important leader and ritual specialist, directs a new sequence of male initiation in 1983 (photo courtesy of C. Roberts).

In addition to ensuring continuity of ritual performance, Gesock organized construction of Bombakan hamlet in the Kam Basin with residentially segregated women's houses and a men's house. By the beginning of 1986 a core of over 30 residents had decentralized from the roadside villages to live with Gesock in Bombakan and others circulated in temporarily, especially from Woktemwanin. The decentralization process gained momentum and, by 1989, most Wopkaimin had abandoned Woktemwanin for hamlets in the Kam Basin (Chris Roberts, personal communication). The Fegolmin, likewise, decentralized from Bolivip for the revitalization of hamlet life based on the Afek cult (Barth and Wikan 1982:51).

The Wopkaimin reinstated old patterns of male controlled sharing (*abipkagup*) in their Kam Basin hamlets and re–established *Colocasia* taro subsistence production. Sharing of hunted game and taro and collective cult traditions provided common purpose and a sense of achievement. Many valued decentralization as a way of preventing loss of cultural knowledge and also of ensuring that boys were initiated. Many were concerned with losing knowledge of their ancestral rain forests and the skills to practice their kinship mode of production. A Telefolmin teenage *pasendia* in Woktemwanin asked me, "Where did you get those animals?" when I arrived with several cages of rodents in 1985. When I explained that we had trapped them in the Hindenburg Mountains and the Kam Basin, the youth replied that "if they come from the bush it is too hard for us to get them." Decentralization prevented loss of cultural knowledge and loss of identification with a sense of place.

PLATE 7.2 Male initiation ceremonies held in Bultem hamlet in 1983 (photo courtesy of C. Roberts).

Continued Prospects for Ideological Protest

The future prospects for the two social protest movements among the Wopkaimin is uncertain. Currently, the indigenous Christian movement started by the *rebaibalists* and the decentralization movement associated with the Afek cult do not interact in common social protest over the intrusion of the Ok Tedi project; rather, they are mutually exclusive. The *rebaibalists* started among peoples in the socio–ecological region more marginal to the Ok Tedi project and they gained their support precisely because they rejected the social order of the past in favor of the supposed benefits of rapid economic change.

Northern Mountain Ok *rebaibalists* lobbied to create a 'pan–Min' province to contain the Ok Tedi project within its new borders (Morren 1986). An alternative Min Association was formed among the Telefolmin in 1981 for the same purpose. In contrast to the *rebaibalists*, the Min Association played on traditions based on the Afek cult for all Mountain Ok to acknowledge their common identity (Jorgensen 1990). They used the *Telefolip* and *Futmanam* cult houses, and the fact that the Mt Fubilan 'pot of gold' sits on top of the Land of the Dead established by Afek's younger brother Umoim, to advocate for a Min province. Neither succeeded and the national government never created a new province. The Western Province encompasses the Ok Tedi project and continues to create an artificial boundary between the southern and northern Mountain Ok in the socio–ecological region.

Previously, the Wopkaimin aggregated only for short–term rituals but the new roadside communities were maintained well beyond the time periods appropriate to short–term rituals and this created significant social stress among those living there. The Wopkaimin did not experience white missionary proselytizing but, in the new roadside villages, Fegolmin Catholic catechists competed with the traditionalists for converts. Through decentralization, the Wopkaimin constructed relationships with the transnational and Christian intruders into patterns comprehensible to them in terms of the established obligations of the Afek cult that supported their own social relationships. Decentralization demonstrated their culture had a limited capacity for exercising social control, especially in the confines of the new roadside aggregate communities.

Instead of contextualizing his generative approach to the study of Mountain Ok religion in the changes ramifying from the creation of a mining frontier, Barth (1987:1) unrealistically presented an unrealistic ethnographic present of "'neolithic' cultivators and hunters in a recently contacted area of Inner New Guinea." Thus, Barth (1987:75) expressed surprise at the "capacity of untrained and pre-trained Ok villagers to function in a modern, high-technology organization" and remarked that "returning individually to their village communities, the scope for them to practice or even express new ideational impulses they brought with them likewise seemed highly restricted".

Unlike previous initiations and refurbishing ceremonies, Wopkaimin celebrations of the Afek cult since the start of the Ok Tedi project have been conducted under full realization of the vast extent of different cultures as a result of exposure to outsiders and strangers. More than ever before, the Afek cult took on enhanced significance as the supreme marker of distinctive Wopkaimin and wider Mountain Ok culture and identity. Using traditional cults like Afek as a form of social protest is a common informal response among indigenous miners and Godoy (1985:207) indicates their use often antedates eruption of strikes. As indicated earlier, this was precisely what occurred among the Wopkaimin.

The Wopkaimin volunteered for work during the infrastructure construction phase at the mine. After the start of gold mining in 1984 it became the "place without work". The Ok Tedi project became an enclave of skilled, outside workers. The bulk of the Wopkaimin did not undergo a voluntary or coercive process of proletarianization. There was no worker solidarity in the roadside villages and they largely became excluded from capitalist relations of production in the mining enclave. Decentralisation to the Kam Basin hamlets became a safely valve from the new stress of life. The Afek cult ideologically endorsed continuity of kinship relations of production.

The Wopkaimin protested against the consequences of rapid economic change through their continuation of the Afek cult. They found little appeal in the *rebaibal* movement because it jeopardized the status they exerted as the indigenous landowners of the mine. Through decentralization and continued commitment to the *Futmanam*, the Wopkaimin carried past traditions forward to retain a sense of place and cultural identity.

Continuity of kinship relations of production in the Kam Basin is ideologically and spatially linked to the clash with capitalist relations of production operating in the roadside villages. Participation in the Afek cult became more important than wage earner participation in the mining enclave. Moreover, as *pasendias* and squatters moved in, they became a demographic minority in their own roadside villages. In December 1984 the Wopkaimin refused to allow OTML to acquire new leases upstream of the project for possible relocation of the tailings dam. They noted their continuing use of the land, that the proposed leases threatened their ancestral rain forests and that compensation was inadequate for the land OTML had already destroyed.

Continued use and proprietorship of their ancestral rain forests remains important to the Wopkaimin. Re-animated Afek traditions and established patterns of hamlet sharing (*abipkagup*) in the Kam Basin hamlets promote collective membership and identity among the Wopkaimin.

8

Freeport and Panguna: Popular Mobilization
and Armed Resistance Against Mining

Regional Political Ecology and Resistance

Across the islands of New Guinea three of the world's largest open–cut gold and copper mines have intruded on the lands and resources of Fourth World Melanesians: the Ok Tedi and Panguna mines in PNG and the Freeport mine in West Papua (Figure 8.1). Indigenous nations in the vicinity of the projects experienced ecocide and ethnocide and responded with movements of social protest. Gerlach and Hine's (1970:xvi) definition of social movements as "a group of people who are organized for, ideologically motivated by and committed to a purpose which implements some form of personal or social change; who are actively engaged in the recruitment of others; and whose influence is spreading in opposition to the established order within which it originated" cross–culturally characterizes the appearance of social movements against mining on New Guinea (Hyndman 1988b, 1991b; May 1982). The volatile articulation between Fourth World nations, colonizers, states and transnationals on the mining resource frontier in New Guinea has erupted into Fourth World wars in West Papua and Bougainville.

Freeport: Mining Invasion of West Papua

There are around 12,000 Amungme (Pogolamun 1985:45), their homeland extends from equatorial glaciers through alpine, sub–alpine,

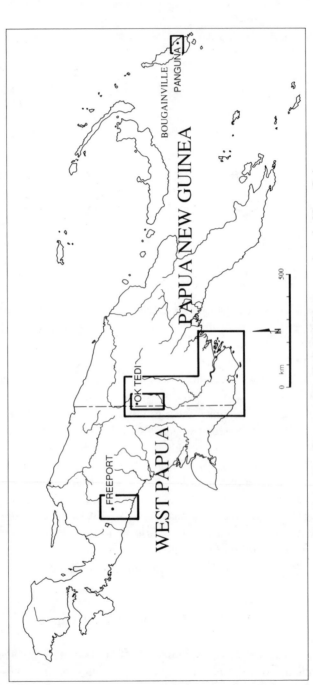

FIGURE 8.1 The Freeport, Ok Tedi and Panguna mines in New Guinea.

montane and lowland rainforest and swamp forest habitats and surrounds the Freeport mining project (Figure 8.2). In the 1950s some Amungme took up the *hai*, a social movement in search of eternal life, and started moving to the southern lowlands of their homeland. Other Amungme were attracted to the Catholic missions, schools and clinics opened in Tsinga and Noemba in 1955. The Dutch established a colonial administration post and a rubber resettlement scheme at Kiliarama in the extreme south of Amungme territory in 1958. Resettlement started between 1961–1963 and stopped in 1970 once West Papua was annexed as another province of Indonesia. Around 2,500 Amungme eventually established a string of villages named Akimuga but they had no resistance to the endemic malaria of the lowlands and many died. The majority of the Amungme remained in their mountain homeland (Pogolamun 1985:46–47) practising kinship relations of production centered on sweet potato cultivation and pig husbandry.

Transnational Mining and the State

Copper on Amungme land was first reported internationally in 1936 by the Dutch geologist J. Dozy who gave the name Ertsberg to the ore mountain of 33 million tonnes of 2.5 percent copper. Based on the Dozy report, J. van Gruisen, managing director of Oost Borneo Maatschappilj, took out a 100,000 ha mining exploration concession in 1959 (White 1983:49) without consulting the Amungme and then passed it on to the US transnational Freeport (Osborne 1985:118). Freeport waited until the withdrawal of Dutch colonialism, then promptly started negotiating a prospecting authority with the Indonesian's in 1963. According to a speech to the Indonesia Council by R. Hopper, an ex–geologist from Standard Oil, Freeport "had been waiting for the right time to enter Indonesia for the development of a long known deposit of copper ore in a remote part of West Irian" (Hook nd:4), the right time deemed to be after Indonesian recolonization of West Papua.

Sukarno's nationalism was a stumbling block to US transnational intervention, and Indonesia was nationalizing Dutch transnationals between 1957–1958 because Holland refused to yield West Papua. From 1958 to 1962 a 'neutral' US mediated the dispute over West Papuan independence. The US was highly critical of West Papuan aspirations for self–determination claiming the Melanesians to be straight out of the Stone Age and the region to be grossly lacking in natural resources. US sponsorship of anthropological projects through Rockefeller and natural

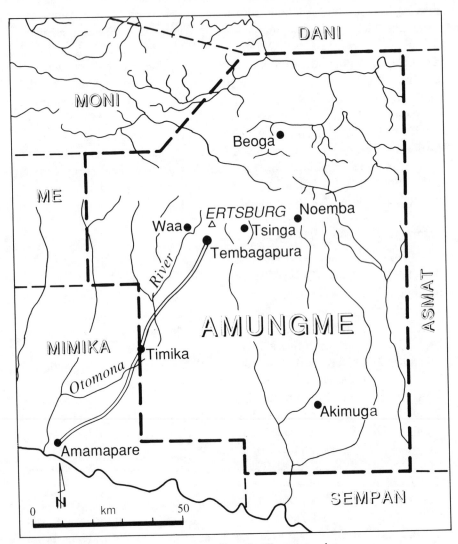

FIGURE 8.2 West Papuans surrounding the Freeport mine.

history projects through Archbold widely publicized and denigrated the West Papuans as still in the Stone Age. The Dani, north of the Amungme (Figure 8.2), became immortalized as warring primitives through the film 'Dead Birds' and the books by Matthiessen (1962) and Heider (1970,1979). The Me, east of the Amungme (Figure 8.2), were portrayed by Pospisil (1978) as the primitive capitalist Kapauku. Yet, the West Papuan school teachers and university graduates espousing independence in 1963 were probably more competent than their Melanesian counterparts in Australian colonial New Guinea who enjoyed their own House of Assembly by 1964 and independence by 1975.

Freeport signed a 'Contract of Work' on 7 April 1967 soon after Indonesia enacted its Foreign Investment Law and became the first transnational to enter Indonesia under the new law. Infrastructure was contracted out to Bechtel in 1970, the same US construction transnational which constructed the Ok Tedi and Panguna projects. The first shipment of copper concentrate went out in late 1972. A tax holiday over the first three years saved them between US$15–25 million dollars (Osborne 1985:119). Not until after the 1969 'Act of Free Choice' that 'legitimated' Indonesian annexation of West Papua did the transnational localize as Freeport Indonesia Inc. (FII).

West Papuan Mobilization and Armed Resistance in the Freeport Socio-ecological Region

Indonesia maintains a policy of oppression and ethnocide against indigenous, Fourth World peoples within the domestic boundaries of the state. All rural communities are categorized according to a 19th century evolutionary progression from traditional (*swadaya*) villages, to transitional (*swakarya*) villages to developed (*swasembada*) villages truly integrated into the Indonesian state with Java at the top (Colchester 1986a:89). But an estimated 800,000 of the some 1.2 million West Papuans are denigrated as pre–villagers so primitive they are classified as isolated and alien peoples (*suka suka terasing*) without legal provisions to safeguard their human and resource rights and sociocultural differences (Colchester 1986a:91). Indonesia utilizes Article 33, section 3 of the 1945 Constitution which states that "Land and water and natural riches therein shall be controlled by the state as the highest authority to manage their utilization for the maximum well–being of the whole people." The Agrarian Law, which permits only shifting cultivators rights to land currently under cultivation (Colchester 1986b:104–105), is used to confiscate land and resources from Fourth World Melanesian nation peoples within the state borders of Indonesia.

For the Amungme, state and transnational collusion to mine gold and copper on their land is nothing short of economic development by invasion. Waa villagers (Figure 8.2) residing close to the mining complex at Tembagapura were the only Amungme to receive compensation and it was a once off payment for direct disruption of current gardens (Mitton 1977:367). Bechtel paid several hundred Amungme and other local Melanesians US$0.10 cents per hour for unskilled construction work but once the mine was operational only 40 continued to be employed and FII is exempted from paying land rent or royalties to the Amungme or assisting the Amungme or the province in economic development (Osborne 1985:119). FII was not obliged to carry out an environmental impact assessment (Mitton 1977:367) and not only is mining causing surface degradation and sediment and water pollution of the Otomona River, but employees are abusing wildlife (Petocz 1984:136).

A massive Indonesian military and police presence paralleled the build up of the mining operation. A civilian pilot named T. Doyle, who flew for eight years between Australia and Freeport, reported that when a FII employee named J. Hansen encouraged the Amungme to start growing vegetables for sale to the mine "he fell foul of the Indonesians because they didn't like anyone having contact with the natives. They felt outsiders might promote the 'false' idea of their owning the land--for which they had received little or no compensation. They dealt with Hansen by firing bullets around his feet, like a cowboy movie. Get out of town or else! We had to fly him out in a bit of a hurry" (Osborne 1985:71).

The Free Papua Movement (Organisasi Papua Merdeka) (OPM) has been fighting a Fourth World resistance movement against Indonesia for West Papuan self-determination for nearly three decades (Nietschmann 1987b; Osborne 1985). Major clashes between the OPM and the Indonesian military occurred in 1977 among the nearby Me and Dani peoples (Figure 8.2) and after the Amungme in the southern Akimuga villages ejected two Indonesian policemen, the Indonesian military retaliated by strafing them on the 22nd of July 1977 from two Bronco OV-10s until they ran out of ammunition (Osborne 1985:69). Indonesian counter-insurgency reprisals and years of resentment against Freeport provoked the Amungme into a major social protest culminating in sabotage against FII. The Amungme, Me and Dani wanted the Indonesians and FII out of the socio-ecological region and they were aided by other OPM fighters under Otto Ondowame. With explosives stolen from FII, they blew up the copper slurry pipe running from the mine down to the portsite of Amamapare and in addition burned fuel installations, blockaded airstrips, destroyed bridges and attacked electricity lines (Osborne 1985:69-70). The Amungme, joined by other OPM, remained in control for several days.

The cost to FII for civil disturbance and property damage was US$11 million, the cost to the Amungme, Me and Dani from the socio-ecological region was a massive military sweep code-named *Operasi Tumpas* (annihilation). The Indonesian military destroyed Amungme gardens, burned down houses and churches and tortured and killed men, women and children. The OPM believes thousands of Me, Dani and Amungme were killed in 1977, while Indonesia claims it was far less, only about 900 (Osborne 1985:72). Petitions and letters of complaint from the Amungme were routinely ignored by the Indonesian authorities (Osborne 1985:122). Amungme living near Tembagapura addressed a long list of grievances and a request for assistance to the governor in May 1980 (Tapol 1984:43-44). The official response four months later was forced resettlement to the lowlands airstrip at Timika where, according to FII (nd:12), the Amungme could become 'farmers'. Timika, with over 15,000 settlers in 1984, was the largest resettlement program of its kind in West Papua but 20 percent of the Amungme infants died in the move because of lack of resistance to malaria (Osborne 1985:123). All residents are threatened by metal oxide pollution of the Otomona River (Petocz 1984:135).

1980 was also the year the FII underground mine came into production (White 1983:46), which further reduced land to the Amungme for gardening, travel and hunting (Pogolamun 1985:49-50). An agreement signed between the Amungme, FII and the state on 8 January 1984 placed Tembagapura and all other FII facilities within the 100,000 ha mining concession completely off limits to the Amungme, in exchange for construction of an unused school in Waa, clinics in Waa and Tsinga and markets used once a week in Waa and Timika (Pogolamun 1985:48).

Not only is the FII 100,000 ha mining concession effectively off limits to the Amungme but 2,150,000 ha of their territory was gazetted in 1978 as the Lorentz Strict Nature Reserve. Half of the reserve is under a petroleum exploration concession and 20 percent is under the FII mining concession and it has been proposed to the International Union for the Conservation of Nature for World Heritage listing as a National Park of

1,560,000 ha (Petocz 1984:79). Fourth World ownership and sustained–yield management of protected areas is not a priority of Indonesian conservation management, which includes only (1) biological importance; (2) relationship to ongoing development projects; (3) threats to integrity of reserves; and (4) location (Petocz 1984:78). Indigenous peoples are usually uninformed if their land has become a protected area; if they are informed it is only after their land has been gazetted and their participation in future management planning is negligible (Petocz 1984:77). FII's lack of a social or environmental conscience, the scale of ecocide and ethnocide and transnational–state abuse of Amungme human rights are major condemnations of the mining project and cast grave doubts on the long–term feasibility of combining conservation and development in the region.

Panguna: Mining Invasion of Bougainville

On Bougainville nineteen distinct languages are spoken in the Panguna socio–ecological region, eleven Austronesian and eight Papuan (Oliver 1973:38). Settled in the foothills and mountains that surround the Panguna mine are some 14,000 Nasioi (Wurm 1982:237; Figure 8.3). The region has been their homeland since 1911 (Ogan 1972:13). For the Nasioi and other Bougainvilleans, identity and tradition are based on their relationship to their land (Oliver 1973:46). Land is owned by co–resident matri–clan members and residence is ideally uxorilocal (Nash 1974:7). Age and gender distinguish certain statuses but emphasis is placed on individual achievement in an undifferentiated society (Ogan 1966b:187). Informal, formal and large–scale exchanges are governed by balanced reciprocity and balanced property exchange is achieved through bilateral cross–cousin marriage (Ogan 1972). Prior to W.W.II Nasioi kinship relations of production focused on *Colocasia* taro (Ogan 1972:23), but after the blight of 1942–44 they produced sweet potato as their staple crop (Connell 1978).

Kinship relations of production on Bougainville was first monetized following W.W.II with cash–cropping of coconuts and cocoa among the men and market vegetables among the women. To Treadgold (1978:16) commoditizing the kinship mode of production was a routine, harmless modernization process because:

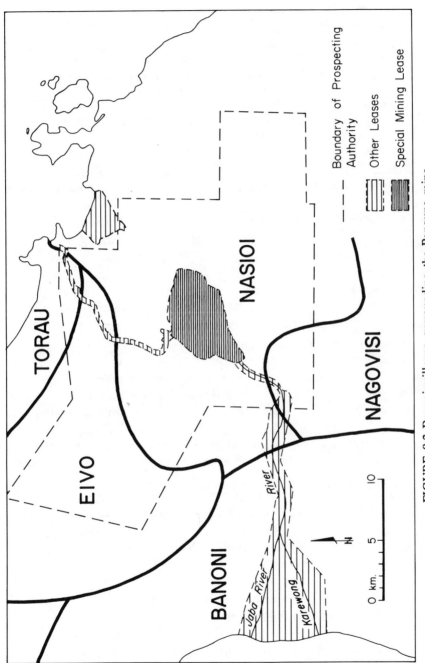

FIGURE 8.3 Bougainvilleans surrounding the Panguna mine.

In terms of resource requirements, it was made possible by the essentially subsistence–affluent state of the indigenous rural economy, which implied the existence of unused surpluses of land and labour. The utilization of these surpluses permitted the expansion of production for export without any significance in terms of subsistence output foregone. Moreover, the methods of cash–crop production were such that little change was needed in traditional methods of economic organization. In short, to apply Myint's (1973:74) phrase, cash–cropping was a virtually riskless operation, requiring no other cost than extra working hours.

In fact, cash–cropping by the Nasioi (Ogan 1972:122,183) and the neighboring Nagovisi (Mitchell 1976:1) was disastrous because it created increasingly serious land shortages at the expense of subsistence production and it provided low returns for labor input. Land acquired for women's market vegetable production followed usual matrilineal patterns (Moulik 1977:32,34; Ogan 1972:116,129), whereas land acquired for men's coconut and cocoa cash–cropping clashed with kinship relations of production. Men already manipulated the marriage system to gain and consolidate status (Ogan 1966b:186). With cash–cropping several men worked together to establish groves but each assumed individual ownership of trees even though the communal land on which they planted belonged to their wives. By continuing to manipulate the marriage system and taking advantage of the Australian colonial administration bias towards patrilineal inheritance, men also passed their trees on to their sons in a matrilineal society that otherwise assigned inheritance to land on which crops are planted to clan daughters (Ogan 1972:116,129). The resulting clash of kinship and capitalist relations of production was not a riskless operation requiring no other cost than extra working hours.

Big–men exchange among the Nasioi is conducted among kin or facilitated by putative kinship relations and is primarily a social activity. After cash–cropping, big–men started competing for prestige in *bisnis*. *Bisnis* became entirely an impersonal economic exchange of commodities for cash (Ogan 1972:39) and clashed with the social exchange of gifts in kinship relations of production. As men manipulated the marriage system it too was monetized (Nash 1981:2). Money entered prestations at marriage. Women became ranked according to purchased prestations and their sexuality was alienated from themselves and controlled by men. The cash–crop/*bisnis* inroads of capitalist relations of production devalued women in the eyes of their men and themselves (Nash 1981).

Far from being a trouble free example of an affluent subsistence society incorporating commoditization into the void of surplus land and labor, cash–cropping and *bisnis* were an acute crisis to established kinship relations of production among Bougainvilleans. They responded to the crisis with *kago* (Melanesian Tok Pisin for cargo cult belief that spiritual and material benefits are obtainable through ritual activity). *Kago* competed with *bisnis* and was widely used as a movement of social protest. The lack of a charismatic leader and Australian colonial administration prosecution of *kago* followers on the southern Bougainville coast prevented a full–fledged *kago* movement from developing among the Nasioi (Ogan 1972:173).

Among the Nasioi and their neighbors, colonial intrusion and behavioral interaction with Europeans was affected through Catholic missions which controlled the dispensation of inappropriate and inadequate schooling until the 1960s (Ogan 1972). The legacy of colonial antagonism between Catholic and Protestant missionaries was reinforced by the Australian colonial administration's division of the Nasioi into progressive Protestants and "cargo–cultist" Catholics (Nash and Ogan 1990:5). Catholic mission schools did not explore the dynamics of colonialism, but Catholic missionization became the focus of *kago* resistance. The clash between kinship and capitalist relations of production among Bougainvilleans was not characterized by the benign use of their surplus land and labor but the expropriation of their land and labor which made the German and Australian colonizers rich and *kago* became a movement of social protest to redistribute the wealth. *Kago* was the first major critique of an alien cultural system and the first social protest for self–determination (Guiart 1951; Worsley 1968).

The Nasioi were against the Australian colonial administration long before mining operations at Panguna. Plantation owners on the Bismarck Archipelago created the '*Buka*' label for the dark–skinned Bougainvilleans (Nash and Ogan 1990:6) and plantations provided "the stereotypes about aliens, whether Europeans, Chinese, Tolai or 'Chimbu', which so strongly affect subsequent inter–group relations" (Chowning 1969:29–30). World War II especially left the Nasioi with a very low opinion of the Australian colonial administration and thereafter they refused plantation wage labor. As Highlanders took over plantation labor work on Bougainville, the menial circumstances of the work led the Nasioi to label them as primitive in the same manner the Europeans had earlier labeled the Bougainvilleans (Nash and Ogan 1990:7). Ogan (1972) notes that agricultural extension officers were not even appointed until 1958 and they contributed little to the expansion of cash–cropping or *bisnis*. Bougainvilleans were neglected by the Australian colonial administration long before the intrusion of the Panguna project (Duncan 1972:27). By the 1960's the Bougainvilleans had symbolically inverted colonially imposed labels and viewed themselves as a progressive people (Nash and Ogan 1990:7). Rather than being incorporated into a colonial political economy, colonial intrusion had emphasized Bougainvillean distinctiveness and separateness. Identification with the colonial state was secondary to Bougainvillean autonomy in land, subsistence, culture, language, social forms and value systems (Hannett 1975).

Transnational Mining and the State

Copper mineralization on Nasioi land was confirmed in 1960 by a geologist of the Australian colonial administration. The transnational Bougainville Copper Limited (BCL), an amalgamation of the Australian based companies Conzinc Rio Tinto and Broken Hill Corporation, began prospecting in 1963. As BCL started test drilling in 1964 the Nasioi reacted to the prospectors as trespassers (Bedford and Mamak 1977:7–10). From 1969–1972 the colonial Australian administration granted BCL leases over 12,500 ha for a mine site, access roads, and waste disposal (Bedford and Mamak 1977:27; Figure 8.3).

By 1964 "helicopters were beating in and out of Panguna valley; prospectors were diamond–drilling deep into the rock; a make–shift precipitous road had been cut to Kieta to take the giant trucks. From the neighboring hills the Nasioi people watched this activity and wondered what was happening to their ancestral land" (West 1972:115). The Nasioi and neighboring landowners (Figure 8.3) vigorously opposed all land acquisition. In interviewing BCL Chairman Don Carruthers (Griffin and Carruthers 1990:59), Professor Jim Griffin stated that Bougainvilleans had every reason to be resentful because:

in 1966 the then Minister for External Territories, Charles Barnes, visited Bougainville and told astonished villagers that, while their traditional land would yield astronomical riches, they themselves would have to be content with damage compensation and spin–off benefits. Minerals belonged to the State.

BCL pushed for a fast track development of the mine with substantial landowner compensation in order to catch a predicted upturn in copper prices but the Australian colonial administration was determined that landowners would only receive occupancy fees even though land 'occupied' by mining would be totally destroyed (O'Faircheallaigh 1990:30).

By the peak of the Bechtel construction phase Europeans demographically accounted for 6.2 percent of the Bougainville population, which was four percent higher than average elsewhere in PNG and the population was 13 percent urban which was also four percent higher than average (Treadgold 1978:37). BCL created rapid urbanization of new towns, by 1988 Arawa reached 15,000 and Panguna 3,500 (Connell 1992) and Bougainvilleans despised these commercial centers. Even more socially drastic was the relocation program started in 1969 for Dapera, Moroni and more recently Kuneka villagers. A new generation of leaders built solidarity between Bougainville peoples by drawing attention to the state and BCL as common enemies. Leo Hannett, a former provincial Premier articulated Bougainvillean ambivalence towards rapid urbanization:

> Arawa, in more ways than one, is everything else except a Bougainvillean town. Arawa is to most Bougainvilleans a strange town ... [which] was born of an unholy wedlock between a multinational corporation and a government that sacrificed Bougainvillean rights and well-being in the names of expediency and the almighty dollar. Arawa is therefore seen as the single towering monument to the twin exploiters of Bougainville: copper and the Papua New Guinea Government (Mamak and Ali 1979:73).

At the time the Panguna mine commenced production, no environmental impact study had been required or carried out (Hughes and Sullivan 1989:37). By 1990 the Panguna mine was 2.5 km across and 400 m deep (O'Faircheallaigh 1990:31). Environmental destruction caused by mining seriously disrupted subsistence and cash–cropping. Expansion of cash–cropping became feasible only at the expense of subsistence production (Mitchell 1976:1; Moulik 1977:44–5; Ogan 1972:122–183; Ward 1975:97–101) which placed an ever greater reliance on *bisnis* as a source of cash earning. Compensation provided cash but was a very contentious issue because of the severe consequences of land appropriation and environmental degradation (Connell 1992). The 1970 Australian colonial administration decision to flush all waste rock, silt and chemical residue down the Karewong and Jaba Rivers (Figure 8.3) continued to be socially and ecologically disastrous. Up until 1989 BCL was dumping about 135,000 tonnes of tailings daily into the Jaba River, according to Hughes and Sullivan (1989:37–38):

> The coarser fraction of the tailings has covered the floor of the 35 km long valley up to 30 m deep and 1 km wide. A delta, now more than 700 ha in area, has accumulated on the floor of Empress Augusta Bay.

Tailings are chemically contaminated with 800–1000 ppb copper and all aquatic life in the Jaba River has been killed. Remobilization of heavy metals ensures ecocide will continue long after the mining is completed (Chambers 1985:180). With an overall population density of 7.6 km^2 (Treadgold 1978:31) and a population growth rate over three percent per annum (Connell 1992), the Nasioi, Nagovisi and Banoni are, by lowland PNG standards (Allen 1983), densely settled near these rivers and rely heavily upon the aquatic and terrestrial resources in their homeland (Mitchell 1976:6). A continuing kinship mode of production alternative for many Nasioi, Nagovisi and Banoni peoples has been ruined (Lafitte 1990:12).

Compensation for the horrendous extent of social and ecological damage was not even standardized before the commencement of mining, nor were the procedures for claims (Bedford and Mamak 1977:30). Separate claims were heard before the Mining Warden's Court until 1969, thereafter a once–off compensation schedule was created for destroyed subsistence crops, pig fences and bush plants. The BCL agreement was renegotiated in the first year of PNG independence, but landowner compensation continued to only come annually. Between 1968–1974 the median amount received was only A$244 and almost 60 percent received less than A$100 (Connell 1992).

BCL signed a Compensation and Occupation Fees Agreement with the Panguna Landowners Association (PLA) in 1980. The PLA was formed under the leadership of Michael Pariu in 1979 and was effectively led by a small group of more educated village men (Connell 1992). The new concept of the Road Mine Tailings (RMTL) Trust Fund was created, but money continued to be distributed very unevenly over a wide number of people and the sums received could have only made a limited impact on people's lives (Connell 1992).

Bougainvillean Mobilization Against Mining in the Panguna Socio-ecological Region

The Nasioi were hostile and active in their resistance to the state and to BCL exploration, construction and operation phases because their rights as landowners were ignored (Dove *et al* 1974:184).

Land is our life. Land is our physical life–food and sustenance. Land is our social life; it is marriage; it is status; it is security; it is politics; in fact, it is our only world. When you take our land, you cut away the very heart of our existence. We have little of no experience of social survival detached from the land. For us to be completely landless is a nightmare which no dollar in the pocket or dollar in the bank will allay; we are a threatened people (Dove *et al.* 1974:182).

When the construction phase peaked at 10,500, 55 percent of the work force were Papua New Guineans. Only 2300 Bougainvilleans worked for BCL (Treadgold 1978:22) and among the landowners only eight percent of the adult Nasioi men worked at the mine (Moulik 1977:47). The process of proletarianization was far from complete by the mid-1980's (Wesley–Smith and Ogan 1992). The Nasioi and their neighbors largely refused to accept mining employment or compensation (Bedford and Mamak 1977:8–11; Stent 1970:7–8). Few landowners were wage–earners and initially they resented northern Bougainvilleans receiving higher paid positions. However, all Bougainvilleans soon shared a common resentment against Europeans (Bedford and Mamak 1974:13) and 'redskins', the term of reference for PNG mainlanders (Griffin 1982:119). From the beginning Bougainvilleans initiated labor unrest at Panguna (Bedford and Mamak 1979:76) and social protest against the large and uncontrolled influx of squatters. The Australian colonial administration called in 100 troops at Rorovana, where they used clubs and tear gas to drive away women protecting their matri–clan land against construction of a recreation area for mine workers (West 1972:117).

Kago and bisnis increased after prospecting started in 1964 (Bedford and Mamak 1977:81). The Nasioi were increasingly forced into *bisnis* because environmental destruction caused by the Panguna project interrupted expansion of subsistence and cash–crop production. The Nasioi had some 50 *bisnis* projects servicing the Panguna mine between 1969 and 1974 before BCL made any substantial compensation payments (Moulik 1977:58–9). Nasioi and Bougainvillean direct participation in the ownership and control of service *bisnis* was a preferred means of autonomy from the state and BCL wage–earning, but most failed because the Nasioi lacked skills in managing costs, profits and market fluctuations in capitalist relations of production (Oliver 1973:169,195). *Bisnis* is financed through cash–crops and compensation payments and is valued more highly than direct wage–earning at the mine. The Panguna project created a demand for service *bisnis*, but Bougainvilleans criticized BCL for becoming too involved in commercial and industrial activities on the island (Connell 1992).

Personal financial gain was rejected for self–determination and autonomous control of land and resources (Moulik 1977:83). Leo Hannett (1975:288–289) voiced Bougainvillean sentiment that:

> Our once peaceful, non–violent living is now forever shattered: we are constantly harried by day and haunted by night with continual acts of violence in our midst. Where we once walked with our heads high, now we move around with our heads hanging low ... never quite knowing what to expect from these outsiders, heartless outsiders with their heartless machines slowly eating out like a cancerous growth the soul of our community; degenerating, humiliating, and dehumanizing us with their 'development' at our expense. We are now made strangers in our own land.

The post–World War II pattern of social protest characterized by rejection of plantation wage labor and the competition between cash–cropping, *bisnis* and *kago* were replicated when mining dissatisfaction culminated in another major social protest movement. Napidokae Navitu became the Nasioi social protest movement for autonomy and identity. It had its inception as a protest meeting against resumption of Arawa plantation in 1969. The Nasioi used Napidokae Navitu as a militant protest movement for autonomy in land and resources. By 1972 the movement attracted 8,000 followers and became the social protest focus for Bougainvillean secession and nationalism (Bedford and Mamak 1977:22; Griffin 1982; Mamak *et al.* 1974:9). The payback killing of two Bougainvillean civil servants after a motor accident in the Highlands in 1973 (Griffin 1982:135) accelerated social protest for secession and repatriation of mainlanders (Hannett 1975:290). Labor unrest and inter–ethnic hostilities culminated in a violent strike against BCL in 1975 causing damage to infrastructure and production. The self–governing PNG administration punitively withheld Bougainville investment royalties.

Proposals were put forward for a post–independence constitution which expressed unity through diversity and regional autonomy but they were inconsistent with the aims of the state. According to Sharp (1975:121), "regionalism now ran counter to a managed neo–colonial state dependent on the free flow of capital from transnational investments." As a result, the Bougainville Provincial Assembly met with 200 village leaders and voted to secede from PNG. On 1 September 1975, a fortnight before PNG independence, the Republic of North Solomons came into being (Sharp 1975:119). Bougainville leader Moses Havini and his father, the paramount chief of the Naboin on Buka, designed the flag:

> The background of the flag is blue, and in the centre is a hat called *upei*. This is a hat worn at initiation ceremonies once upon a time throughout the whole province. The *upei* is set on a star carved out of a turtle shell which was the badge worn by paramount chiefs on the island. The background is green, signifying the rich resources of the island, and the blue, signifying the sea. The same flag is used today as the flag of the NSP Provincial Government (Havini 1990:23).

The United Nations refused to extend recognition and within a year Bougainville was encapsulated as the new North Solomons Province (NSP) within PNG. Bougainville affiliation was accomplished with restoration of their royalties and creation of provincial government autonomy (Bedford and Mamak 1977:88–89; 1979:74–85). During these developments Napidokae Navitu continued as a Bougainvillean focus for development, education and autonomy (Griffin 1982; Oliver 1973:172–176).

When kinship relations of production clashed with cash–cropping the Bougainvilleans responded with *kago* and when they clashed with the Panguna mining project they responded with Napidokae Navitu, a more successful protest movement achieving compromise, modifying the power of BCL and providing a degree of local autonomy. Griffin (1982:138) concludes that by the mid–1970's Napidokae Navitu followers had achieved many of their social protest objectives:

> land disputes of 1969 and other compensatory issues were adequately settled; a moral victory was scored over the colonial Administration; the mining agreement was drastically renegotiated to the chagrin of the intrusive transnational company (another moral victory); the full one and a quarter per cent royalties were paid to the provincial government; the North Solomons

was united under a provincial government with real powers; local government councils were abolished and traditional authority sanctioned through village government; attempts were being made to foster traditional culture in schools and through provincial agencies; education came under substantial provincial control and North Solomonese maintained a high level of access to positions throughout Papua New Guinea in tertiary institutions, public service, church and business, and privileged access on the North Solomons itself; the elections of 1977 and 1982 saw Mola and Lapun eliminated and all four MPs committed to the one party, the radical Melanesian alliance, led by John Momis.

The Bougainville Revolutionary Army

Through the 1980s the people realized how they were economically neglected (Connell 1990:33) and a distinctive Bougainvillean identity flourished (Nash and Ogan 1990). Loss of land and pollution destroyed the mode of subsistence in portions of Nasioi, Nagovisi and Banoni homelands, but there is continuity in peoples' lives, they live close to their ancestral homelands, speak Bougainvillean languages and their values, ceremonies and kinship relations of production remain important.

Through the same period compensation money from BCL that the PLA received for family heads and the RMTL Trust Fund increasingly became the focus of dispute among landowners. Compensation was rarely channeled into long-term investment either in the 1970s (Bedford and Mamak 1977:81–85), or the 1980s (Connell 1992). The RMTL Trust Fund became associated with PLA leadership too directly linked to BCL rather than landowner interests. In August 1987 a new–PLA replaced the old led by younger, more educated Nasioi men and women who opposed the BCL mining operation. A woman, Perpetua Serero, led the new–PLA and claimed that:

We don't grow healthy crops any more, our traditional customs and values have been disrupted and we have become mere spectators as our earth is being dug up, taken away and sold for millions. Our land was taken from us by force: we were blind then, but we have finally grown to understand what's going on (Hiambohn 1989:18).

The new–PLA immediately placed demands on BCL. In March 1988, 500 landowners organized by the new–PLA marched on BCL with a petition of demands for increased basic services, localization of employment and greater control of erosion and pollution perceived as threatening the health and livelihood of Bougainvilleans (May 1990). With no response from BCL they closed the mine during a one day sit-down protest in May 1988. BCL brought in Applied Geology Associates as consultants and in a public meeting in November 1988 they used their report to refute claims by Bougainvilleans that the mine was responsible for loss of wildlife, declining agricultural production or a range of human illnesses. Francis Ona, a vocal new-PLA leader, declared BCL's environmental inquiry to be a 'whitewash' and stormed out of the meeting, while landowners present at the meeting disagreed violently with BCL's conclusion (Connell 1992).

Before she died, Perpetua Serero commented that from Richard West's (1972) book *River of Tears: The Rise of the Rio Tinto Zinc Corporation, Ltd*, "We knew we could expect the worst." A few days after the 'whitewash' public meeting of November 1988, armed Bougainvilleans took a large quantity of explosives from the BCL magazine (May 1990). BCL shut down the Panguna mine in December 1988 as fires and explosions destroyed mine installations valued at K850,000. In a formal communication to the North Solomons Provincial Premier Joseph Kabui, Francis Ona declared that the Bougainvilleans meant business and were prepared to die for their cause. The chairman of BCL responded with investment threats, indicating they might pull out of their new gold ventures at Hidden Valley and Mt Kare.

In the following weeks Panguna mining installations were professionally blown up with the assistance of Bougainvillean Sam Kauona, an explosives expert trained in Australia who left the Papua New Guinea Defense Forces (PNGDF) to join armed struggle with Francis Ona. Early in 1989 the armed Bougainvilleans began referring to themselves as the Bougainville Revolutionary Army (BRA). In radio broadcasts of 3 and 25 November 1988 and in letters to the PNG *Post Courier* on 28 April and to the NSP Peace and Justice Committee on 29 April 1989, Francis Ona set down what the BRA was fighting for:

To Members of the Panguna Landowners' Association

I am writing to you in regard to the demands to both BCL and the national government. The original issues were:
(1) K10 billion environmental compensation payment.
(2) BCL to be closed.
(3) Break away from PNG.

There was no answer to all these demands by BCL or the National Government.
Our only option now is (3): break away from PNG. Only then we will be able to save the lives of our people in Bougainville.

To make you aware:

BCL Prospecting Authorities (PAs): There are now nine Prospecting Authorities. We had only seven [previously], but without the knowledge of NSP landowners, BCL and the Government added two more. This means that the whole of Bougainville Island is a great enlargement of Panguna. Life will not exist on our Island. Our very government is hiding this fact. It will sacrifice our lives for the sake of PNG economy. You mothers of this nation must talk it out in order save our childrens' lives. We, your men folk, are doing our part in the jungle.

Please don't just sit and wait for us, campaign and talk to the authorities about the matter. We will die here in the jungle fighting for you. There are no two ways about it. Our leaders are frightened to speak out for all of us. Please be united and walk side by side. Forget about your differences and struggle for only one goal: to save the lives of our future generations. Keep talking to the radio and newsman. Tell the Government that the time for round-table talks is over. We want only to break away from PNG so that we will rule our own lives and economy.

Shooting by the Government forces: The behaviour by security forces must be condemned. They have been shooting at unarmed landowners. Also, the report over the radio that we are smuggling guns is not true. It is only a campaign by the Government to get Australian assistance. Don't believe what is said over the radio by the Government.

We have blocked all the Government forces and they can't advance, that's why they are asking me time and time again to surrender.

Please stay firm because I will only surrender in a coffin. This is because of my children and your children of generations to come. If I don't win this war it means the lives of our future generations will not be secured.

Please always pray that our Almighty Father may help us to win the war.

Government: Members of the PNG Government are blind to our people and their livelihood. Mr Kabui has fallen into the same pit with Father Momis, because he could not speak for himself. To make it worse, this so-called democratic nation has now become a second South Africa.

This leads us to the root cause and it is, of course, that this country is run and administered by BCL. There are in this company people in top management who have South African identities and ideologies.

This is why, on the principles of apartheid, there are two nations in one White and Black.

FACTS: Two hospitals, two schools, two drinking clubs, worst of all, two living standards.

The Government of PNG is not run to safeguard our lives but rather to safeguard the few rich leaders and white men. This is why there will never be any peace in PNG. Our leaders are like clouds that fly over the mountains, not knowing where they will turn into rain and eventually disappear.

Our Government has no economic foundation, that's why it borrows from other countries. All the money raided in the country goes back to pay these loans and leaves nothing for the nation, so it goes on borrowing again.

This will never end, it will go on and on until they suck our blood and economic death is followed by an instant human disappearance from this island.

Our country is losing billions every year because our leaders are selfish and negotiate with big companies at the cost of our people.

Invading

The outside domination of the business sector in the North Solomons is a clear picture that we are losing a grip on our island and our freedom. We are living on land which is actually owned by foreigners. BCL and PAs account for two-thirds of the area of land in NSP, while another third is covered by [palm] oil plantations owned by Kina Securities, a company owned by outsiders.

This is the fact that most people of NSP will never see until it is too late.

Under this situation I don't see why our leaders are tongue-tied and will not stand up and fight for our people's rights.

All I can see in the future for our children is pain, fatigue and death. I wish that some leaders would open their eyes, ears and mouths that we must stand as one and defend our island and safeguard the lives of our future generations. Maybe it's too late now but it is worth trying. With Almighty god, nothing is impossible. So pray each day, all of you, for our victory and success.

Lastly, please sister, take care of my family and be kind to them everyday. God knows what comes next.

Until then, dear, it's goodbye and God bless you all.

Yours sincerely
Francis Ona.[1]

Dear Bart Kigina

I wish to thank your committee you have set up to express Justice in this time of problems on Bougainville. May I also extend my sincere thanks to our Bishop who represents the Catholic Community. You have received numerous complaints about the inhuman treatment by [PNG] Security Forces towards our people. This, I have to say that, it is only a starting point of the inside rottenness of the whole colonially manipulated government system of Papua New Guinea. There is more to be uncovered for the whole world to hear and our access is through your committee. Our communications system has been strictly controlled by [the] Government restricting us from expressing our true feelings. In our constitution 'Freedom of Speech' is a fake, if our news interviews have to be cut by certain factors of the government. To us, the constitution of Papua New Guinea is just a cover–up of what leaders at high offices profess day and night about the democratic government of Papua New Guinea. These same leaders are corrupt and dictators.

These same leaders ordered the Security Forces shoot to kill when we are fighting for our true democratic rights in this country. This government is not for our people which would secure their freedom of their rights. It is a fact a government for the economy of Papua New Guinea and Australia. What we are fighting for is to get out of this government which is about to sacrifice the democracy at the mercy of the economy. The pressure from CRA is too much for the government to exercise its own power. Further to this, the Australian government is taking a deep stand to assist [the] Papua New Guinea Government and its Defence Forces to fight us. [The] Namaliu Government is telling lies saying that Bougainville militants are smuggling weapons from overseas. This is only a cover–up of cold blood murdering of innocent people fighting for their rights.
What I see there is that our human race is under threat with the existence of BCL through this major factors:

(1) The use of dangerous chemicals in its production line.

(2) The environmental damage caused by the Panguna mine and [the impact] that nine Prospecting Authorities would bring about when mining continued ahead.

(3) A fifth of our total area of Bougainville is already damaged. No creature will ever exist on it again. Another four-fifths when covered will completely restrict our people from subsistence farming which in return will mean the life of [the] entire province.

(4) Social unrest is continuing to increase with the presence of outside influence.

With this in mind, I am deeply concerned for the lives of our future generations.

These concerns have never been addressed to the world community. That's why they don't know what we are fighting for.

To conclude, I wish to make you aware that we don't trust [the] Papua New Government any more. We feel no way a part of Papua New Guinea. We have already broken away from Papua New Guinea; however, we are finding it hard to declare it to [the] Papua New Guinea Government. We have asked Joseph Kabui ... [but] he is too cowardly to express our demand to [the] Papua New Guinea Government. We are ready to fight for our people until we all die. This is the only way left for us and our future generations.

We wish that you give us the blessing by exposing our message to the whole world so that they may understand and support us to gain independence.

I wish you all our Almighty God's blessing and success in your work for his people. Thank you.

Yours sincerely,
Francis Ona.[2]

Anthropologist Eugene Ogan (1990:36) initially misinterpreted the nature of the armed conflict as an "issue of compensation, especially as this produced disagreements among Nasioi themselves, *not* an attempt to overthrow the provincial or national governments, which is the proximate cause of violence against the mine." Ogan (1990:37–38) trivialized Ona's letters as merely personal pronouncements of an individual and cautioned:

While no one can know for sure whether his motivations might have changed since his initial 'retreat to the bush', it is much more likely that his apparently political pronouncements represent tactics to extricate himself from a personal dilemma (he has been accused of murdering his patrilineal uncle, Matthew Kove) than a coherent plan to supplant any government authority. In this sense, then, Ona's talk of a 'Bougainville Revolutionary Army' is just that--talk ... dissatisfaction has not been able (as of September 1989) to produce the degree of political consensus required to mount a rebellion, revolution, civil war or insurrection as legally defined.

The Bougainvilleans were profoundly dissatisfied after two decades of having their natural resources converted into national resources and through their BRA they proceeded to mount a very successful Fourth World resistance movement against the state and BCL. Media and academic focus on Ona as an individual and on state controlled notions of legally defined conflict ignored what the BRA was fighting for and that the Bougainvilleans were united as a people. It is a nation vs state (Nietschmann 1987b) armed conflict over autonomous control of land and resources, not an insurgency to overthrow the PNG National government.

According to Moses Havini (1990:25), who had designed Bougainville's first secession flag and had gone on to act as NSP Executive Officer, Ona was hailed by Bougainvilleans as their new hero and his broadcasts were recorded and played constantly in homes, shops and villages:

> There is widespread support throughout Bougainville for Ona's three demands, namely: a better deal for the landowners affected by the mine (including compensation for environmental damage); a better deal for Bougainville (that is, the profits from the mine staying in Bougainville rather than going to the PNG Government); and secession. In my experience, everywhere you go, people will express support for Ona. People say that the only way to solve the problems with Papua New Guinea is to give North Solomons its independence.

Other politicians who had pragmatically sought revenue provided by the Panguna project, increasingly became politically supportive of the Bougainvillean struggle against BCL expressed through the new-PLA. By October 1988 the former MP for South Bougainville and Minister for Mines, Paul Lapun, had completely changed his views on BCL:

> At the time I signed the agreement allowing BCL to commence mining operations here on Bougainville, you didn't tell me what would happen to my environment. You capitalise on my ignorance and after 18 years here much of my land has been depleted. what happens when the gold and copper

finishes? You will leave with your money and I will be left with a barren wasteland. The government stays in Port Moresby and says BCL knows what it is doing, and yet we see our environment dying daily. When I was young they fooled me and now I am old and still alive to see the result of my decision, I weep. Who cares about a copper mine if it kills us? (*Times of Papua New Guinea* 26 October 1988).

In December 1988 the Melanesian Alliance party called for a renegotiation of the BCL agreement to better favor the interests of the landowners. Party chairman Chris Bengko said the "agreement was drawn up during the colonial era by foreigners to protect the foreigners and their companies" (quoted in Hyndman 1988a).

Shoot to kill orders were issued by Police Commissioner Paul Tohian against 'saboteurs'. The BRA succeeded in closing the Panguna mine in May 1989 and it had immediate economic implications to PNG. Bougainvilleans were labeled as 'rebels' and 'Rambo style terrorists' by then Prime Minister Namaliu and he ordered PNGDF troops into the conflict while announcingto the PNG parliament that:

The priorities of the Government are clear. First, we will rid Bougainville of this terrorist scourge. Second, we will restore peace to the island. Third, and vital, for the whole nation, we will reopen the Bougainville copper mine (Senge 1990:12).

Namaliu broadcast over the radio a State of Emergency on Bougainville to become effective from 26 June 1989 in which he stated that:

If this disruption continues, the standard of living of all our people will suffer and our strong economy, and our bright future as a young, developing nation, will be placed in real peril. We cannot allow a militant minority, resorting to murder, violence and sabotage, to destroy our achievements and our future. My government hopes that the Emergency declaration, and the operations which will begin next week, will bring an early end to this crisis, and will do so with the minimum of loss of life or injury (Namaliu 1990:16).

In September 1989 a leaked cabinet document was published, which said "Cabinet is now firmly of the view that a state of insurgency exists" (*Niugini Nius* 22 September 1989). In unleashing counter–insurgency reprisals code–named Operation Footloose (Bougainville Information Service 1990) against the BRA the PNG National government failed to meet any of its priorities. Operation Footloose further drained the PNG economy, the PNGDF failed to defeat the BRA and only succeeded in becoming an army of occupation against Bougainvillean civilians.

The PNGDF lost the war with the BRA and Operation Footloose resulted in more than 200 casualties (*Pacific Islands Monthly* February 1991:12). In early March 1990 the PNGDF withdrew from Bougainville and BRA Supreme Commander Francis Ona declared an independent Republic of Bougainville in May 1990. The BRA took control of every district in Bougainville, set up its headquarters at the Panguna mine site and established an interim government. No states have recognized the Republic of Bougainville and PNG blockaded the island to cut off all essential services in May 1990. However, there is widespread Melanesian nationalism support, especially from the adjacent Solomons Islands, for the Bougainvillean self–determination struggle.

The media misunderstood the nature of the armed resistance movement on Bougainville. It is illustrative to note that the PNG *Post Courier* almost never referred to the conflict as a war or to those fighting in Bougainville as the BRA. Rather labels were used like: 'arsonists' and 'landowner strongman Francis Ona' (2 December 1988), 'saboteurs' and 'Rambo–style terrorism' (6 December 1988), 'Panguna rebel landowners' (21 March 1989), 'rebel villagers' (22 March 1989), 'Ona and his rebels' (5 April 1989), 'minority cult groups' (10 April 1989), 'rebel landowners' (11 April 1989), 'Bougainville rebellion' (19 April 1988), 'bunch of vicious killers, cruel thugs, and violent criminals who believe in cargo cult ideology, secession and hero mentality' (17 July 1989), 'illegal army' (1 August 1989), and 'Ona a rascal' (2 August 1989). When the war started the PNG *Post Courier* referred to PNGDF 'heros laid to rest' (17 April 1989), but as atrocities accumulated in the counter–insurgency reprisal it was the PNGDF committing 'rape, beatings, humiliation, physical assault, terror tactics and deaths against innocent villagers' (27 April 1989).

PNGDF counter–insurgency tactics used in Operation Footloose generated ever greater Bougainvillean support for the BRA. According to Callick (1990:19), PNGDF "troops have been for substantial periods out of control and openly disdainful of civil authorities. They have carried guns––and fired them––while drunk, they have stripped and beaten villagers at checkpoints, they have destroyed more than 1000 houses, and several young Bougainvilleans, not provably rebels, have died after military questioning." Civilians were forcefully "relocated" from their homelands to coastal camps using strategic hamletting tactics to cut BRA supply lines (Bougainville Information Service 1990:2; Robie 1989:16). Several suspected members of the BRA, including a Uniting Church pastor, were reportedly murdered by PNGDF troops and their bodies dropped into the sea from a helicopter (*Sydney Morning Herald* 8 March 1990). An Amnesty International report confirmed claims of human rights violations and PNG police and army brutality (May 1990:176).

The Logic of Violence

PNG resists acknowledging that the Bougainville interim government incorporates all the broadly based institutions on Bougainville which have won popular support, including the elected provincial government and all Christian denominations on the island. The military operation launched in September1990 was codenamed Operation Cleric, with the two bishops and the pastor who all hold ministries in the interim government as its targets. While the public stance of the PNG government is to not refer at all to the interim government of Bougainville, but only to its military wing, the BRA, the PNG government invests considerable energy in trying to discredit the priests who have felt called, as an act of Christian witness, to take ministries. Recent attacks have focused on Bishop Gregory Singkai, Catholic bishop of Bougainville, who has been publicly likened to Hitler. That produced a response from the PNG Catholic Bishops conference, declaring such a parallel to be offensive.

PNG strategy assumes the interim government is only a handful of fanatical teenage militants with guns, and that many Bougainvilleans are keen to escape their tyranny. If the existence of an interim government can be ignored, a direct appeal can be made to the Bougainville people, and their loyalty to the government undermined.

Health, Order and Morale on the Island

Reliable reports from Bougainville indicate that this strategy is not working. Despite deteriorating health and nutrition, and isolation caused by the blockade denying fuel and communications, morale appears to be steady, and no widespread breakdown of order has occurred. Young hotheads in local BRA commands have alienated local leaders by interrogating their elders and on a few occasions beating or killing people. There have been further attacks on property in September and October 1990, notably the sacking of the Aisitavi girls secondary school, which had been run by the Catholic church and was the only secondary school on the island for girls.

These incidents do not appear to have shifted the loyalties of most villagers, except on Buka, where there have long been tensions between island and coastal peoples, between Buka islanders and mainland Bougainville, and sectarian rivalries between Catholic and Adventist villages.

These rifts were serious enough to enable PNG Defence Forces to re-establish control of Buka with a limited force of no more than 400 men, meeting little resistance from local BRA commanders. The main BRA force was heldback from engaging the PNGDF until soldiers attempt the next stage of Operation Cleric, which is expected soon.

While morale may be holding, the interim government is unable to establish a presence in all villages. Bougainville has basically reverted to a traditional society, including religious explanations of how they have survived. Villagers today tell of crops which grow quicker than usual, harvest seasons which are longer than usual, an extraordinary abundance of seafood. All this is attributed to the beneficial intervention of ancestors, pleased that villagers have stood up to defend their land.

Villagers do not see the struggle for Bougainville in the terms as used in the media. To them it is less a struggle for sovereignty, regional security or national integrity than a sacred struggle for land, empowered by the ever present spirits of ancestors.

PNG police and Defence Force reputations are seriously damaged and national government authority and control over its security forces were seen to be very limited. In an effort to create dialogue and trust, PNG and BRA signed the Endeavor Accord aboard a New Zealand warship in August 1990, and later the Honiara Declaration in January 1991. These peace attempts failed because neither side could get backing from their governments.

Within weeks of signing the accord, PNG launched Operation Cleric and sent troops into Buka and armed a civilian counter-insurgency militia, the Buka Liberation Front (BLF). The BLF hamletted over 12,000 into "care centres" and created a free-fire zone over the island and smashed BRA military resistance. By mid-1992 PNG still imposed a media restriction on Buka and vigilante chairman Thomas Anis claimed the BCL still acted as an "authorised unauthorised security force" (Spriggs 1992).

The second phase of Operation Cleric in April 1991 was the supposedly unsanctioned reoccupation of northern Bougainville by Colonel Leo Nuia.

Coastal villages were shelled and machine-gunned from patrol boats and helicopters supplied by Australia. By January 1992 the area between Wakunai and Arawa was a contested no-man's land. During celebrations for the second year of the newly declared Republic in May 1992 there was a reported massacre of Aita villagers. Also in May of 1992 the PNGDF landed in southern Bougainville and started hamletting the Siwai into "care centers" (Spriggs 1992).

The PNG government is attempting a military, rather than a negotiated settlement. So far they have succeeded in dividing the South and North from other Bougainvilleans. Bougainvilleans are even more united against the PNG blockade and increased military option and insist that fighting will not stop until the PNGDF pulls out of North and South Bougainville. Meanwhile, Bougainvilleans feel they have won their independence with or without PNG recognition. The new Paias Wingti government of July 1992 should recognize that Bougainville nationalism will not go away and that a military option will only create an occupation army in an ungovernable Bougainville.

Notes

1. The letter of 28 April 1989 to the PNG *Post Courier* (Ona 1990:7–10) is presented without editing or paraphrasing to convey a Bougainvillean voice.

2. The full letter of 29 April 1989 to the Justice and Peace Committee, Kieta, NSP (Ona 1990:10–12) is presented without editing or paraphrasing to convey a Bougainvillean voice.

3. Only portions of text are presented without editing or paraphrasing to convey a Bougainvillean voice. For full text see the Bougainville Information Service.

9

The Other Side of the Volatile Mining Resource Frontier in New Guinea

Melanesian Indigenous Nations

Declining territorial colonialism and emerging recolonization, internal colonialism and transnational mining has conscienticized indigenous nations in Melanesia to mobilize themselves and work for autonomous resource control and self–determination. West Papuans, Bougainvilleans and Kanaks have been particularly influential in promoting Melanesian nationalism. They are prominent in internationalizing the Fourth World autonomy movement in Asia–Pacific and they attend as indigenous nations to the United Nations Working Group on Indigenous Populations (UNWGIP).

States and international organizations like the United Nations, however, carefully avoid referring to the Fourth World nations as indigenous *peoples*, but use minorities and ethnic groups because peoples carries the notion of self–determination. Widely adopted by states and other international organizations is the UNWGIP definition of the Fourth World as indigenous *populations*:

> composed of the existing descendants of the peoples who inhabited the present territory of a country wholly or partially at the time when persons of a different culture or ethnic origin arrived there from other parts of the world, overcame them and, by conquest, settlement or other means, reduced them to a non–dominant or colonial situation; who today live more in conformity with their particular social, economic and cultural customs and traditions than with the institutions of the country of which they now form

172

a part, under a State structure which incorporates mainly the national, social and cultural characteristics of other segments of the population which are dominant (UNWGIP 1982a).

The Fourth World widely accepts the definition of indigenous peoples as incorporated into the Charter of the World Council of Indigenous Peoples which states that:

Indigenous peoples are such population groups as we are, who from old–age times have inhabited the lands where we live, who are aware of having a character of our own, with social traditions and means of expression that are linked to the country inherited from our ancestors, with a language of our own and having certain essential and unique characteristics which confer upon us the strong conviction of belonging to a people, who have an identity in ourselves and should be thus regarded by others (UNWGIP 1982b).

In a charter–signing ceremony in the Hague in February 1991, West Papuans, with 20 other indigenous nations from around the world, founded the Unrepresented Nations and Peoples Organization (UNPO). Spokesperson Catherine Ingram indicated the UNPO "will be an independent body for peoples and nations that can't get into the United Nations. The body aims to promote the peaceful resolution of conflicts and offers diplomatic training, advise on dealing with the UN, public relations counsel and expertise on environmental issues" (*The Daily Globe* 6 February 1991). Asia Pacific nations are well represented in the UNPO, with representation from West Papuans, East Timorese, Aboriginal Australians, Palauans, Hawaiians, Tibetans, Cordillerans from the Philippines and indigenous nations from Sarawak, Taiwan and Inner Mongolia and East Turkestan in China.

Socio–Ecological Regions as Social Time Bombs

Filer (1990:5) argues that "landowning communities" developed a "social time–bomb" relationship to the Panguna mining project and that this and all other mining company–community relationships in PNG are misunderstood because of the "myth of Bougainvillean nationalism" and the "myth of Melanesian communism". The alternative offered to Melanesian nationalism is a class analysis focused on the compensation package, to which Filer (1990:26–27) attributes a:

process of social disintegration engendered by the economic relationship between the company, the government and the community. The trouble is that there may be no economic relationship between the landowners and the developers which will curtail the process. ... Panguna landowners seem to have experienced a loss of social harmony and a relationship of economic dependency as a result of the compensation package accepted by their predecessors.

It is the clash of states and nations and the clash of kinship and capitalist relations of production, not selfish individuals competing over mining compensation packages, that turn mining projects into social time–bombs in New Guinea.

Where Filer (1990) only finds a myth, Nash and Ogan (1990:9–13) assert that dealing with the Panguna mining project, in fact, created Bougainvillean identity and nationalism. According to Nash and Ogan (1990:13):

Bougainvilleans have had to contend for years with very real violence to themselves and their way of life, committed by colonizers, by a multinational mining firm, and presently by other Papua New Guineans, including riot police whose brutality under the guise of pacification is being investigated by the PNG government. Their creation of a Bougainvillean ethnic identity has precisely sustained "collective cooperative efforts" in self–defense against forces that might otherwise overwhelm them.

Symbolic inversion and boundary maintenance have been creative processes in the formation of Bougainvillean nationalism. Skin color became a focal symbol of their identity as a people and in using it they symbolically inverted the ideological fiction of colonialism for their own political ends. Boundary maintenance was further enhanced by contrasting Bougainvillean peacefulness with the violence of other New Guineans. As explained by one sixteen–year–old Bougainvillean girl "I think all Niuginians are bad because they want to make trouble between themselves. ... Bougainvilleans are like brothers and sisters" (quoted in Nash and Ogan 1990:11).

Not just the immediate "landowning communities" but entire socio-ecological regions have become the focus of social time–bombs on the frontier of mining expansion in New Guinea. Anthropologists have long acknowledged the link between descent, land and peoples in New Guinea. Melanesian indigenous nations are not expansionist like states, group boundaries and territorial limits are thought of as coterminous. Increasingly on the volatile mining frontier in New Guinea, Melanesian indigenous nations are developing their common potential to resist transnational and state encapsulation. The Wopkaimin have initiated an ideological movement of social protest against the Ok Tedi project through revitalization of identity attached to homeland, the men's cult and their kinship relations of production. The Amungme with the OPM and the Bougainvilleans have initiated Fourth World armed resistance against mining projects in their socio–ecological regions.

Fourth World wars are not fought over a myth. Fourth World indigenous nations asserting their right to control their own lives within their own territories is as significant a social movement of our time as was territorial decolonization following World War II. Global conflict has changed from massive armies of states fighting one another to the Third World War (Nietschmann 1987b) of insurgencies against states created by decolonization and of state invasions to annex Fourth World nations externally and internally. Of the 120 wars in the world today, 98 percent are in the Third World and the majority, 72 percent, are between states and Fourth World nations (Nietschmann 1987b). Fourth World wars are above all else over land and resources, and autonomy is the umbrella term for territorial–political solutions to the conflicts.

The Freeport project is the most extreme example in New Guinea of the Third World using mining transnationals for economic invasion of Melanesian indigenous nations. The Amungme and other West Papuans from the socio–ecological region took up armed resistance with the OPM against the Freeport project and the Indonesian state, and thousands have died in the conflict. The Bougainvilleans experienced a long history of fragmentation caused by German and Australian colonialism. Colonialism, cash–cropping, *bisnis* and *kago* differentiated interests among the Bougainvilleans but they retained their autonomy in land, resources, culture and language. They perceived the Panguna project as a common threat and Napidokae Navitu stimulated wider Bougainvillean identity and unification for self–determination throughout the socio–ecological region. A decade later the BRA took up armed resistance against the Panguna project and the state of PNG to defend Bougainvillean land rights and identity and hundreds have already died in the conflict.

According to Filer (1990:9):

Once upon a time there was a community whose members lived in complete harmony with each other and with their natural environment, who jointly owned the land to which they had a mystical attachment, who chose their leaders by consensus, settled their arguments by compromise, and redistributed the products of their labor to ensure that everyone enjoyed the same condition of subsistence affluence.

This "village which exists everywhere and nowhere" has "always been on the verge of disintegration" and is nothing more than the "Melanesian village in the sky" that "Europeans had invented long before they came to Melanesia" (Filer 1990:9). By substituting instability for communism, Filer (1990:9) encapsulated diverse Melanesian indigenous nations "in a national identity which cannot be distinguished from a hundred other national identities created by the same colonial experience."

Prior to mining in the Freeport, Ok Tedi and Panguna socio–ecological regions, surrounding Melanesian indigenous nations practiced kinship relations of production with virtually no experience of survival detached from the land. Cooperative well–being was not a utopian dream but a reality in their kinship relations of production and they conflict profoundly with the individualized monetization of capitalist relations of production.

Land underlies the grievances behind all social time–bombs in the mining socio–ecological regions of New Guinea. Land is both the basis of production and of a sense of tradition, place and identity. Mining has not eliminated kinship relations of production and access to land and resources in New Guinea (Wesley–Smith and Ogan 1992:261). Moreover, the emergence of true classes in the mining socio–ecological regions has been complicated by ethnicity (Wesley–Smith and Ogan 1992:261). Identity construction, nationalism and kinship relations of production conflict with class formation and are certainly more relevant to comprehending the land–based aspirations behind social time–bombs on New Guinea's mining frontier.

Worsening environmental degradation and pollution and the realization that when the mining monetary lifeline disappears the land will be gone forever have been pivotal in igniting the social time–bombs. Making Melanesian communism a myth denies the land–based aspirations and clash of relations of production occurring between nations and states on the mining frontier in New Guinea. These land–based mode of production conflicts require political solutions for the control of land and resources.

Polomka (1990:3) judges that "the future of Bougainvilleans would be best secured through working out a lasting, mutually beneficial relationship with Port Moresby within the framework of the Papua New Guinea nation–state" and is optimistic about the future of mining in PNG because "as in all societies, a declining role for land as a livelihood for the majority is an unavoidable price of rising living standards and a flourishing nation–state." Polomka would like to pronounce PNG safe for the penetration of transnational capital, and unfortunately, as pointed out by Filer (1990:16) "if we keep our eyes focused on the mining industry, we can see that the government and the mining companies are still proceeding on the assumption or in the hope that other mining projects will continue to sustain the national economy, even if Panguna is closed for a long time." PNG cannot afford to ignore that their future is land–based and that Melanesian nations on the mining frontier are already empowering themselves and demanding sustainable development. Continued transnational mining based on Polomka's optimism will bring a succession of social time–bombs in New Guinea.

Ancient Futures and Sustainable Development

Third World colonialism has replaced First World colonialism as the principal global force that tries to subjugate indigenous peoples and their ancient nations. First World colonial empires became rich and powerful through forced incorporation of distant peoples and territories. The island of New Guinea is dismembered between the Third World states of PNG and Indonesia. Economic development is used to invade Melanesian indigenous nations. What is called nation–building actually becomes state expansion by nation–destroying. Capture and control of resources, not extension of politics or economic philosophy, is the objective of the mineral extraction invasion in New Guinea.

The mining frontier expands in Indonesia and PNG by dispossessing indigenous nations from their land and resources and degrading the environment. Nations manage resources and states consume them. Melanesian indigenous nations maintain the quality of their lands, waters and resources but Third World states like Indonesia and PNG do not. A system that does work is being destroyed to maintain a system that does not work.

As the latest expansive phase of mining reaches indigenous nations on the frontier of transnational and state penetration, Howard (1988:10–11) questions whether we are witnessing the last stand of what he terms 'tribalism'. Contrary to Howard's pessimistic appraisal that mining will lead to the demise of indigenous nations, Godoy (1985:210) indicates that indigenous miners in Malaysia, Sierra Leone, Brazil and Bolivia are currently shifting back and forth between kinship and capitalist relations of production as mining there undergoes a process of involution. The lesson from the Quechua tin miners (Nash 1979; Taussig 1980) is valuable for describing the clash of modes of production and the process of ideology translated into action leading to change.

Melanesian indigenous nations have rejected the Freeport, Ok Tedi and Panguna mines as imposed development projects and have initiated social movements for sustainable development with retention of cultural and environmental diversity. For Bougainvilleans this does not mean that it is back to "year Zero of autonomous subsistence existence" (Callick 1990:18) or that they have "reverted to traditional society" (Bougainville Information Service 1990:3). Present Melanesian indigenous nations on the New Guinea mining frontier do not live as their ancestors did. As mining brought about ever greater resource depletion and environmental degradation, the Wopkaimin responded with past ways of living that ensured more permanence and sustainability of their ancestral rain forests. Social time–bombs developed on the mining frontier of New Guinea because indigenous nations rejected wholesale transformation of nature and culture for sustainable development of their homelands and themselves as distinct peoples.

Sustainable development for threatened peoples, habitats and resources is on the top of the political agenda throughout the world today. Present and future mining projects in New Guinea need to meet the challenge of sustainable development from the perspective of indigenous resource managers, for as recently posed by Baines (1989:273):

Independent Pacific Island governments accept that these systems, being expressions of social structure itself, are basic to the continued welfare of their societies. At the same time these governments are proceeding to implement forms of economic development which are in conflict with these traditional systems. This poses a development dilemma which is crucial for the future of the people of the South Pacific islands. To what extent can the traditional systems accommodate future change? Will serious efforts be made to adjust approaches to economic development so as to ease those disruptions to traditional resource–management systems which are eroding Pacific island societies?

Local systems of resource knowledge guide subsistence production and, as so provocatively asserted by Pernetta and Hill (1982), this production is a critical subsidy to the development and market sector of the state economy. Lands of Melanesian nations have attracted the mining developers. In New Guinea transnational mining under the state as resource owner insults the resource rights of Melanesian indigenous nations. As this process is repeated across New Guinea the real prospect is one of continuing degradation of physical and biotic resources and extinction of the people's capacity for self–reliance (Grant 1987; Morren 1984). PNG and Indonesia have the opportunity to learn from the the Bougainvillean and West Papuan Fourth World wars and the mounting protests in the Fly River socio–ecological region. Sustainable development is not nice rhetoric the state can afford to ignore, indigenous nations are already demanding it on the volatile mining frontier of New Guinea.

The implication for resource rights of indigenous peoples and sustainable development, so well expressed in a series of cogent essays by Clarke (1973, 1976, 1977, 1990), is that the only way indigenous and Western resource management can be incorporated into state policy in Melanesia is by requiring that "economic development" be based on how people are already using the environment. There is no indication that Indonesia intends to alter their economic development program of state invasion of West Papua. However, as an independent state in Melanesia, PNG has responsibilities other than profits. The state must also consider quality of life so that Melanesians can control their future through sustainable development.

Togolo (1982) made it abundantly clear a decade ago, during the "Traditional Conservation in Papua New Guinea: Implications for Today" conference held over six days on Port Moresby in October 1980 (Morauta et al. 1982), that the transnational Panguna project cannot be accommodated to local needs of the Bougainvillean people and that the conflict can only be resolved through equity and distributive justice. It is possible that equity can be generated through people–centered sustainable development, an argument similarly shared by Bulmer (1982).

On this spaceship earth cultural and environmental diversity under autonomous resource management of indigenous peoples is a precious resource. Clarke (1990:246) has elegantly presented how the ever reconstructed past can serve as an authoritative guide for the present:

> Anyone who has lived in a traditional society knows how the economy is integrated into the whole landscape and daily life. The economy is not an abstraction that determines how the land and resources are to be used; it is not a method whereby human activities and the landscape are divided into abstract sectors of forestry, agriculture, industry, fisheries. The environment's immediacy and the absence of the distancing veil of money keep "economic factors" from driving people to environmentally damaging actions. To stress the holism of the landscape is not to say that it is homogenous; it is made up of many component biotic domains—all finely known by the human inhabitants. But each of these domains is clearly part of a larger whole and none draws heavily on outside sources of matter or energy (other than the evenly spread gifts of rain and sunshine). Not using extrasystem inputs, the yields of agricultural systems were strongly positive in energy terms. In other words, the whole landscape of a particular human community was largely self-sufficient even though certain kinds of trade were well developed traditionally. Everyone in the community was aware of the ecosystemic processes taking place and aware that none could be exceeded without danger.

Sustainable development is highly desirable but emphasizing satisfaction of human needs—development—rather than sustainability is nothing more than an apology for having lost the ability to live with nature.

The Wopkaimin do not live in Rousseauian harmony with nature, rather they are subtle environmental manipulators. Living resources of their ancestral rain forests are under good hands in their kinship relations of production. As mining spread communal well-being based on *abipkagup* sharing became threatened. The Ok Tedi project also changed the rules according to how the Wopkaimin and other peoples of the socio-ecological region interact with their environment. Responding to the mode of production clash in the roadside villages and the ever increasing environmental degradation, the Wopkaimin revitalized their Afek cult and returned to their Kam Basin homeland. The Wopkaimin empowering themselves to have their ancestral rain forests under their resource management and control makes good sense. It helps prevent the destruction of their kinship mode of production and subsistence capacity. Such a strategy of maintaining self-sufficiency, instead of dependency on compensation which can never be adequate and disappears when the Ok

Tedi project closes, should only be to the long term advantage of the Wopkaimin and PNG.

The Wopkaimin provide lessons on how to live with their ancestral rain forests. Unfortunately, only a few people, privileged anthropologists like me, are able to appreciate and learn their accumulated wisdom. We can only hope resource management under their kinship relations of production is passed on to future generations because their survival, not our wants, is what is at stake. The impact on resources is a matter of degree. Let us not lose sight of the Wopkaimin. They are not "culturally frozen" by tradition, rather, they will continue to evolve with tradition provided self–sufficiency remains an option to dependency. Their resource management knowledge based on long–term familiarity with place and biota represents an achievement of considerable magnitude worthy of continuation in itself as well as an opportunity for cooperative research to study its local effectiveness and applicability for transfer to sustainable development elsewhere in New Guinea. Wopkaimin, Bougainvillean and West Papuan resistance against the relentless expansion of the mining resource frontier are important expressions of a socio–ecologically sustaining and empowering Melanesian nationalism.

References

Aisbett, J. 1958a. *Report of Patrol to Wopkaimin Territory.* Telefolmin Patrol Report 5/1957–58.

_____. 1958b. *Report of Patrol to Wopkaimin Territory.* Telefolmin Patrol Report 2/1958–59.

Allen, B. 1983. "Human Geography of Papua New Guinea." *Journal of Human Evolution* 12: 3–23.

Anderson, J. 1973. "Ecological Anthropology and Anthropological Ecology," in J. Honigmann, ed., *Handbook of Social and Cultural Anthropology.* Pp.179–240. Chicago: Rand McNally.

Austen, L. 1923. "The Tedi River District of Papua." *Geographical Journal* 62: 335–49.

Australian Mineral Development Laboratories. 1984. *Interim Tailings Disposal Scheme (Ok Tedi Mining Limited). Impacts and Legislation.* Boroko: Papua New Guinea Department of Minerals and Energy.

Baines, G. 1989. "Taditional Resource Management in the Melanesian South Pacific: A Development Dilemma, in F. Berkes, ed., *Common Property Resources: Ecology and Community–Based Sustainable Development.* Pp.273–295. London: Belhaven Press.

Barr, J. 1983. "A Survey of Ecstatic Phenomena and 'Holy Spirit Movements' in Melanesia." *Oceania* 54: 109–132.

Barr, J., and G. Trompf. 1983. "Independent Churches and Recent Ecstatic Phenomena in Melanesia: A Survey of Materials." *Oceania* 54: 48–50.

Barrau, J. 1958. *Subsistence Agriculture in Melanesia.* Bernice P. Bishop Museum Bulletin No. 219. Honolulu: Hawaii.

Barth, F. 1971. "Tribes and Intertribal Relations in the Fly Headwaters." *Oceania* 41: 171–91.

_____. 1975. *Ritual and Knowledge among the Baktaman of New Guinea.* New Haven: Yale University Press.

_____. 1987 *Cosmologies in the Making: A Generative Approach to Cultural Variation in Inner New Guinea.* Cambridge: Cambridge University Press.

Barth, F. and U. Wikan. 1982. *Cultural Impact of the Ok Tedi Project.* Boroko: Institute of Papua New Guinea Studies.

Bayliss–Smith, T. 1985. "Subsistence Agriculture and Nutrition in the Bimin Valley, Oksapmin sub–district, Papua New Guinea." *Singapore Journal of Tropical Geography* 6: 101–15.

Bedford, R., and A. Mamak. 1974. "Bougainvillean Students: Some Expressed Attitudes Towards Non Bougainvilleans, Arawa Town and the Copper Mining Company." *New Guinea and Australia, the Pacific and South-east Asia* 9: 4–15.

_____. 1977. *Compensating for Development.* Bougainville Special Publication No. 2. Christchurch: University of Canterbury.

_____. 1979. "Bougainville," in A. Mamak, and A. Ali, eds, *Race, Class, and Rebellion in the South Pacific.* Pp.69–85. Sydney: Allen and Unwin.

Bell, H. 1966. *Report of Patrol to Wopkaimin Territory.* 1 PIR Patrol Report 2/1965–66.

Berger, T. 1985. "The Fourth World," in *Village Journey.* Pp.172–183. New York: Hill and Wang.

Black, J. 1970. "The Hagen/Sepik Patrol 1938–39." *Journal of the Anthropological Society of South Australia* 8: 12–27.

Blaikie, P., and H. Brookfield, eds. 1987. *Land Degradation and Society.* London: Methuen.

Bodley, J., ed. 1988. *Tribal Peoples and Development Issues: A Global Overview.* Mountain View: Cummings.

Booth, I. 1957. *Report of Patrol to Wopkaimin Territory.* Telefolmin Patrol Report 2/1957–58.

Bougainville Information Service. 1990. *Bougainville Situation Report: November 1990.* Victoria, Australia: P.O.Box 1091, Collingwood.

Bowers, N. 1968. The Ascending Grasslands: An Anthropological Study of Ecological Succession in a High Mountain Valley of New Guinea. Ph.D. Thesis, Columbia University, New York.

Boyd, D. 1975. Crops, Kiaps and Currency: Flexible Behavioural Strategies among the Ilakia Awa of Papua New Guinea. Ph.D. Thesis, University of California, Los Angeles.

Brillante, C. 1972. *Report of Patrol to Wopkaimin Territory.* Ningerum Patrol Report 14/1971–72.

Brookfield, H. 1969. "On the Environment as Perceived." *Progress in Geography* 1: 51–80.

Brookfield, H., and P. Brown. 1963. *Struggle for Land: Agriculture and Group Territories among the Chimbu of the New Guinea Highlands.* Melbourne: Oxford University Press.

Brookfield, H., and D. Hart. 1971. *Melanesia: A Geographical Interpretation of an Island World.* London: Methuen.

Brown, C. 1977. "Folk Botanical Life-Forms: Their Universality and Growth." *American Anthropologist* 79: 317–342.

_____. 1979. "Folk Zoological Life-Forms: Their Universality and Growth." *American Anthropologist* 81: 791–817.

Brown, P. 1978. "New Guinea: Ecology, Society and Culture." *Annual Review of Anthropology* 7: 263–291.

Browne, N., ed. 1983. *Ok Tedi 24:00*. Brisbane: Ok Tedi Mining Limited.

Buchbinder, G. 1973. Maring Microadaptation: A Study of Demographic, Nutritional, Genetic, and Phenotypic Variation in a Highland New Guinea Population. Ph.D. Thesis, Columbia University, New York.

_____. 1977. Nutritional Stress and Postcontact Population Decline among the Maring of New Guinea," in L. Greene, ed., *Malnutrition, Behaviour, and Social Organisation*. Pp.109–141. London: Academic Press.

Buchbinder, G., and R. Rappaport. 1976. "Fertility and Death among the Maring," in P. Brown, and G. Buchbinder, eds, *Men and Women in the New Guinea Highlands*. Pp.13–34. Washington DC: American Anthropological Association.

Bulmer, R. 1968. "The Strategies of Hunting in New Guinea." *Oceania* 38: 302–18.

_____. 1976. "Selectivity in Hunting and in Disposal of Animal Bone by the Kalam of the New Guinea Highlands," in G. Sieveking, I. Longworth, and K. Wilson, eds, *Problems in Economic and Social Archaeology*. London: Duckworth.

_____. 1982. "Traditional Conservation Practices in Papua New Guinea," in L. Morauta, J. Pernetta, and W. Heaney, eds, *Traditional Conservation in Papua New Guinea: Implications for Today*. Pp.59–78. Boroko: Institute of Papua New Guinea Studies.

Bulmer, S. 1982. "Human Ecology and Cultural Variation in Prehistoric New Guinea," in J. Gressitt, ed., *Biogeography and Ecology of New Guinea*. Pp.169–206. The Hague: W. Junk.

Bulmer, S., and R. Bulmer. 1964. "The Prehistory of the Australian New Guinea Highlands." *American Anthropologist* 66: 39–76.

Burger, J. 1987. *Report from the Frontier: The State of the World's Indigenous Peoples*. London: Zed Press.

Busse, M. 1991. "Environment and Human Ecology of the Lake Murray–Middle Fly Area," in D. Lawrence, and T. Cansfield–Smith, eds., *Sustainable Development for the Traditional Inhabitants of the Torres Strait Region*. Pp.441–450. Townsville: Great Barrier Reef Marine Park Authority.

Buttimer, A. 1980. "Home, Reach, and the Sense of Place," in A. Buttimer, and D. Seamon, eds, *The Human Experience of Space and Place*. Pp.166–187. London: Croom Helm.

Callick, R. 1990. "The War Port Moresby Lost." *Islands Business*, March: 18–22.

Campbell, S. 1938. "The Country Between the Headwaters of the Fly and Sepik Rivers." *Geographical Journal* 92: 232–58.

Cattani, J., T. Taufa, W. Anderson and J. Lourie. 1983. "Malaria and Filariasis in the Ok Tedi Region of the Star Mountains, Papua New Guinea." *Papua New Guinea Medical Journal* 26: 122–126.

Chambers, M. 1985. "Environmental Management Problems in Papua New Guinea." *The Environmental Professional* 7: 178–85.

Champion, I. 1966. *Across New Guinea from the Fly to the Sepik*. Melbourne: Landsdowne Press.

Chowning, A. 1969. "Recent Acculturation between Tribes in Papua New Guinea." *Journal of Pacific History* 4: 27–40.

_____. 1982. "Physical Anthropology, Linguistics and Ethnology," in J. Gressitt, ed., *Biogeography and Ecology of New Guinea*. Pp.131–168. The Hague: W. Junk.

Clarke, W.C. 1971. *Place and People: An Ecology of a New Guinea Community*. Canberra: Australian National University.

_____. 1973. "The Dilemma of Development," in H. Brookfield, ed., *The Pacific in Transition*. Pp.275–298. Canberra: Australian National University.

_____. 1976. "Maintenance of Agriculture and Human Habitats within the Tropical Forest Ecosystem." *Human Ecology* 4: 247–59.

_____. 1977. "The Structure of Permanence: The Relevance of Self–Subsistence Communities for World Ecosystem Management," in T. Bayliss–Smith and R. Feachem, eds, *Subsistence and Survival*. Pp.363–384. London: Academic Press.

_____. 1990. "Learning from the Past: Traditional Knowledge and Sustainable Development." *The Contemporary Pacific* 2: 233–53.

Colchester, M. 1986a. "Unity and Diversity: Indonesia's Policy Towards Tribal Peoples." *Ecologist* 16: 89–98.

Colchester, M. 1986b. "The Strugle for Land: Tribal Peoples in the Face of the Transmigration Programme." *Ecologist* 16: 99–110.

Connell, J. 1978. *Taim Bilong Man: The Evolution of Agriculture in a Solomon Island Society*. Development Studies Centre, Monograph No. 12. Canberra: Australian National University.

_____. 1990. "Perspectives on a Crisis (4)," in P. Polomka, ed., *Bougainville: Perspectives on a Crisis*. Pp.43–53. Strategic and Defence Studies Centre, Research School of Pacific Studies. Canberra: Australian National University.

_____. 1992. "Compensation and Conflict: The Bougainville Copper Mine, Papua New Guinea," in J. Connell, and R. Howitt, eds, *Mining and Indigenous People in Australasia*. Pp.55–76. Sydney: Oxford University Press.

Connor, W. 1978. "A Nation is a Nation, is a State, is an Ethnic Group, is a ... ." *Ethnic and Racial Studies* 1: 379–88.

Cosgrove, D. 1978. "Place, Landscape, and the Dialectics of Cultural Geography." *Canadian Geographer* 12: 66–72.

186

Craig, B. 1967. "The Houseboards of the Telefolmin Sub–District in New Guinea." *Man* n.s. 2: 260–73.

_____ 1969 . Houseboards and Warshields of the Mountain Ok of Central New Guinea: Analysis of an Art Style. M.A. Thesis, University of Sydney, Sydney.

_____ . 1988. "Relic and Trophy Arrays as Art among the Mountain Ok, Central New Guinea," in L. Hanson, and A. Hanson, eds, *Art and Identity in Oceania*. Pp.196–210. Bathurst: Robert Brown.

_____ . 1990. "The Telefomin Murders: Whose Myth?" in B. Craig and D. Hyndman, eds, *Children of Afek: Tradition and Change among the Mountain Ok of Central New Guinea*. Pp.115–150. Sydney: Oceania Monographs.

Dent, G. 1966. *Report of Patrol to Wopkaimin Territory*. Olsobip Patrol Report 1/1965–66.

Dornstreich, M. 1973. An Ecological Study of Gadio Enga (New Guinea) Subsistence. Ph.D. Thesis, Columbia University, New York.

Douglas, M. 1969. *Purity and Danger: An Analysis of Concepts of Pollution and Taboo*. London: Rutledge, Kegan, Paul.

Dove, J., T. Miriung, and M. Togolo. 1974. "Mining Bitterness," in P. Sack, ed., *Problems of Choice: Land in Papua New Guinea's Future*. Pp.181–189. Canberra: Australian National University.

Downs, R., and D. Stea. 1977. *Maps in Minds: Reflections on Cognitive Mapping*. New York: Harper and Row.

Duncan, H. 1972. The Regional Economic Impact of the Bougainville Copper Project. B.Ec. (Hons) Thesis, Flinders University, Adelaide.

Dwyer, P. 1982. "Prey Switching: A Case from New Guinea." *Journal of Animal Ecology* 51: 529–42.

_____ . 1983. "Etolo Hunting Performance and Energetics." *Human Ecology* 11: 145–73.

Dwyer, P., and D. Hyndman. 1983. "'Frog' and 'Lizard': Additional Life–Forms from Papua New Guinea." *American Anthropologist* 85: 890–96.

Eagle, M. and R. Higgins. 1991. "Environmental Investigations of the Effects of the Ok Tedi Copper Mine in the Fly River System." *The Australian Institute of Mining and Metallurgy Bulletin* 5: 46–56.

Eggleton, M. 1968. *Report of Patrol to Wopkaimin Territory*. Olsobip Patrol Report 4/1968–1969.

_____ . 1969. *Report of Patrol to Wopkaimin Territory*. Ningerum Patrol Report 17/1969–70.

Ellen, R. 1982. *Environment, Subsistence and System: The Ecology of Small–Scale Social Formations*. Cambridge: Cambridge University Press.

Fabian, J. 1983. *Time and the Other: How Anthropology Makes its Object*. New York: Columbia University Press.

Fairthorn, E. 1975. "The Concept of Pollution among the Kafe of the Papua New Guinea Highlands," in R. Reiter, ed., *Toward an Anthropology of Women.* Pp.127–140. New York: Monthly Review Press.

Feil, D. 1984. *Ways of Exchange: The Enga Tee of Papua New Guinea.* St. Lucia: University of Queensland Press.

Filer, C. 1990. "The Bougainville Rebellion, the Mining Industry and the Process of Social Disintegration in Papua New Guinea." *Canberra Anthropology* 13: 1–39.

Fenton, J. 1959. *Report of Patrol to Wopkaimin Territory.* Telefolmin Patrol Report 7/1958–59.

Fitzer, D. 1963. *Report of Patrol to Wopkaimin Territory.* Kiunga Patrol Report 9/1962–63.

Frankel, S. 1976. "Mass Hysteria in the New Guinea Highlands." *Oceania* 48: 106–33.

Freeport Indonesia Inc. nd. Tantangan Pertambangan Mining Challenge.

Friedman, J. 1974. "Marxism, Structuralism and Vulgar Materialism." *Man* n.s. 9: 444–69.

Frodin, D. and D. Hyndman. 1982. *Ethnobotany of the Ok Tedi Drainage. In Ok Tedi Environmental Study.* Vol.5, Pp.209–340. Melbourne: Maunsell and Partners.

Gardner, D. 1990. "Mianmin Leadership." Paper presented to the Mek and their Neighbors: Man and Environment in the Central Highlands of New Guinea Conference. October, Andechs, Germany: Max Planck Institute of Human Ethology.

Gelber, M. 1986. *Gender and Society in the New Guinea Highlands: An Anthropological Perspective on Antagonism Towards Women.* Boulder: Westview Press.

Gerlach, J. and V. Hine. 1970. *People, Power and Change.* New York: Bobbs-Merrill.

Godelier, M. 1972. *Rationality and Irrationality in Economics.* New York: Monthly Review Press.

_____. 1979. "The Appropriation of Nature." *Critique of Anthropology* 4: 17–27.

_____. 1986. *The Making of Great Men: Male Domination and Power among the New Guinea Baruya.* Cambridge: Cambridge University Press.

Godoy, R. 1985. "Mining: An Anthropological Perspective." *Annual Review of Anthropology* 14:199– 217.

Gould, P., and R. White. 1974. *Mental Maps.* London: Penguin Books.

Grant, J. 1987. "The Impact of Dependent Development on Community and Resources." *Human Ecology* 15: 242–60.

Gregory, C. 1982. *Gifts and Commodities.* London: Academic Press.

Gressitt, J., and N. Nadkarni. 1978. *Guide to Mt. Kaindi: Background to Montane New Guinea Ecology.* Handbook No. 5. Wau: Wau Ecology Institute.

Griffin, J. 1982. "Napidakoe Navitu," in R. May, ed., *Micronational Movements in Papua New Guinea*. Pp.113–138. Department of Political and Social Change: Australian National University.

Griffin, J., and D. Carruthers. 1990. "The Bougainville Mine Impact (2): Dialogue with the Chairman, Bougainville Copper Limited," in P. Polomka, ed., *Bougainville: Perspectives on a Crisis*. Pp.54–66. Strategic and Defence Studies Centre, Research School of Pacific Studies. Canberra: Australian National University.

Grossman, L. 1977. "Man–Environment Relationships in Anthropology and Geography." *Annals of the Association of American Geographers* 67: 126–44.

―――― . 1981. "Cultural Ecology of Economic Development." *Annals of the Association of American Geographers* 71: 220–36.

―――― . 1984. *Peasants, Subsistence Ecology, and Development in the Highlands of Papua New Guinea*. Princeton: Princeton University Press.

Guiart, J. 1951. "Forerunners of Melanesian Nationalism." *Oceania* 22: 81–90.

―――― 1970. "The Millenarian Aspect of Conversion to Christianity in the South Pacific," in S. Thrupp, ed., *Millennial Dreams in Action*. Pp.136–137. New York: Schoken.

Hannett, L. 1975. "The Case for Bougainville Secession." *Meangin Quarterly* 34: 286–93.

Hardesty, D. 1977. *Ecological Anthropology*. New York: Wiley.

Harrison, J. 1962. "The Distribution of Feeding Habits among Animals in a Tropical Rainforest." *Journal of Animal Ecology* 31: 53–63.

Havini, M. 1990. "Perspectives on a Crisis (3)," in P. Polomka, ed., *Bougainville: Perspectives on a Crisis*. Pp.17–27. Strategic and Defence Studies Centre, Research School of Pacific Studies. Canberra: Australian National University.

Healey, C. 1988. "Hunting Horticulturalists: Pleasure, Profit and Pot." Paper Presented to the Fifth Conference on Hunting and Gathering Societies. August, Darwin: Australia.

Heider, K. 1970. *The Dugum Dani: A Papuan Culture in the Highlands of West New Guinea*. Chicago: Aldine.

―――― . 1979. *Grand Valley Dani: Peaceful Warriors*. New York: Holt, Rinehart and Winston.

Hiambohn, W. 1989. "Landowners Resort to Sabotage in Panguna." *Pacific Islands Monthly* January: 16–19.

Hide, R., J. Pernetta and T. Sanabe. 1984. "Exploitation of Wild Animals," in R. Hide, ed., *South Simbu: Studies in Demography, Nutrition and Subsistence*. Pp.291–380. Boroko: Institute of Applied Social and Economic Research.

Hipsley, E., and F. Clements. 1947. *Report of the New Guinea Nutrition Survey Expedition, 1947*. Canberra: Department of External Territories.

Hipsley, E., F. Clements, and N. Kirk. 1965. *Studies of Dietary Intake and the Expenditure of Energy by New Guineans.* South Pacific Commission Technical Paper No. 147. Noumea, New Caledonia.

Hoad, R. 1964. *Report of Patrol to Wopkaimin Territory.* Olosibip Patrol Report 1/1964–1965.

Holmberg, A. 1969. *Nomads of the Long Bows. The Siriono of Eastern Bolivia.* New York: Natural History Press.

Hook, C. nd. *Treachery in West Papua.* Deventer: Foundation Workgroup New Guinea.

Hope, G., J. Golson and J. Allen. 1983. "Paleoecology and Prehistory in New Guinea." *Journal of Human Evolution* 12: 37–60.

Howard, M. 1988. *The Impact of the International Mining Industry on Native Peoples.* University of Sydney: Transnational Corporations Research Project.

Hughes, I. 1970. "Pigs, Sago and Limestone." Symposium: Agriculture in New Guinea, 42nd ANZAAS Congress, Port Moresby, Papua New Guinea.

_____ . 1977. *New Guinea Stone Age Trade.* Canberra: Australian National University.

Hughes, P. and M. Sullivan. 1989. "Environmental Impact Assessment in Papua New Guinea: Lessons for the Wider Pacific Region." *Pacific Viewpoint* 30: 34–55.

Hyndman, D. 1979. Wopkaimin Subsistence: Cultural Ecology in the New Guinea Highland Fringe. Ph.D. Thesis, University of Queensland, St. Lucia.

_____ . 1982a. "Biotope Gradient in a Diversified New Guinea Subsistence System." *Human Ecology* 10: 219–59.

_____ . 1982b. "Population, Settlement, and Resource Use," in *Ok Tedi Environmental Study.* Vol.5, Pp.1–71. Melbourne: Maunsell and Partners.

_____ . 1984a. "Hunting and the Classification of Game Animals among the Wopkaimin." *Oceania* 54: 289–309.

_____ . 1984b. "Ethnobotany of Wopkaimin Pandanus: A Significant Papua New Guinea Plant Resource." *Economic Botany* 38: 287–303.

_____ . 1985. "The Good Go to Heaven and the Bad Go to Hell: Doing Patienthood on the Orthopaedic Ward," in L. Manderson, ed., *Australian Ways: Anthropological Studies of an Industrial Society.* Pp.113–126. Sydney: Allen and Unwin.

_____ . 1987. "Mining, Modernisation and Movements of Social Protest in New Guinea." *Social Analysis* 20–38.

_____ . 1988a. "Ok Tedi: New Guinea's Disaster Mine." *Ecologist* 18: 24–9.

_____ . 1988b. "Melanesians Resisting Ecocide and Ethnocide: Transnational Mining Projects and the Fourth World on the Island of New Guinea," in J. Bodley, ed., *Tribal Peoples and Development Issues: A Global Overview.* Pp.281–298. Mountain View: Cummings.

190

_____ . 1991a "The Kam Basin Homeland of the Wopakimin: a Sense of Place," in A. Pawley, ed., *Man and A Half: Essays in Pacific Anthropology and Ethnobiology in Honour of Ralph Bulmer*. Pp.256–265. Auckland: The Polynesian Society.

_____ . 1991b. Digging the Mines in Melanesia. *Cultural Survival Quarterly* 15: 32–39.

_____ . 1992a. "Wopkaimin Landowners, the Ok Tedi Project and the Creation of the Fly River Socio–ecological Region," in D. Lawrence, and T. Cansfield–Smith, eds, *Sustainable Development for the Traditional Inhabitants of the Torres Strait Region*. Pp.355–366. Townsville: Great Barrier Reef Marine Park Authority.

_____ . 1992b. "Zipping Down the Fly on the Ok Tedi Project," in J. Connell, and R. Howitt, eds, *Mining and Indigenous People in Australasia*. Pp.77–90 Sydney: Sydney University Press.

Hyndman, D., and D. Frodin. 1980. "Ethnobotany of Schefflera (Araliaceae) in the Ok Tedi Region, Papua New Guinea." *Ethnomedizin* 6: 101–126.

Hyndman, D., and J. Menzies. 1980. "Aproteles bulmerae (Chiroptera: Pteropodidae) of New Guinea is not Extinct." *Journal of Mammology* 61: 151–60.

Hyndman, D., and J. Menzies. 1990. "Rain Forests of the Ok Tedi Headwaters: An Ecological Analysis." *Journal of Biogeography* 17: 241–73.

Hyndman, D, and G. Morren. 1990. "Human Ecology of the Mountain Ok of Central New Guinea: A Regional and Inter–Regional Approach," in B. Craig, and D. Hyndman, eds, *Children of Afek: Tradition and Change among the Mountain Ok of Central New Guinea*. Pp.9–26. Sydney: Oceania Monographs.

Hyndman, D., S. Ulijaszek, and J. Lourie. 1989. "Variability in Body Physique, Ecology and Subsistence in the Fly River Region of Papua New Guinea." *American Journal of Physical Anthropology* 79: 89–101.

Jackson, R. 1975. "Social and Regional Implications of Mine and Infrastructure Developments." Appendix II, in Rendel and Partners, *Transportation Systems for Frieda, Ok Tedi and Tifalmin Mineral Projects*. Port Moresby: Department of Transport.

_____ . 1982. *Ok Tedi: The Pot of Gold*. University of Papua New Guinea: Word Publishing.

Jackson, R., C. Emerson, and R. Welsch. 1980. *The Impact of the Ok Tedi Project*. Boroko: Papua New Guinea Department of Minerals and Energy.

Jackson, R., and T. Ilave. 1983. *The Progess and Impact of the Ok Tedi Project*. Report No. 1. Waigani: Institute of Applied Social and Economic Research.

Jansen, A. 1963. "Skinfold Measurements from Early Childhood to Adulthood in Papuans from Western New Guinea." *Annals of the New York Academy of Science* 110: 515–31.

Jones, B. 1980. Consuming Society: Food and Illness among the Faiwol. Ph.D. Thesis, University of Virginia, Charlotte.

Jorgensen, D. 1976. *The Telefolmin Village, Now You See It, Now You Don't.* Northwest Anthropological Conference, Melanesian Symposium. Ellensburg: Washington.

_____. 1981a. Taro and Arrows: Order, Entropy and Religion among the Telefolmin. Ph.D. Thesis, University of British Colombia, Vancouver.

_____ 1981b. "Life on the Fringe: History and Society in Telefolmin," in R. Gordon, ed., *The Plight of Peripheral Peoples in Papua New Guinea.* Pp.59–80. Occasional Paper No. 7. Cambridge: Cultural Survival.

_____. 1990. "The Telefolip in Telefolmin: Architecture of Identity," in B. Craig and D. Hyndman, eds, *Children of Afek: Tradition and Change among the Mountain Ok of Central New Guinea.* Pp.151–160. Sydney: Oceania Monographs.

_____. 1991. "Big Men, Great Men and Women: Alternative Logics of Gender Difference," in M. Godelier and M. Strathern, eds, *Big Men and Great Men.* Pp.256–271. Cambridge: Cambridge University Press.

Josephides, L. 1985. *The Production of Inequality: Gender and Exchange among the Kewe.* London: Tavistock.

Kienzle, W., and S. Campbell. 1937. "Notes on the Natives of the Fly and Sepik Headwaters." *Oceania* 8: 463–81.

Kirsch, P. 1989. "The Yonggom, the Refugee Camps along the Border, and the Impact of the Ok Tedi Mine." *Research in Melanesia* 13: 30–61.

Kreye, O., and L. Castell. 1991. "Development and the Environment: Economic–Ecological Development in Papua New Guinea." *Catalyst* 21: 1–119.

LaFitte, G. 1990. "Bougainville: A River of Tears." *Arena* 91: 11–17.

Langness, L. 1976. "Discussion," in P. Brown, and G. Buchbinder, eds, *Men and Women in the New Guinea Highlands.* Washington D.C.: American Anthropological Association.

Lea, D. 1964. Abelam Land and Sustenance. Ph.D. Thesis, Australian National University, Canberra.

_____. 1972. "Indigenous Horticulture in Melanesia," in R. Ward, ed., *Man and the Landscape in the Pacific Islands.* Pp.252–279. London: Clarendon.

Lindenbaum, S. 1984. "Variations on a Sociosexual Theme," in G. Herdt, ed., *Ritualized Homosexuality in Melanesia.* Pp.337–361. Berkeley: University of California Press.

Linares, O. 1976. "'Garden Hunting' in the American Tropics.' *Human Ecology* 4: 331–350.

Lourie, J., ed. 1987. *Final Report. Ok Tedi Health and Nutrition Project 1982–1986.* Port Moresby: University of Papua New Guinea.

Lourie, J., T. Taufa, J. Cattani, and W. Anderson. 1986. "The Ok Tedi Health and Nutrition Project, Papua New Guinea: Physique, Growth, and Nutritional

192

Status of the Wopkaimin of the Star Mountains." *Annals of Human Biology* 13: 517–36.

Luhrs, G. 1966. *Report of Patrol to Wopkaimin Territory*. Olsobip Patrol Report 3/1965–66.

Majnep, I. and R. Bulmer. 1977 *Birds of My Kalam Country*. Auckland: University of Auckland Press.

Mamak, A., and A. Ali, eds. 1979. *Race, Class and Rebellion in the South Pacific*. Sydney: Allen and Unwin.

Mamak, A., and R. Bedford, with L. Hannett, and M. Havini. 1974. *Bougainville Nationalism: Aspects of Unity and Discord*. Special Publication No. 1. Christchurch: University of Canterbury.

Manuel, G. and M. Posuns. 1974. *The Fourth World: An Indian Reality*. New York: Free Press.

Matthiessen, P. 1962. *Under the Mountain Wall: A Chronicle of Two, Seasons in the Stone Age*. New York: Viking.

May, R., ed. 1982. *Micronationalist Movements in Papua New Guinea*. Department of Political and Social Change: Australian National University.

_____. 1990. "Papua New Guinea's Bougainville Crisis." *The Pacific Review* 3: 174–77.

McAlpine, J., G. Keig, and R. Falls. 1983. *Climate of New Guinea*. Canberra: Australian National University.

McArthur, M. 1977. "Nutritional Research in Melanesia: A Second Look at the Tsembaga," in T. Bayliss–Smith and R. Feachem, eds, *Subsistence and Survival*. Pp.91–128. New York: Academic Press.

McCall, G. 1980. "Four Worlds of Experience and Action." *Third World Quarterly* 2: 536–45.

McGrath, G. 1972. *Report of Patrol to Wopkaimin Territory*. Ningerum Patrol Report 16/1971–72.

McGregor, J. 1968. *Report of Patrol to Wopkaimin Territory*. Olsobip Patrol Report 2/1967–68.

Mitchell, D. 1976. *Land and Agriculture in Nagovisi, Papua New Guinea*. Boroko: Institute of Applied Social and Economic Research.

Mitton, R. 1975. "Development of the Freeport Copper Mine," in J. Winslow, ed., *The Melanesian Environment*. Pp:365–372. Canberra: Australian National University.

Modjeska, N. 1982. "Production and Inequality: Perspectives from Central New Guinea," in A. Strathern, ed., *Inequality in New Guinea Highlands Societies*. Pp.50–108. Cambridge: Cambridge University Press.

Morauta, L., J. Pernetta, and W. Heaney, eds. 1982. *Traditional Conservation in Papua New Guinea: Implications for Today*. Boroko: Institute of Papua New Guinea Studies.

Morren, G. 1974. Settlement Strategies and Hunting in a New Guinea Society. Ph.D. Thesis, Columbia University, New York.

_____ . 1984. "Review of: Traditional Conservation in Papua New Guinea: Implications for Today." *Archaeology in Oceania* 19: 39.

_____ . 1986. *The Miyanmin: Human Ecology of a Papua New Guinea Society.* Ann Arbor: UMI Research Press.

Morren, G., and D. Hyndman. 1987. "The Taro Monoculture of Central New Guinea." *Human Ecology* 15: 301–15.

Moulik, T. 1977. *Bougainville in Transition.* Development Studies Centre, Monograph No. 7. Canberra: Australian National University.

Namaliu, R. 1990. "Perspectives on a Crisis (2)," in P. Polomka, ed., *Bougainville: Perspectives on a Crisis.* Pp.13–16. Strategic and Defence Studies Centre, Research School of Pacific Studies. Canberra: Australian National University.

Nash, J. 1979. *We Eat the Mines.* New York: Columbia University Press.

Nash, J. 1974. *Matriliny and Modernization: The Nagovisi of South Bougainville.* New Guinea Research Bulletin, No. 55. Canberra: Australian National University.

_____ . 1981. "Sex, Money and the Status of Women in Aboriginal South Bougainville." *American Ethnologist* 8: 107–126.

Nash, J., and E. Ogan. 1990. "The Red and the Black: Bougainvillean Perceptions of other Papua New Guineans." *Pacific Studies* 13: 1–17.

Nelson, M. 1964. *Report of Patrol to Wopkaimin Territory.* 1 PIR Patrol Report 18/1965–66.

Nietschmann, B. 1970. *The Study of Indigenous Food Producing Systems: Mere Subsistence or Merrily Subsisting?* Conference of Latin American Geographers. Muncie: Indiana.

_____ . 1973. *Between Land and Water: The Subsistence Ecology of the Miskito Indians, Eastern Nicaragua.* New York: Seminar Press.

_____ . 1974. "When the Turtle Collapses, the World Ends." *Natural History* 83: 34–41.

_____ . 1984. "Indigenous Island Peoples, Living Resources and Protected Areas," in J. McNealy and K. Whiler, eds, *National Parks, Conservation and Development.* Pp.333–343. Washington DC: Smithsonian.

_____ . 1987a. "The New Pacific: Geopolitics of Pacific Island Fisheries." *Cultural Survival Quarterly* 11: 7–9.

_____ . 1987b. "The Third World War." *Cultural Survival Quarterly* 11: 1–16.

Norgan, N. and J. Durnin. 1974. "The Energy and Nutrient Intake and the Energy Expenditure of 204 New Guinea Adults." *Philosophical Transactions of the Royal Society of London B* 268: 309–48.

North Fly Clinico–Epidemiological Pilot Study. 1978a. *First Report of Teams 2 and 3.* Port Moresby: Medical School, University of Papua New Guinea.

_____. 1978b. *Second Report of Teams 2 and 3*. Post Moresby: Medical School, University of Papua New Guinea.

O'Faircheallaigh, C. 1990. "The Bougainville Crisis." *Policy Organisation and Society* (Winter): 30–35.

Ogan, E. 1966a. "Drinking Behavior and Race Relations." *American Anthropologist* 68: 181–88.

_____ . 1966b. "Nasioi Marriage: An Essay in Model Building." *Oceania* 22: 172–93.

_____ . 1972. *Business and Cargo: Socio-economic Change Among the Nasioi of Bougainville*. New Guinea Research Bulletin No. 44. Canberra: Australian National University.

_____ . 1990. "Perspectives on a Crisis (5)," in P. Polomka, ed., *Bougainville: Perspectives on a Crisis*. Pp.35–39. Strategic and Defence Studies Centre, Research School of Pacific Studies. Canberra: Australian National University.

Ohtsuka, R. 1977a. "The Sago Eaters: An Ecological Discussion with Special Reference to the Oriomo Papuans," in J. Allen, J. Golson, and R. Jones, eds, *Sunda and Sahul*. Pp.465–492. London: Academic Press.

_____ . 1977b. "Time-space Use of the Papuans Depending on Sago and Game," in H. Watanabe, ed., *Human Activity System*. Pp.231–260. Tokyo: University of Tokyo Press.

Ok Tedi Mining Limited. 1984. *Addendum No. 1, October*. Report to the Department of Minerals and Energy, Papua New Guinea.

_____. 1985. *PA/03/85–5*. Report to the Department of Minerals and Energy, Papua New Guinea.

Oliver, D. 1973. *Bougainville: A Personal History*. Melbourne: Melbourne University Press.

Ona, F. 1990. "Perspectives on a Crisis (2)," in P. Polomka, ed., *Bougainville: Perspectives on a Crisis*. Pp.7–12. Strategic and Defence Studies Centre, Research School of Pacific Studies. Canberra: Australian National University.

Oomen, H. 1971. "Ecology of Human Nutrition in New Guinea: Evaluation of Subsistence Patterns." *Ecology of Food and Nutrition* 1: 3–18.

Osborne, R. 1985. *Indonesia's Secret War: The Guerilla Struggle in Irian Jaya*. Sydney: Allen and Unwin.

Pacific Island Regiment No. 1. 1963. *Report of Patrol to Wopkaimin Territory*. 1 PIR Patrol Report 53/1962–63.

_____ . 1966. *Report of Patrol to Wopakimin Territory*. 1 PIR Patrol Report 16/1966–1976.

Paine, R. 1985. "The Claim of the Fourth World," in J. Brosted, *et al.*, eds., *Native Power: The Quest for Autonomy and Nationhood of Indigenous Peoples*. Pp.49–66. Olso: Universitetsforlaget.

Parker, F. 1972. *Local Government Survey*. Ningerum Patrol Report 4/1972–73.

Paijmans, K. 1976. *New Guinea Vegetation*. Canberra: Australian National University Press.

Pernetta, J. and L. Hill. 1982. "International Pressures and Internal Resource Management in Papua New Guinea," in L. Morauta, J. Pernetta, and W. Heaney, eds, *Traditional Conservation in Papua New Guinea: Implications for Today*. Pp.319–332. Boroko: Institute of Papua New Guinea Studies.

Pernetta, J., and D. Hyndman. 1982. "Ethnozoology of the Ok Tedi Drainage," in *Ok Tedi Environmental Study*. Vol. 5, Pp.73–207. Melbourne: Maunsell and Partners.

Perey, A. 1973. Oksapmin Society and World View. Ph.D. Thesis, Columbia University, New York.

Petocz, R. 1984. *Conservation and Development in Irian Jaya: A Strategy for Rational Resource Utilization*. Gland: WWF/IUCN.

Pintz, W. 1984. *Ok Tedi: Evolution of a Third World Mining Project*. London: Mining Journal Books.

Pogolamun, M. 1985. "Akimuga to Timika: All that Glitters is not Copper." *Kabar Dari Kampung* 1: 45–50.

Polier, N. 1990. "Migrant Min, Miners, and Gardeners: Social Movement and Social Transformation among the Faiwolmin of Golgpbip." Paper presented to the Mek and the Neighbors: Man, Culture and Environment in the Central Highlands of West New Guinea Conference. October, Andechs, Germany: Max Planck Institute of Human Ethology.

Polomka, P. 1990. "Overview: Land as 'Life', Security and Impediment to Unity," in P. Polomka, ed., *Bougainville: Perspectives on a Crisis*. Pp.1–4. Strategic and Defence Studies Centre, Research School of Pacific Studies. Canberra: Australian National University.

Poole, F. 1981. "Transforming 'Natural' Woman: Female Ritual Leaders and Gender Ideology among Bimin–Kuskusmin," in S. Ortner, and H. Whitehead, eds, *Sexual Meanings*. Pp.116–165. New York: Cambridge University Press.

_____ . 1982. "The Ritual Forging of Identity: Aspects of Person and Self in Bimin–Kuskusmin Male Initiation," in G. Herdt, ed., *Rituals of Manhood: Male Initiation in Papua New Guinea*. Pp. 99–154. Berkeley: University of California Press.

Pospisil, L. 1978. *The Kapauku Papuans of West New Guinea*. Second Edition. New York: Holt, Rinehart and Winston.

Pouwer, J. 1964. "A Social System in the Star Mountains: Towards a Reorientation of the Study of Social Systems." *American Anthropologist* 66: 133–61.

Powell, J. 1976. "Ethnobotany," in K. Paijmans, ed., *New Guinea Vegetation*. Pp.106–183. Canberra: Australian National University.

Quinlaven, P. 1954. "Afek of Telefomin: A Fabulous Story from New Guinea which Leads to a Strange Story." *Oceania* 25: 17–22.

Rand, A., and T. Gilliard. 1967. *Handbook of New Guinea Birds*. London: Weidenfeld and Nicolson.

Ransley, G. 1975. *Report of Patrol to Wopkaimin Territory*. Ningerum Patrol Report, May–June 1975.

Rappaport, R. 1968. *Pigs for the Ancestors*. New Haven: Yale University Press.

_____. 1984. *Pigs for the Ancestors*. A New Enlarged Edition. New Haven: Yale University Press.

Reynders, J. 1964. "A Pedo–ecological Study of Soil Genesis in the Tropics from Sea Level to Eternal Snow: Star Mountains, Central New Guinea." *Geology, Nova Guinea* 6: 159–317.

Richards, M. 1970. *Report of Patrol to Wopkaimin Territory*. Ningerum Patrol Report 1/1970–71.

Richards, P. 1966. *The Tropical Rainforest: An Ecological Study*. Cambridge: Cambridge University Press.

Robie, D. 1989. "Bougainville: One Year Later." *Pacific Islands Monthly* November: 10–18.

Rodman, W., and D. Counts, eds. 1983. *Middlemen and Brokers in Oceania*. ASAO Monograph No. 9. Ann Arbor: University of Michigan Press.

Rogers, D., and M. Miner. 1963. "Amino Acid Profile of Manioc Leaf Protein in Relation to Nutritive Value." *Economic Botany* 17: 211–16.

Sahlins, M. 1963. "Poor Man, Rich Man, Big Man, Chief: Political Types in Melanesia and Polynesia." *Comparative Studies in Society and History* 5: 285–303.

Schieffelin, E. 1975. "Felling the Trees on Top of the Crop: European Contact and the Subsistence Ecology of the Great Papuan Plateau." *Oceania* 46: 25–39.

Schmink, M., and C. Wood. 1987. "The 'Political Ecology' of Amazonia," in P. Little, and M. Horowitz, eds, *Lands at Risk in the Third World: Local–Level Perspectives*. Pp.38–57. Boulder: Westview Press.

Schwartz, T. 1962. "Systems of Areal Integration: Some Considerations Based on the Admiralty Islands of Northern Melanesia." *Anthropological Forum* 1: 56–97.

Senge, F. 1990. "Counting the Losses in a State of War." *Pacific Islands Monthly* February: 12–13.

Sexton, L. 1986. *Mothers of Money, Daughters of Coffee: The Wok Meri Movement*. Ann Arbor: UMI Research Press.

Shapiro, J. 1988. "Gender and Totemism," in R. Randolph *et al*, eds, *Dialectics and Gender: Anthropological Perspectives*. Pp.1–19. Boulder: Westview Press.

Sharp, N. 1975. "The Republic of the Northern Solomons." *Arena* 40: 119–27.

Sheridan, T. 1988. *Where the Dove Calls: The Political Ecology of a Peasant Corporate Community in Northwestern Mexico*. Tucson: University of Arizona Press.

Short, N., S. Freden, and W. Finch. 1976. *Mission to Earth: Landsat Views of the World*. Washington DC: NASA.

Sinnett, P. 1977. "Nutritional Adaptation among the Enga," in T. Bayliss–Smith, and R. Feachem, eds, *Subsistence and Survival*. Pp.63–90. London: Academic Press.

Sorenson, E., and C. Gajdusek. 1969. "Nutrition in the Kuru Region. 1. Gardening, Food Handling and Diet of the Fore People." *Acta Tropica* 26: 281–330.

Spicer, E. 1971. "Persistent Cultural Systems." *Science* 174:795–800.

Spriggs, M. 1992. "Bougainville's Crisis Explained." *The Independent Monthly* August: 28–9.

Stanley, B., and O. Lewis. 1967. "The Protein Nutritional Value of Wild Plants Used as Dietary Supplements in Natal (South Africa)." *Plant Foods for Human Nutrition* 1: 253–58.

Stent, W. 1970. "What is Truth?" *New Guinea and Australia, the Pacific and South–east Asia* 5: 6–12.

Strempel, I. 1966. *Report of Patrol to Wopkaimin Territory*. 1 PIR Patrol Report 28/1965–66.

Stone, B. 1984. "Pandanus from the Ok Tedi Region, Papua New Guinea, Collected by Debra Donoghue." *Economic Botany* 38: 304–13.

Strathern, A. 1971. *The Rope of Moka*. Cambridge: Cambridge University Press.

_____ , ed. 1982. *Inequality in New Guinea Highlands' Societies*. Cambridge: Cambridge University Press.

Stretton, H. 1976. *Capitalism, Socialism and the Environment*. Cambridge: Cambridge University Press.

Swadling, P. 1983. *How Long Have People Been in the Ok Tedi Impact Region?* National Museum Record No. 8. Boroko: Papua New Guinea.

Tapol. 1984. *West Papua: The Obliteration of a People*. London: Tapol.

Taufa, T., J. Lourie, J. Mea, V. Sinha, J. Cattani, and W. Anderson. 1986. "Some Obstetrical Aspects of the Rapidly Changing Wopkaimin Society." *Papua New Guinea Medical Journal* 29: 301–07.

Taukuro, B., et al. 1980. "The World Health Organization North Fly Clinico-Epidemiological Pilot Study." *Papua New Guinea Medical Journal* 23: 80–86.

Taussig, M. 1980. *The Devil and Commodity Fetishism in South America*. Chapel Hill: University of North Carolina Press.

Terra, G. 1964. "The Significance of Leaf Vegetables, Especially of Cassava, in Tropical Nutrition." *Tropical and Geographical Medicine* 16: 97–108.

Thornton, R. 1980. *Space, Time, and Culture among the Iraqw of Tanzania*. London: Academic Press.

Tierney, I. 1960. *Report of Patrol to Wopkaimin Territory*. Telefolmin Patrol Report 9/1959–60.

_____ 1961. *Report of Patrol to Wopkaimin Territory*. Telefolmin Patrol Report 6/1961–62.

Togolo, M. 1982. "The Conflict of Interests Facing the Individual in Decisions about Conservation," in L. Morauta, J. Perneta, and W. Heaney, eds, *Traditional Conservation in Papua New Guieea: Implications for Today*. Pp.339–348. Boroko: Institute of Papua New Guinea Studies.

Townsend, P. 1969. Subsistence and Social Organization in a New Guinea Society. Ph.D. Thesis, University of Michigan, Ann Arbor.

Townsend, B. 1988. "Giving Away the River: Environmental Issues in the Construction of the Ok Tedi Mine, 1981–1984," in J. Pernetta, ed., *Potential Impacts of Mining on the Fly River*. UNEP Regional Seas Report and Studies No. 99 and SPREP Topic Review No. 33. Pp.107–119. Nairobi: United Nations Environment Programme.

Treadgold, M. 1978. *The Regional Economy of Bougainville: Growth and Structural Change*. Development Studies Centre, Occasional Paper No. 10. Canberra: Australian National University.

Tuan, Y. 1975. "Place: An Experiential Perspective." *Geographical Review* 65: 151–65.

Ulijaszek, S., D. Hyndman, J. Lourie, and A. Pumuye. 1987. "Mining, Modernisation and Dietary Change among the Wopkaimin of Papua New Guinea." *Ecology of Food and Nutrition* 20: 13–56.

United Working Group on Indigenous Populations. 1982a. *Report on the Study of the Problem of Discrimination against Indigenous Populations*. Chapter 11, paragraph 19 (E/CN.4/Sub.2/L.566). Geneva: United Nations Economic and Social Council, Commission on Human Rights.

_____ . 1982b. *Study of the Problem of Discrimination against Indigenous Populations*, submitted by the Special Rapporteur J. Martinez Cobo, Chapter V, p.5. (E/CN.4/Sub.2/Add.6). Geneva: United Nations Economic and Social Council, Commission on Human Rights.

Vayda, A., and B. McCay. 1977. "Problems in the Identification of Environmental Problems," in T. Bayliss–Smith and R. Feachem, eds, *Subsistence and Survival*. Pp.411–418. London: Academic Press.

Venkatachalam, P. 1962. *A Study of the Diet, Nutrition and Health of the People of the Chimbu Area (New Guinea Highlands)*. Port Moresby: Department of Public Health Monograph No. 4.

Vines, A. 1970. *An Epidemilogical Sample Survey of the Highlands, Mainland and Island Regions of the Territory of Papua New Guinea*. Konedobu: Papua New Guinea Department of Public Health.

Voorhoeve, C. 1975. "The Central and Western Area of the Trans–New Guinean Phylum," in S. Wurm, ed., *Papuan Languages and the New Guinea Linguistic Scene*. Pp.264–281. Canberra: Australian National University.

Waddell, E. 1972. *The Mound Builders: Agricultural Practices, Environment and Society in the Central Highlands of New Guinea*. Seattle: University of Washington Press.

Ward, M. 1975. *Roads and Development in Southwest Bougainville*. New Guinea Research Bulletin No. 62. Canberra: Australian National University.

Watson, J. 1980. "Forward," in K. Pataki–Schweizer, *A New Guinea Landscape*. Seattle: University of Washington Press.

Weaver, S. 1984. "Struggle of the Nation–State to Define Aboriginal Ethnicity in Canada and Australia," in G. Gold, ed., *Minorities and Mother Country Imagery*. Pp.182–210. St. Johns: New Foundland Memorial University.

Wesley–Smith, T. 1989. "Precapitalist Modes of Production in Papua New Guinea." *Dialectical Anthropology* 14: 307–21.

Wesley–Smith, T., and E. Ogan. 1992. "Copper, Class, and Crisis: Changing Relations of Production in Bougainville." *The Contemporary Pacific* 4: 245–67.

West, R. 1972. *River of Tears: The Rise of the Rio Tinto Zinc Corporation Ltd*. London: Earth Island Limited.

Weyler, R. 1984. "The Fourth World," in *Blood on the Land*. Pp.212–250. New York: Vintage.

Wheatcroft, W. 1975. The Legacy of Afekan: Cultural Symbolic Interpretation of Religion among the Tifalmin of New Guinea. Ph.D. Thesis, University of Chicago, Chicago.

White, L. 1983. "Freeport Indonesia's Ertsberg Project Sets Sights on Expanded Concentrate Production." *Engineering and Mining Journal* September: 46–55.

Whiting, M., and J. Morton. 1965. "Tropical Plant Foods with Exceptional Nutritional Value." *Proceedings of the Seventeenth International Horticultural Congress* 4: 99–105.

Whyte, H. 1958. "Body Fat and Blood Pressure of Natives in New Guinea: Reflections on Essential Hypertension." *Australian Annals of Medicine* 7: 36–46.

Wolf, E. 1982. *Europe and the People Without History*. Berkeley: University of California Press.

Woodburn, J. 1968. "Introduction to Hadza Ecology," in R. Lee, and I. De Vore, eds, *Man the Hunter*. Pp.49–55. Chicago: Aldine.

Worsley, P. 1968. *The Trumpet Shall Sound: A Study of 'Cargo' Cults in Melanesia*. London: Macgibbon and Kee.

_____ . 1984. *The Three Worlds*. London: Weidenfeld.

Wurm, S. 1982. *Papuan Languages of Oceania*. Tubingen: Gunter Narr Verlag.

Young, C. 1966. *Report of Patrol to Wopkaimin Territory*. Olsobip Patrol Report 1/1966–1967.

About the Book and Author

The ancestral rain forests for the Wopkaimin people have long been a sacred geography, a place that has allowed them to act out the obligations of the male cult system and social relations of production based on kinship. Today the people and their place are suffering disastrous consequences from the sudden imposition of one of the world's largest mining projects, which has brought about severe social and ecological disruptions.

Based on fieldwork spanning more than a decade, David Hyndman's book traces the extraordinary socioecological transformation of a traditional society confronting modern technological risk. Across the island of New Guinea, the clash between the simple reproduction and subsistence production system of indigenous peoples and the expanded production and private accumulation system of mining has resulted in environmental degradation.

Mining extracts a surplus to link the State with the international market, and therefore the State has not been an objective arbiter of conflicting claims. Faced with a debt crisis, the State has favored mining investors, condoning the plunder of the island's natural resources for gold and copper. The hegemony of this dominant ideology of private accumulation has cast indigenous peoples in the role of subversives. Indigenous landowners have had to struggle for social justice and equity, at times even taking up arms against mining projects to protect their culture and their ancestral homeland.

David Hyndman is senior lecturer in the Department of Anthropology and Sociology at the University of Queensland, Australia.

Index